INTO THE GREAT UNKNOWN

BY THE SAME AUTHOR

Shooting the Globe*

Reading the Funny Bible and other Stories

*Winner of the Daystar Award for best book of its genre.

INTO THE GREAT UNKNOWN

Adventures in Africa, Eastern Europe, and Asia

MAURICE HARVEY

iUniverse, Inc.
Bloomington

INTO THE GREAT UNKNOWN
Adventures in Africa, Eastern Europe, and Asia

PHOTO CREDITS
All photographs by the author except front cover—author's photographs by Julian Phillips in Ethiopian war zone and back cover by James Li Hing, Ruanda-Burundi—Tanzania borders—albeit using my cameras and settings!

Email: mauriceharvey35@gmail.com
Phone +64 21 626 992

iUniverse books may be ordered through booksellers or by contacting:

iUniverse
1663 Liberty Drive
Bloomington, IN 47403
www.iuniverse.com
1-800-Authors (1-800-288-4677)

ISBN: 978-1-4620-6299-7 (sc)
ISBN: 978-1-4620-6300-0 (hc)
ISBN: 978-1-4620-6301-7 (ebk)

Library of Congress Control Number: 2011919556

Printed in the United States of America

iUniverse rev. date: 11/16/2011

CONTENTS

DEDICATION

To my loving faithful family Lorraine, Rosanne and Clive

Preface

This is not a travel guide, more like a historical document. I have written in the main of the 1960-90 eras. Every country is changing all the time and things are different now in most countries. Some changes are for the better but in many cases, the situation is much worse.

Over the years the Internet has changed the world drastically and cell phones have been revolutionary. Corruption in its various forms continues to spoil countries that were once stable albeit still colonies or newly independent. Twenty years of self-rule in some places has not brought true freedom for everyone, but often it is a case of the strong becoming stronger and richer, and the poor and weak remaining so. More than one president can be described as 'the leader of a brutal dictatorship and kleptocracy. He enriched himself and his family and friends at the expense of the people.' Sadly this is true of a number of countries.

I have not attempted to update the political and economic conditions of the places mentioned in this book.

My work as an international photojournalist took me all over the world (see the appendix for a list of countries and territories visited). Because of the great changes that have taken place, one would like to revisit them all once again. Some countries were visited only once and many others a number of times. I had over 40 trips to Thailand and there were about 85 visits to India. As a family, over a period of 37 years, we lived in Northern Rhodesia, Nigeria, Fiji, Indonesia, Philippines, Hong Kong and England.

I came across a poem by the Psalmist David that expresses my feelings about the life I have lived especially when people say that I have been very lucky.

'You bless those who trust in you, Lord . . .
You Lord have done many wonderful things, and you have planned many marvelous things for us.
No one is like you!
I would never be able to tell all that you have done.' Psalm 40 v 4 & 5 (CEV)

This book is not based on memory, mine would be too unreliable, but on diaries and reports. Most of the material is from reports of visits made for the United Bible Societies, the worldwide Bible publishing organization.

Thanks are due to my wife Lorraine and children Rosanne and Clive who were willing to let me travel so often and extensively when there were no instant communication services available and even telephone calls were often not possible.

Leaving New Zealand isolated and far away from everywhere else, was for a young man in 1960, truly an adventure into the unknown. But with the strong assurance that God was with me, it became an adventure of excitement and great enjoyment.

This is not a continuous narrative of living and travelling around the world, but a smorgasbord of experiences, each chapter designed to stand on its own.

My thanks to Andrew Killick of Castle Publishing Services for his expert editorial work and to the proofreaders Bev Perreau, Eileen Smyth and Lorraine. The team at universe was only a phone call away and always available with their encouragement and support. especially Nikolai Ronalds, Joy Hansen, Hope Davis . . . .

Maurice Harvey
November 2011

1

TO AFRICA—THE JOURNEY

July 1960

I made my way along a passage that seemed to rise and fall before me as I entered the dining room. A young woman was clinging to a pillar heaving her stomach out, lunch all over her pretty dress as the floor tipped and rolled beneath her.

Aboard the good ship *Monowai*, having departed New Zealand on the 9th July 1960, I was bound for the newly independent nation of the Congo, formerly the Belgian Congo. I had seven steel cabin trunks and had painted them bright green. Inside were packed all the things I had been told to bring. These included such exotic items as a hurricane lamp, mosquito net, canvas tent, ten changes of clothing, a compass, typewriter, insect repellent, a set of Rawleigh medicines and notes of useful but unpublished books including *Where there is no Doctor* and *Where there is no Dentist*.

A crowd of about 200 family and friends came to see me off. As was the custom in those days when seeing missionaries off by ship, they sang for about an hour. A cloth bag of letters and telegrams was handed to me just before I boarded with instructions to read one a day. All of the boys in my class at the Bible Training Institute and nearly all of the girls had written, plus there were 24 telegrams and many other letters. I managed to make them last for the 50 days of my journey to Africa.

Two folding chairs were provided for my parents to sit on during the farewell ceremony. Mum and Dad enjoyed the occasion with the usual mix of parental joy and sadness. My mother had said that she had asked God to take one of her nine children to the mission field but never expected he would choose two. My eldest sister, Edna, had already been in the Congo for 12 years. When I said farewell to my father, who was a sick man at the time, I knew that I could not expect to see him again. He wrote me a note that read, 'the tears flow . . . but I am very proud and happy.' At the last minute he dug into his jacket pocket and produced a handful of half crown silver coins saying, 'It's not much'. But I knew it was a sacrifice for him as a pensioner. I asked my brother Frank to bank them for me.

Finally, at 8.00 p.m. the steamer gave a loud hoot and we threw our coloured paper streamers to the people on the wharf. Our loved ones caught and held the long ribbons of paper. As the ship slowly moved away the streamers tightened then broke. It was a marvellous sensation, a slow moving 15-minute farewell. As we headed towards the open sea it was truly a voyage into the unknown. I felt a sense of excitement with the future being dreadfully unknown. All I could do in those circumstances was to follow the Psalmist's instruction, 'Commit your way unto the Lord, and rest and trust in Him'.

I was sure I was doing the right thing by going to Africa. All I had was a one-way ticket, $300 in travellers cheques, no fixed income or promises of support—just faith that God would provide. We passed through the harbour entrance and out into the open sea. I stood on the deck and watched my homeland disappear. When darkness fell I found the Southern Cross in the night sky and wondered when I would see it again. In my youthful naivety somehow assuming that by the following night it would have disappeared over the horizon. What would my father have thought of me if he knew that? He had a much better knowledge of astronomy than I did.

Two days of eating, resting and sleeping followed—then came the storm. Thankfully I wasn't sick. I met another passenger, May Roy of CIM (or

OMF as it is now known) who was a worker in the Philippines. We had tea together and she emphasised the importance of learning the local language as soon as I could.

The Second Engineer had dinner with us one night and regaled us with the story of the ship. The *Monowai* was built in 1925 and weighed about 11,000 tons. She was a troop carrier during the war, described as an Armed Merchant Cruiser. She was attacked by a submarine near Fiji and later took part in the Normandy landings after being converted to a Landing Ship. 'She's a great old girl, see how well she rides,' he said as he grabbed the salt-cellar before it could roll off the table.

Australia

On arrival in Sydney, I discovered that serious trouble was developing in the Congo. On the 10th of July, the day after I had left New Zealand, the Congolese army had revolted and, among other things, turned on the Belgians who had remained after independence had been declared. Many of the white missionaries had also been targeted. Leaders of the Brethren mission work in Sydney told me in no uncertain terms that the Congo was a bloodbath. They said that there was no way I could go there and that I should turn around and go home. My response was immediate. 'Well in that case,' I said, 'I'll go to the country next door.' I decided to push on with my journey, making Northern Rhodesia my destination for now. I thought perhaps I could engage in language study there while I waited for the Congo to settle down. The Brethren leaders in Sydney had no authority over me so I kept going. My diary records the contradictory remark, 'The future seems quite dark and gloomy, but I am sure all will be well.'

I had a week in Sydney staying with a retired customs officer who drove me around the city so that I could speak at various church meetings. He had a Morris Minor and when he stopped at intersections he would put the car into neutral and yank on the handbrake for all he was worth. Then, when the lights changed, he would put the car into gear and struggle to release the brake he had so fiercely applied. Before long, horns would blare behind us and he would mutter with annoyance about discourteous drivers.

I was booked on the 28,000-ton P&O Liner *Oronsay*, which would take me as far as Bombay. En route we called at Melbourne, Adelaide and Fremantle. In each port there were people from a local church to meet and entertain me for the day. In Perth they put on a big lunch as well as a tour of the city. Dr Victor Williams and his bride Daphne going to Ireland for their honeymoon were with me me at the purser's table. One night, my diary notes, that after a busy day in Melbourne, Victor and I went through the entire menu. On another day I wrote that our waiter was 'not very cooperative but today he began the day with a smile. We must work him too hard because Victor and I usually go through the menu.'

During the three-day layover in Freemantle I caught up with correspondence. I kept a note of the number of letters I had written. It was customary to write an acknowledgement for every gift received, whether large or small, and I was quickly finding out that this was one of the banes of missionary life. According to my record, by the 3rd December 1960 I had written 796 letters that year, all by hand.

After leaving Fremantle, I came across a couple of missionary ladies returning to East Africa. As soon as they heard where I was going, they set about teaching me Swahili. I worked hard at this new task for the rest of the voyage—only to find out much later that East African Swahili was a little different from Congo Swahili. Nevertheless it was a good introduction to Bantu languages. We crossed the equator on Tuesday 2nd August at 9.48 a.m. Little did I know that this would be the first of numerous crossings in the future. Next day we arrived at Colombo, Ceylon (now Sri Lanka).

Sri Lanka, India and the Seychelles

We were taken ashore by ship's launch and I spent the day wandering around the markets and streets of this fascinating city. At the Post Office I met a young man who attached himself to me as a guide. He was useful in that he chased off the marauding beggars and rickshaw drivers who continually surrounded us, like one little girl of about 7 with a tiny baby on her back, who looked at me with large black pleading eyes crying, "Eeenglish money."

The first person I met when I disembarked was a Buddhist monk who was on the wharf handing out literature. He courteously encouraged me to read it carefully. This in itself was a challenge and an eye-opener to me and I was surprised to find that it was apparently not only Christians that engaged in evangelism.

Back on board, while we waited to leave the harbour, we were surrounded by small boats full of people selling fruit and curios. One young fellow held up a handful of British silver change. I swapped it for a pound note and he sent up by rope a small carved elephant as an added extra.

At noon the next day we arrived in Bombay (now Mumbai). As we moved slowly against the wharf I could see scores, actually it seemed like hundreds, of uniformed coolies all yelling for business. As soon as the gangway was down they rushed on board and I was surrounded by a dozen grinning, yelling men pleading for work. I chose seven of them. The luggage had been brought out of the baggage room and stacked up on the deck. It was not a little disconcerting to see my bright green tin trunks snatched up, placed on the heads of the porters and quickly leaving the ship. I watched the trunks bobbing up and down in the sea of black heads of the people on the wharf and wondered if I would ever see my luggage again.

I took my turn at customs and immigration and was soon down on the wharf, where New Zealand missionary Harold McGregor was waiting to receive me. He led me to the customs shed and behold, there were my trunks neatly piled up with seven smiling porters holding out their hands for their fee.

The McGregors had a typical Bombay apartment, with a flat roof and painted with a yellow wash, in the suburb of Bandra. On arrival, we sat down to drink several cups of tea and then set off to the market. Once we had purchased some cloth, we took it to a tailor who made up a suit and some shorts for me within a couple of days.

I had a seven-day stay in Bombay and had my first experiences of working with an interpreter while I preached. I was invited to speak at several church services and Bible studies. One day, I spoke at an open-air meeting in Bandra bazaar where we had an audience of over 200 people. My message was interpreted into the local language, Marathi. Harold said that I 'spoke like a professional as though I had been doing this all my life.'

I already knew a little about Bombay from the stories my father had told about the place. He had worked at sea as a young man and served in the merchant navy during the First World War. It was when his ship was replenishing its coal supplies in Bombay that he heard that he had become a father for the first time. I had always entertained a secret wish to visit the place one day. My father would tell us of the way hundreds of coolies would file aboard, each with a basket of coal on his head and tip it into the coal bunker. There were two gangplanks—one up and one down. The coal was usually quite fine and very dusty. As a result, the dust would rise up out of the bunker, enveloping everything and everyone. The coaling went on continuously throughout the night until the bunkers were full. On completion, the ship was in a filthy condition with coal dust everywhere.

What really amazed me about Bombay, were the countless numbers of people. So many living in huts and shacks made of every type of material imaginable, many in a wretched condition. But I soon learned that the poor shacks made of bits of tin, plastic and wood, were not necessarily a sign of poverty. There was such a shortage of housing that many people had to resort to makeshift dwellings. From these simple huts emerged men, women and children in spotless clothes as they set off to work and school.

Another day I went to town on my own and had a great time at the bazaar. As my diary records:

A walk around the Bandra bazaar was a real experience—the yelling of meat vendors as they cheerfully patted slim joints of goat and mutton urging me to buy, the flies, the smells of the fish market and the beefy smell of the beef market. These enterprising 'butchers' had about a four-foot section of the bench and sat in the middle of their piles of meat. It was not laid out according to the way we cut up a carcase, but simply chopped up into small pieces. Roast whole leg of lamb was apparently not included in Indian cuisine. Cows and pigs wandered around along with mangy scabby dogs.

The next day I caught the train into the city where I spent a long time in Crawford Market and bought a few clothes and a suitcase. Later, back at the railway station, I opened my new case to put something away, and a large crowd of people immediately gathered around to see what was inside it! A tout approached me and asked if I had seen Crawford Road yet. No only Crawford market. 'Ah, but you must see the Crawford Road and see the girls in their cages.' I had never heard of this tourist attraction and fortunately declined. Later I learned that this is where young women prostitutes are held, and Harold very gravely said, 'that was wise not to go there.'

As I took in all the suffering and poverty, the beggars, people bathing, eating and sleeping on the streets, the blind and lame, tiny babies lying naked asleep on dirty footpaths, the gabble of a strange language, I was thankful I didn't have to stay in India. I watched a man with neither fingers nor toes rolling through mud in an effort to attract attention and gain a few coins. When I arrived back at the McGregors' apartment, Harold was astounded and a little angry that I had bought the suitcase, telling me that it would have been so easy to be cheated. He was all the more surprised when I told him that I had paid only 30 Rupees for it. The price had started at 300! He sat down and muttered, 'Well I suppose you'll do all right in Africa,' which I took to mean that I knew how to look after myself in a foreign culture.

The Bombay suburban trains deserve a mention. I was advised to go into the city after the morning rush hour. The 10.00 a.m. train was crowded but, I was told, at 8.00 a.m. it would be jam-packed. I went back to the station next morning just to see how packed the trains really were. Every carriage had four doors on either side, and there were usually six to eight men hanging on to and out of each doorway, well beyond the profile of the carriage. Some passengers were riding the buffers between the carriages. There were so many people on the roofs of the trains that I couldn't count them—all riding perilously close to overhead wires that carried 1,500 volts DC.

Here's a quote from a recent article that shows the situation hasn't changed that much:

'The current problem of over-crowding is so grave, and the pressure on the infrastructure and facilities so high, that 4,700 passengers are packed into a 9-rake (nine carriages) during peak hours, as against the rated capacity of 1,700. It is now not uncommon to see 14 to 16 passengers per square meter of floor space, causing what is known as 'super dense crush' load. In other words, 550 people crammed into a carriage built to carry 200.

'There are approximately 3,500 deaths on the Mumbai suburban rail track on a yearly basis—that's about 9 every day! Many of these deaths are caused by people attempting to cross the railway tracks on foot, and avoid taking the overhead bridges that are provided for their use, hence they get hit by the trains. Some passengers die when they sit on the roofs and are electrocuted.'

I took many photographs, which was not easy because of the way people would crowd around wanting to get in the photo. Later that day, the tailor called me to come and collect my new clothes. One suit, three pairs of trousers and two pairs of shorts cost me nine pounds Sterling.

I received four letters from my sister Edna Lind. She told me that they had fled from the Congo and were now in Lusaka, Northern Rhodesia. I was not to worry, she said. I should continue my journey and perhaps stay with them for language study. Another letter informed me that they planned to move to Ndola, a town on the Copperbelt—an area with a vast number of copper mines.

After six days, my ship for East Africa was ready to sail. This was the S.S. *Karanja* of the British India Line. It was a three-class vessel and Thomas Cook had booked me into First Class, assuring me that this was the only class a European may travel. After obtaining my luggage from the bond store where I had left it during my stay, there was the usual scramble and scuffles among the porters for the 'honour', well at least the job, of taking my luggage aboard. Once I had embarked, I quickly settled into single cabin No. 24, on the promenade deck. It had a porthole and was fitted out beautifully in highly polished mahogany. It must have been specially designed as a man's cabin because it had a washbasin and urinal. I was assigned to the Second Engineer's table along with a couple of young ladies bound for a holiday in the Seychelles. This missionary life was getting better and better!

I took a look at the third class area, or what they called the 'bunked cabin'. It was one huge space with bunks, three-high, all around the walls and up the centre, accommodating 850 people. All the passengers here were Indians. The place was lined with washing and, here and there, small cooking fires had been set up directly on the steel floor planking—surely these were illegal! The First Mate, the officer in charge of the passengers and cargo, explained that before the bunk cabin had been converted from a hold, they carried 2,208 people on the open deck. 'It was a tight fit, but they are better off being bunked.'

First stop was Port Victoria on the island of Mahe, capital of the Seychelles. This tropical paradise is made up of more than 100 islands. The coconut and banana palms against the rich blue sky were so beautiful. For lunch I bought a dozen Lady Finger bananas, tiny and sweet, and resisted the temptation to buy a beautifully cured tortoise shell. The people fascinated me. They were a mixture of Indian, French, African and Chinese. An Indian trader struck up a conversation with me and explained that the people wanted their independence from Britain. I was a little uncomfortable when he began to get quite excited about this. 'I tell my wife, 'cause she's the boss,—all the women are the boss—that we have to do something!' I found out later that this was a largely matriarchal society, and unwed motherhood is the norm. Then he suddenly changed the subject. 'Have you seen our special coconut?'

I shook my head. 'Ok, come with me. You must see the woemuns buttum.'

'What on earth is that?'

He grabbed my hand and, holding on tightly, led me to the other side of the market. Now that was something new—holding hands with a man, I was not used to that. He took me to a stall and waving his hands said, 'There's our most famous, most rare woemauns buttum. She is only here not anywhere else, she makes us famous.'

I had no idea what he was talking about. On the table lay what looked like two coconuts joined together. It turned out that they were a species of palm called the *Coco de mere,* that when husked, look like a woman's bottom.

I hired a taxi to drive me around the island and loved the small houses built along the hillsides among luxuriant fruit trees. They were mostly made of corrugated iron with large wooden shutters propped open to let in the cool breeze.

Africa

Back on the voyage, August 17th arrived and Africa was only a day away. I wondered what this great continent had in store for me. A French-speaking fellow passenger gave me my first French lesson but I spent the afternoon on Swahili, breaking off only to watch a whale, and a large school of flying fish. There were hundreds of these fish gliding about a metre above the water and travelling faster than our ship. Their fins spread out like wings and they come down and touch the water with their tails wriggling at a tremendous speed to give them lift once again for another longhop. A crewman explained that the whale was a Brydes whale. It was about 12 metres long and after a few blows disappeared beneath the surface of the ocean.

At 6.45 a.m. the next day, the coast of Africa appeared before me. This was Thursday 18th August. There was a spectacular sunrise and I used my sunglasses as a filter for my camera lens as I captured the scene on film as it streamed through the porthole. We were soon into Kilindi, the Mombasa Harbour where we were to stay for two days. A Kenyan friend, Michael Lomax, a fellow student from BTI, had given me a cheque for 1,000 shillings. They had recently sold their farm in the Kenyan highlands and this was part of the tithe. When I went to cash the cheque, the bankers were a little surprised to see such a large cash cheque and spent several minutes looking up their huge ledgers that measured about a yard across. All the details of the transaction were entered by hand. 'We have werry much complications here,' said the Indian teller, 'because we have to give not the Kenya Shillings but the English pounds.' After that I rented a car that cost 30/—a day. After dinner I drove along the coast for about 15 miles. On the top of a rise, I witnessed a most beautiful sight. The sky was ablaze with stars and the numerous palm trees made lovely silhouettes. I can't remember if I spotted the Southern Cross, but the night sky of Africa would always be a joy to behold in the coming years.

The next day, I spent time in the market practising my Swahili. I could greet the people, ask for food and drink, check prices and respond with 'too expensive'. I would tell them where I was from and make a comment about the weather. It was great fun and a wonderful sensation to communicate with people. It was like another world opening up. It certainly gave me a taste for languages, something that I had feared for most of my life. A few years before, when I was about to start secondary school, I begged my parents not to send me to Wellington College because I would be required to learn French and Latin. Wellington Technical College had no foreign language classes. Given my track record, the idea of going to the Congo, where English was not spoken, and being required to learn two languages simultaneously, appeared quite ridiculous. But somehow I believed the Lord would enable me to cope with language study.

In the market, I soon discovered that a little knowledge could be a dangerous thing. You only have to say a few words and someone will let loose a barrage of conversation, leaving you utterly stranded. 'No, no I don't know very much. I'm still learning.' In fact I soon found out that one of the first sentences to learn in any language is, 'I cannot speak your language.'

Zanzibar was the ship's next stop. I tried to find out the meaning of the word and discovered that Arab traders called it *Zinj-el-Barr*, which means 'coast of the black people'. Again we arrived early in the morning and were greeted by another spectacular sunrise. Zanzibar is famous for its spices, and it really is true what they say about the place—you can smell the cloves way out at sea. We anchored in the harbour and I took the ship's launch to the wharf where I hired a rickshaw and asked to see the sights. My driver was a good guide and took me down all sorts of streets and lanes. One thoroughfare was so narrow that a young girl coming in the opposite direction could not squeeze past, and had to step into a carved wooden doorway. I hired a taxi for a drive around the island. I stopped to take a photo of an old Arab, with a large cane knife, who was working in his garden. He was angry and came running at me, waving it around. I beat a hasty retreat, blessing Ron Hewetson who had advised me to buy a

Pentax camera with its fast moving range finder—I stood my ground and got a beautiful shot of his grizzly bearded face.

Zanzibar is a beautiful island that produces huge quantities of cinnamon, nutmeg, pepper and cloves. Many of the people lived in mud and wattle houses or small huts. When I arrived back at the central market, a policeman approached me and offered to be my guide for half an hour. The streets in the locality were a complete maze. I watched a man with two huge baskets of oranges on his bike: he could hardly hold it upright—the produce must have weighed 200 lbs.

I wandered through narrow streets that snaked here and there, and some of the houses had carved wooden balconies that reached over the street. Electricity cables were looped from house to house, some so low that I could touch them. Talk about dangerous. There were many Indian curio shops selling old silver bracelets, antique nautical instruments and strings of cowrie shells. There was food on sale everywhere. Street vendors were grilling chunks of squid or lobster and all kinds of fish over charcoal fires. I didn't want to speak with any of the Indians; I wanted to practise my few words of Swahili, like the very first foreign words I uttered, '*Nina taka mia,*' I want some water.

Eventually I came across David Livingstone's house. I would be going to some of the places he had explored in the 19th century, but what would take me a few days of travel had taken him many months, indeed years. The Anglican Cathedral on Zanzibar is built on the old slave market to commemorate the end of the Arab-dominated African slave trade. Many thousands of people from East and Central Africa were sold as slaves here—although not nearly as many as the tens of millions sold in West Africa. It was a moving experience to read about this terrible trade. Arab slavers had penetrated deep into the interior to bring out as many as seven to ten thousand people a year.

The slave chamber, which still exists for people to visit, is horrific. The ceiling was too low for the prisoners to stand up and, we were told by the caretaker at the site, they were jammed in so tightly they couldn't lie down. There were only two small openings in the wall to allow in light and air, and many slaves died of suffocation. Inside the church, there are many reminders of the trade including a stained glass window of Livingstone, who campaigned for the abolition of slavery. Right next to the altar is a red circle that marks the spot of the whipping post. Apparently, slaves were whipped to test their strength and resilience before being offered for sale.

I watched with fascination a procession of Indian people carrying Hindu idols of wood and stone and felt that this was pathetic to see them worshiping gods that have ears but can't hear. The ship left port at one 1.00 a.m., but I was well asleep by then after a tiring but exhilarating day of discovery. Many years before, I had dreamed of visiting five exotic places on earth: Kathmandu, Timbuktu, Mandalay, Bombay and Zanzibar. I now had two of them under my belt.

We sailed overnight to Dar-es-Salaam, Tanganyika that, after independence, combined with Zanzibar to become Tanzania. A local missionary, Mr Dalton, met me and whisked me off to the Sunday morning service in a brand new chapel. There were about 30 people of several races in attendance, including missionaries from four countries who were passing through. Mr and Mrs Williams from the Congo were visiting on their way home to Australia. It was encouraging to hear that some Congo missionaries were returning to their stations.

Before returning to the ship, some of the local missionaries tried to convince me to disembark right there and stay on in Tanzania. They said I would never be able to work in the Congo. One even said that the Lord had told him to tell me this, and assured me of a warm welcome. The fact that I had learned so much Swahili in such a short time convinced him that I was their man. As I thought about this later, they certainly needed help. Here they were with an assembly of 30 people that included only a handful of Africans—the rest were all local Indians and foreigners. They did need someone to work with the Swahili-speaking people. But it was too late to disembark here with my luggage, although I was assured that it could be sent back from Beira.

Another days sailing and we reached the port of Beira, Portuguese East Africa (now Mozambique), my final destination aboard the *Karanga*. That night I spent an hour on the First Class deck thanking God for the safe journey and his guidance, and looking forward with great expectation to a lifetime of service in Africa. In those days, if you were called to serve in a particular place, that's where you stayed for the rest of your life. There was a beautiful sunset followed by the rising of the Evening Star. It was brilliant. I began to ask the Lord to make me a 'star of light' in Africa. I had been reading in Philippians where Paul wrote about being a 'burning and shining light in a dark place'. The future looked so exciting and I was looking forward to being on African soil.

We disembarked at 9.30 a.m. and the luggage followed an hour later, lifted off the ship in rope slings, my seven bright green trunks all topsy-turvy. I wondered about my packing. I hired two taxis to take me to the railway station and kept a sharp eye out for the second one to make sure he was following closely behind. There were no custom inspections or immigration formalities whatsoever. This is Portuguese East Africa, explained the captain, this place was not a colony of Portugal. Rather, it was officially part of the 'pluricontinental and multiracial nation of Portugal'.

I left my luggage at the station, stacked up in the Station Master's office, and went into the city for lunch. He was very happy to help a 'railway man'. I found a completely deserted restaurant and the waiter suggested corned beef sandwiches. Thinking about of the normal size of a sandwich back home in New Zealand and feeling hungry, I ordered six. The waiter looked at me strangely, confirmed that I meant six and off he went. He returned a few minutes later with six huge doorstep sandwiches of which I could only manage three. They were made up of 12 very thick slices of bread with a generous amount of beef. My first lesson: don't take anything for granted, everything is different from what it is back home.

A young, good-looking Mulatto woman came into the restaurant and walked over to my table. Her English wasn't that good but she was able to say rather hesitatingly, 'Your friend told me you were here waiting for me.' A Mulatto, as my pre-politically correct dictionary puts it, is 'the offspring of a white and a Negro'. She stood beside the table, brushed her hair back, undid the top button of her blouse and sat down, leaning forward so that it opened slightly. That's strange, I thought, I have no friend here. Then the waiter appeared and standing behind her began to make internationally understood hand signals that I shouldn't have anything to do with her. I rearranged the remaining sandwiches on my plate, pushed it towards her and said, 'Try these they are very nice. Ciao.' And made my exit.

According to my pre-arranged travel plans, I was to take a train that evening for Salisbury (now Harare) in Southern Rhodesia (now Zimbabwe). Back at the station I had a chat with the fireman of the huge Garrett locomotive assigned to our train of 10 coaches. This was an articulated 4-6-2 + 2-6-4 steam engine. He spoke no English and I no Portuguese but we could converse in railway locomotive language. The driver invited me to ride with them on the footplate but I declined fearing for the safety of my unprotected luggage. I was the sole occupant of a nicely appointed six-berth cabin.

This railway began its life in 1898 as a two foot narrow gauge right through to the Rhodesian border but was soon changed to 3' 6" gauge (1067 cm). It became the lifeline of the port and for many years carried much of the cargo and passengers to and from the central African countries of the Rhodesias (now Zimbabwe and Zambia) as well as Nyasaland (now Malawi).

We left on time at 6.30 p.m. and I marvelled at the accuracy of my travel bookings. It had taken me 46 days to get to this stage of the journey but I was right on target to catch the train. We proceeded into the night, which was brilliantly lit with a stunning display of a myriad of bright stars overhead, the like of which we never see in New Zealand. I could see the Southern Cross low on the horizon and remembered how on the first night out of Wellington, I took a good look at that star formation thinking that I may not see it again.

The countryside was undulating, to say the least, with severe grades and curvature making the trip slow going. I loved the clusters of little huts made of mud and wattle that we passed along the way.

Twenty hours later we were In Salisbury. Dr Glenn met me and took me to her home, where she took care of 20 children whose parents were missionaries. She showed me the sick bay and, as I noted in my diary, 'gave me the warmest and most sincere and definite invitation to come and stay in this sick bay if ever I should become ill and needed treatment or rest.'

I thought about this and realised that there was a fairly high chance of becoming ill in Africa.

Another 24-hour train ride, and I was In Bulawayo. John and Mary Albury took me to their home. They were ex-Congo missionaries. John was sure that it wouldn't be possible for me to enter the Congo. They had lots of stories about mission life, all of which were helpful. The main point they impressed upon me was that missionaries are normal people—not saints.

I was booked on the fast train to Lusaka, capital of Northern Rhodesia. Even at express speed it took 24 hours. An Afrikaans farmer sharing my compartment had lots to say about dealing with the black man. 'Treat him like your dog. Feed him well, house him, give him medicine when he needs it, demand obedience or be punished, and he will serve you forever!' I wasn't sure how that would work in a church situation! It goes without saying that this level of racism was astonishing.

Lusaka was my final destination and my sister and brother-in-law Edna and Richard Lind and their three boys Raymond, Peter and Warwick were at the station to meet me when the train arrived on time at 7.05 p.m. It was now 28th August; a 50-day journey from New Zealand and the Thomas Cook timetable had been accurate all the way.

2

A NEW LIFE IN AFRICA—Freedom in their souls

1960-1969

When I left New Zealand, the Linds had still been in Elizabethville (now Lubumbashi) expecting me to join them. Throughout my journey, I had been unable to discover exactly what had gone wrong in the Congo. Now it was all explained to me.

The Belgian Congo had become independent on 1st July 1960. The army at that time was still under the control of Belgian officers. Four days later, there was a disciplinary problem with soldiers in the capital. The new Prime Minister dismissed the Belgian General, and the entire officer corps was immediately replaced with ethnic Africans, keeping some Belgians on in an advisory role. Shortly thereafter, the decision was made to promote all enlisted men to the next higher rank, thereby eliminating all privates from the army. Then the soldiers turned against their remaining European officers. On 5th July, bands of army mutineers could be seen roaming through the streets of the capital, causing panic among both Africans and Europeans. The unrest persisted and by 9th July the mutiny had reached the Equateur and Katanga provinces. Panic-stricken Europeans began to arrive in Léopoldville and poured across the border into Northern Rhodesia telling their own grisly stories.

The Belgians sent in paratroops, and on 11th July their navy bombarded the port of Matadi. The Congolese thought that the Belgians were trying to reclaim the country, and on the same day, amid all the chaos, the rich province of Katanga, in the south of the country, formally proclaimed its own independence. They had exceedingly large deposits of copper, cobalt and uranium—worth fighting for!

When Congolese troops began attacking Belgian settlers, the United States and the Soviet Union turned the troubles into a Cold War conflict by supporting rival factions of the government, such as Moise Tshombe of Katanga who had declared secession with the support of the Belgian-owned mining company and a comic-opera army led by European mercenaries.

Government troops moved towards Katanga in August 1960 but were waylaid in the diamond-mining state of Kasai where they massacred thousands of Baluba tribes people. The United Nations sent troops to restore order in Congo and eventually managed to land a force in the capital of Katanga, Elizabethville, where they were soon fighting Tshombe's mercenaries.

Richard Lind told of meeting a man just over the border. He was a Belgian trader who had lost everything. He had probably lived in the lap of luxury all his life. He was so hungry he said to Richard, 'Have you got a piece of bread?'

There followed a period of instability, and we listened closely to both the news broadcasts of Rhodesian Radio and the BBC. Joseph Mobutu led a military coup in September 1960, which overthrew Prime Minister Patrice Lumumba and expelled the staff of the Soviet embassy. Lumumba, a courageous but unstable man, was murdered in mysterious circumstances the following February. He was captured while fleeing from his rivals. A newspaper photo showed that his arms and legs were bound with barbed wire, and he was thrown into the back of an army truck, taken into the bush and slaughtered.

In September 1961, UN Secretary General Dag Hammarskjold led a mission to try to reconcile Tshombe with the central government.

Hammarskjold was killed in a plane crash about six miles from where we were living. We heard the DC-6 fly over our house just before it crashed into the bush.

In later years, top UN personnel boasted in their public speeches and various books about how they pretended to be merely preserving law and order, while actually carrying out a military operation to crush the new nation—all in the name of 'peace'. The great irony was that the free world had been told that the UN army was sent to the Congo to 'protect it from Communism'. In reality, the Americans were desperate to keep their access open to the valuable minerals, such as uranium, diamonds, copper, tantalum and 298 other types of minerals that lay beneath the rich red soil of the Congo.

At the beginning of September some missionaries returned to their stations in the Congo. Ray Morris decided to return as well, but only so he could pack up and leave Africa altogether. 'I've had enough and am getting out while I can,' he said. Richard and I decided that the best course of action was for me to travel with Ray up to his station in Kiolo, Congo. The idea was that I could look around the Congo for a couple of weeks, and then return to the Linds in Ndola. Richard and Edna were expecting a baby, and they planned to live in Ndola until the baby was born. After that, they would look into the opportunities that existed in Northern Rhodesia.

Ray Morris drove me up to Elizabethville. The border officials gave us little trouble, but they were surprised to see Europeans going *into* the Congo. 'Babwanas [sirs], you are going the wrong way!' one of them said.

The Brethren Mission work throughout Central Africa, known as the 'Beloved Strip', was quite extensive. There were 114 missionaries in Northern Rhodesia alone. But the mission had no central headquarters or committee that directed the work. Each person was left to decide where he or she would like to work—or, in mission parlance, 'where the Lord leads'. So even though I had come from New Zealand and been 'commended' by my sending assemblies (i.e. 'home churches'), it was up to me to decide what to do.

I sent the fastest communication available in 1960, an airmail letter, to the assemblies that had sent me out—Queen Street, Palmerston North, and Newtown, Wellington—explaining my situation. I didn't ask them to tell me what to do, but simply to pray that I would make the right decision. I knew it would take about three weeks before I heard back from them by return mail. It didn't even occur to me to make a phone call. By the time my call was manually directed through Lusaka, Johannesburg, Capetown, London, and goodness knows where else, the quality of the line would have made communication extremely difficult. Telegrams were available, but were not suitable for long messages.

The way the mission worked as a whole was a mystery to anyone not involved. How could it operate without a director and home board, or even a local committee? What about personal support? There was no visible organisation whatsoever. The procedure though was really quite simple. Take my own case for example: When I felt that I was called to serve the Lord in the Congo, I went to the elders of my home churches and told them. They all agreed with me that because of my upbringing, work experience and, involvement in local Christian work like Bible in Schools, Every Boys Rally, Bible teaching and preaching, song leading and two years at the Bible Training Institute, I was a suitable person to go to the foreign mission field. They then took the step of commending me to the work of the Lord. Commendation has the same legal status as ordination, so upon being commended I legally became a 'minister of the gospel'.

My diary entry of 3rd November 1959 reads, 'I now feel certain that [God] wants me to go to the Congo.' Two days later: 'No I am not at all sure.' But then on Friday 13th November: 'I feel that I can honestly say that I am sure that the Lord wants me for the Congo.' So I wrote to my elders and asked for a meeting with them in the New Year after BTI graduation. I announced my plans to my parents on 26th January 1960. The following day I hitchhiked to Wellington and made a booking for Africa with Thomas Cook & Son. I had about $25 to my name. My next move was to apply for a passport, then a visa, for the Belgian Congo through the Belgian embassy.

I received my official 'Letter of Commendation for the Lord's work in Africa' on 31st January 1960. The elders might have been a bit surprised to hear that I had already made my bookings!

As for financial support, I was expected to trust the Lord to provide for me. There was no salary system. Each commending assembly would undertake to support me as they were able, but this probably wouldn't amount to much more than a couple of gifts per year. All the assemblies in the country would be notified of my calling and some of them would take it upon themselves to send me money from time to time. These transactions were mostly handled by an office in Palmerston North that acted as a kind of bank, dealing with the transfer of money on behalf of the churches. Sometimes this office was given money to distribute as they saw fit.

When I went to Thomas Cook to make my bookings for Africa, it was simply a giant step of faith. A day after making the booking, a lady in Gisborne sent me quite a large cheque with a note saying, 'I have the feeling that you are going to need this.' I had never met her or even heard of her and had no idea how she could have known about me. But that was the first example of the many amazing ways the Lord provided for me in the years to come. It wasn't the done thing to mention a personal need to anyone. Instead, you simply told the Lord about it and let him provide.

Once Ray Morris and I had arrived in Elizabethville, a long-serving missionary named Mr Rew acted as my guide around the city. Elizabethville had once been a beautiful place. The streets were lined with trees (especially jacarandas), there were comfortable houses for the Belgians and fine shops. But the Congolese army had destroyed much of it; there were entire streets of shops completely burned out. I met several missionaries from various places. One fellow strongly advised me against staying on Elizabethville. Several others felt that the Lord was telling them that I should work with them—they each came from different language areas. If the missionaries were hearing from God, it seemed like the Lord was as confused as everyone else!

I was asked to deliver a Renault Dauphine car to a missionary in Bunkeya, north of the capital, travelling in a convoy with three others to Jadotville.

Jadotville was a nice little town that had been severely ravaged by the army—most of the European establishments had been destroyed. For the next few days, I found myself acting as cook to a houseful of missionaries who had stopped over on their way back to their various mission stations. Several of them offered me a job. Maybe they were impressed with the icecream I made every day. My host, Mr Nock, began teaching me Congolese Swahili, correcting all the East African usages I had learnt from the missionary ladies aboard the *Oronsay*. For example, the greeting 'Jambo' in the East became 'Yambo' in the Congo. East African Swahili was influenced by English, whereas the Congolese dialect was influenced by French.

On the Sunday afternoon, Mr Nock loaded up his old VW Combi with Bibles and New Testaments in about 40 different languages and we headed to the local market. I was amazed at the way the people crowded around to see these books and at the number that we sold in such a short time. I decided there and then that I wanted to become a distributor of God's Word. During the day I had spoken at two church services and, that evening, Mr Nock suddenly said, 'They have accepted you.' I didn't know what he was talking about. He explained that every missionary has a local nickname, and many never discover what their nickname is. However, the people had already told him that this new bwana was ok, and I was named *Wa Mutende*—'a man of peace'. My host was glowing with happiness about this because he had visions of me staying on and working with him in Jadotville. As far as I know, this name stuck with me throughout my time in Central Africa, though people rarely called me that to my face.

Later, when we lived in the Luapula Valley, there was a local customs inspector known by the people as *Tata wa luse* or 'Father of mercy'. But this carried an air of sarcasm because of the ulterior motives inherent in the fact that he apparently only ever offered rides to women, not men as well, in his Landrover. Another missionary, Mr Ernest Salisbury from New Zealand, had a name the native people found difficult to pronounce. It came out as something that sounded awfully like 'Bwana Scratchibelly'—'Salisbury' proving too strange for the local speech patterns. So his sister decided that, to preserve his dignity, he would be known to his face as Bwana James. My surname came out as 'Afi'. Once the formal prefix 'Ba' was added, I became 'BaAfi'.

During my few days in Jadotville, I was able to capture many photographs of what remained of the town, and found practically no resistance from the local people. Unfortunately these photographs were lost when our car was broken into in South Africa a few years later. One morning I found a small black eight-legged creature in my bedroom. Thinking that it was a type of local earwig, I showed it to my hostess and she immediately cried out in fright. It was a scorpion. It is said that pound for pound, this nocturnal invertebrate has a deadlier set of jaws than the great white shark. Its tail injects poison at lightning speed, which can result in death after suffering excruciating pain. Whether you die or not, it is an utterly agonising experience. No wonder the household was upset! I got rid of it very quickly.

It was time to complete the delivery of the little Dauphine Renault, so a young fellow by the name of Kitanda was assigned to accompany me for the rest of the journey north. He had about as much English as I had Swahili, so this was my first real foreign linguistic experience. We managed though, and got through the bush to one of the most famous villages in Southern Congo. Bunkeya was the home of the former Paramount Chief, Mushidi. It was exciting to get off the beaten track, travelling over many miles of rough unpaved bush tracks.

Once I arrived, I was given the task of taking a series of photographs of the village for an elderly missionary named Miss Lily Myers, who was soon to return to Australia for furlough or perhaps retirement. I was escorted around this huge village that hadn't changed much in 200 years. The houses were made of mud bricks and grass thatched roofs. The women were preparing food for their families by making a stiff porridge made of manioc or cassava flour. Manioc is a plant with tuberous roots, which grow as thick and long as a man's forearm. They are peeled and then taken to the river. A hole is dug at the edge of the water and the tubers are left to soak. This process, I was told, 'takes out the poison'. After a few days they are removed and placed in the sun to dry. Once they are dried, they begin to look like large lumps of fibrous chalk. These are then pounded by the women using large wooden wooden mortars carved from tree trunks that look a bit like a very large eggcup. The resulting flour is sifted and porridge is made from it.

This porridge, I soon discovered, was not the most exciting of foods. Water is put on to boil then removed from the fire. Manioc flour is added and the woman stirs it until it becomes thick and gluey—and that's it. They don't put it back on the fire, so it is neither boiled nor cooked. It was amazing to see how they would take a pot of boiling water off the fire, add the flour and, holding the pot between their unshod feet, stir away until the right constituency had been reached—all without burning their feet!

I was longing to see inside one of their houses and, after some time, a friendly old man, whose grin featured a solitary tooth, invited me in. With no windows, and no lighting of any kind, it took a few minutes for my eyes to adjust to the darkness of this one-roomed dwelling. There were a few sleeping mats in one corner, some cooking pots in another, a small bag of flour and a pile of twigs. Knowing that I would be a Christian, the man reached up to a simple shelf that held his most precious possessions, and took down his well worn Luba-Sanga Bible and hymnbook. He proudly handed these to me with both hands, indicating that they were very special to him. I turned to the first hymn that was printed in Roman script. I was able to recognise the song because the English title was written next to it in small print. So I began to hum the tune. The man danced up and down with joy, which increased when I began to sing the Luba Sanga words that were written there, reading them phonetically. I had greeted him in Swahili but when he saw I could sing in Luba-Sanga, his own language, he let forth a flood of joyful verbiage—of which, of course, I could not understand a single word. When I left him, he sat in the doorway of his hut shaking his head in wonder, no doubt muttering to himself, 'How can a foreigner like him sing my language but not speak it?'

Miss Myers asked me to give her a driving lesson in her old Kombi; she needed it. We swept around a corner and smashed into a mud house, nearly demolishing it. Then she fought with the gear lever to get the thing into reverse saying, 'I've just had this fixed but they didn't put the gear box in straight!'

The grave of the Paramount Chief Mushidi was an important feature of the village. He had been a great and powerful king over much of the Katanga province, and had allowed the first missionary to enter the area.

This first missionary was Fredrick Arnot who, in 1881, followed David Livingstone into Central Africa. He began what became the Brethren missionary work, under the banner of the Garanganze Evangelical Mission. Across the borders in Northern Rhodesia and Angola, the mission became known as Christian Missions in Many Lands.

Next day Kitanda and I returned to Elizabethville in a local taxi. The taxi was a big Customline Ford V8 station wagon that the driver packed with 16 adults, plus a few babies, and a heavy load on the roof including a live goat, one man and a number of chickens. The weight of the load on the roof caused it to cave in so that it was only just possible to find enough headroom to sit inside the car. I managed to get a front seat, but only just. I perched on the edge of the seat and held the door open, as I could not close it. As we travelled, to the delight and encouragement of our fellow passengers, Kitanda gave me lessons in Swahili. The potholes and deep ruts kept the vehicle to a speed of 50 km/h but it was enough to stir up the soft, fine talcum powder-like red dust that swept up from the road covering us completely. We stopped five times to clean out the petrol line.

During this time, I read the biography of Fred Arnot, *From the Hands of the Wicked*, which recorded some of the gruesome violence that had occurred in the region. I was soon given cause to wonder if anything at all had changed over the century that had passed. On arriving back in Elizabethville, I learned that Katanga Province had been raided by the Congolese forces and there were dreadful stories of the atrocities that were committed. Cruel beatings and torture of the most horrific kind had taken place—the descriptions of which have no place in this book. The perpetrators were called *Simba*—the lions—and were to be greatly feared.

Here's a quote from the prologue of *From the hands of the Wicked*:

Chief Mushidi's daughter Ngulewe, had falsely accused a young man by the name of Kalanda of attempted rape and had him arraigned before her father who condemned him to death. 'Immediately the guards undid the cords binding Kalanda to the stake. They pushed him to his knees 'midst the crowds jeering and shouts of anger. Then, with several inaccurate and inefficient blows the executioner hacked at Kalanda's head. It was a disgusting and gruesome affair and by the time the head had been completely severed, the executioner and guards were covered in blood. The body that had been Kalanda's was twitching in its own deep red pool. From the neck stump two long jets of blood were spurting out and spraying the feet of some of the onlookers. One of the guards made an attempt to pick up the head. But before he could do so, Ngulewe ran forward and grabbed it by its hair. Holding it up high so that the people could see her actions, she swung the ghastly trophy towards her father who gave no impression of being moved in any way. Then someone from the royal gathering came forward with a spiked pole. The head was transfixed and followed by the grinning princess it was carried to adorn the outside of her house. Watching his daughter skipping along behind the procession Mushidi began to chuckle. It was then that he looked across at Arnot.'

'These are momentous days,' records my diary. The guesthouse where I was staying (*Restawhile*) was filled to capacity with missionaries who had fled their stations after being threatened with attack. One Pentecostal group was in tears as they heard of the way some of their stations had been destroyed by the marauding forces of the Congolese army. A day or two after I had left Bunkeya, the army had advanced within a few miles of Elizabethville. Local people had burned out all the shops owned by Greek traders in the city, and when I went to take photographs, the few people standing around applauded, telling me to send the photos away and 'show the world that we hate these whites!'

On 26th October, Richard Lind wrote, 'Our senior missionaries from Elizabethville are still on the Copperbelt and they do not know when they will be able to return to their work. During the battle between the United Nations and the Katanga forces they were in the very centre of the fighting that took place in the suburb where the missionary home *Restawhile,* the European Chapel, and two other houses for workers are situated. One of these was our home before we came to Ndola. Bullets actually entered the house. We are thankful that our children did not have to see something of the terror and terrible horror of the Elizabethville battle, of which the newspaper reports were certainly not exaggerated.'

The situation in which I found myself was quite unusual. Here I was, a brand new missionary recruit, with no place to go. It did not seem to be the right thing to stay in Elizabethville, and with all mission stations in outlying areas needing help, the job opportunities were many. But Mr Rew wanted me to stay on and work with him. He told me about a young Scottish woman who was arriving soon and who would perhaps make a nice wife for me. I chose not to tell him about a certain young New Zealand lady named Lorraine who was also en route to Africa, and in whom I already had some interest.

Finally I decided that the best thing to do was to accept the Lind's offer to stay with them for six months of intensive language study in Northern Rhodesia. Richard was an excellent teacher and could preach in French, KiLuba, KiSwahili and ChiBemba.

Back in Ndola, I moved in as planned with Richard and Edna. They presented me with a book on the ChiBemba grammar and I began work. ChiBemba is a language with strict rules and was considered by linguists at that time to have 79 different tenses of the verb. I was supposed to learn the first 20 for the elementary examination. In an attempt to encourage people to learn the language, the government offered a reward of ten pounds for passing this exam. You received 20 pounds for passing the advanced exam with all its 79 tenses. I passed the elementary exam but was fortunate because I didn't know the very common verb 'to dry something in the sun.' As I sat in the examination room trying to figure it out, I realised I knew the words for 'water' and 'without', so I concocted the phrase 'that they might be without water'. The examiner said he gave me marks for initiative!

The importance of knowing about the verb 'to dry something out in the sun' has to do with the problem of the *putsi* fly that is common in many parts of southern Africa. Clothes put out into the sun to dry must always be ironed thoroughly because of a fly that would lay minute eggs on the cloth. If it is not ironed, then after the clothes had been worn for an hour or two, the heat of the body would cause the eggs to hatch and a tiny grub emerges and burrows its way underneath the skin. After a few days a pricking sensation could be felt which looked as though a boil was developing. It was the tiny maggot that was feeding on your flesh.

They could be removed by blocking off the area with sticking plaster or Vaseline, thus suffocating the creature. Otherwise you had to let it grow to full size over a period of about 8 days, then, using tweezers, pull the thing out completely. Not a pleasant site to see a young baby covered in these, so ironing was a major industry in any home.

At the end of my first week of language study on 30th September, I wrote, 'I find I can speak 120 words. That might not sound very many, but it's an awfully hard job to cram them all in! There are some that are identical in spelling but they must be pronounced correctly, like, *ukupepa* and *ukupepa*. They mean 'to pray' and 'to smoke'. So you see there is quite a difference there.' Another pair is *ukufyala* and *ukufyala*, 'to dress' and 'give birth'. The first few weeks of learning a foreign language can be difficult, but after a while, when the sounds become familiar, the learning process speeds up. The ChiBemba language is rich in verbs and nouns many of which we do not have in regular English. The main dictionary is a book of 830 pages with about 20 entries to a page—that's over 16,000 words.

It was the end of the rainy season and a strange phenomenon takes place. Not long before the rains arrive, after eight months of dry weather without any rain at all, the trees in the bush begin to turn green. The jacaranda trees that line the streets burst into a blaze of brilliant purple. Then the weather changes into what was known locally as 'suicide' month—an extremely hot month that is broken when the rains come in November.

A few months into my study, I went to join Mr and Mrs Morse at Lwela Mission. Their assignment was to teach me a particular group of tenses. This place was surrounded by bush and one night there was a lightning storm. I set up my camera at the bedroom window and left the shutter open for several minutes. When the film was processed, it wasn't possible to tell which photo had been taken that night. The sheet lightning had been so even and bright that it lit up the bush as though it was daylight. Mr Morse was a good teacher and I learned much from him, but he was not a well man. He couldn't endure the slightest excitement after supper, as he would not be able to sleep as a result. Therefore the rule was that there was to be no laughter, no conversation, nothing exciting at all—only quiet reading until bedtime. This was not so easy for a young fellow like me, full of enthusiasm about everything.

On Saturday afternoons I liked to go for a walk in the bush. The bush in this area was thick and impenetrable, but quite easy to navigate if you kept to the regular paths. After walking for about an hour I would leave the path and find a nice spot to sit quietly. There were no sounds at all except perhaps the breeze rustling the leaves and the occasional birdcall. After a few minutes it was fascinating to observe what creatures would emerge. There were very few animals—the local people boasted that they had eaten them all. If an animal was reported to be in the area, the whole village would be out after it and not rest until the creature was slaughtered. One time I saw a small antelope, like a duiker, and another day I saw a bushbuck, but I kept the information to myself.

One Saturday afternoon I was walking in the bush and heard the sound of children laughing. I made my way through the undergrowth, along a narrow path, and came across all the girls from the mission boarding school skinny-dipping in the river. On seeing me, they shrieked with laughter and disported themselves about. I beat a hasty retreat. How was I to know that this was the 'women only' section of the river?

I always called this part of Africa 'the land of the living'. There were creepy-crawlies everywhere. The total number of varieties of insect has never been catalogued, although there are supposed to be 2,000 varieties of ants. There are also 66 kinds of lizards.

After the first language exam, I went to Kawama mission in the Luapula valley for further language study with Ken Kruse, a noted expert in the language. Upon my arrival, one of the elders greeted me then turned to Ken and said something that made Ken laugh. Ken then explained: 'He has just said "You can't pick a louse out of your hair with one finger." 'Meaning, 'two are better than one'. The elder was clearly pleased that Ken now had company. Ken advised me to learn all the proverbs and riddles I could because they are a major element of any conversation.

Here are some of my favourites, some of which have obvious meanings . . . some less so.

'Trees in the forest rub together.'

'The children dance but the mother doesn't.' Meaning, the grass on an anthill sways in the breeze but the anthill itself does not move.

'Bampundu balelila the twins are crying.' That is, the two nostrils are craving for snuff.

'You don't ask a chameleon to stretch a drum.' A chameleon moves with sudden steps, whereas you need a strong, firm, steady hand to stretch a wet goatskin over a drum.

'Adultery is like dung, one goes far to do it.'

'Spilled water is not picked up.'

'He who was busy with two things, drowned.'

'If there are many roosters, the day will be long.'

'What women say is nonsense.' (Clearly feminism hadn't made any inroads there.)

Some are very earthy: 'She struts around like a woman who thinks her fine breasts will never wither.'

The following saying is probably used by the people to describe us foreigners who, try as we may, never seem to understand everything that is going on: 'The stranger draws water from a dirty pool.' Meaning, a stranger may be ignorant of local customs, therefore his mistakes can be excused.

And there were a whole lot that can't be told here, just for men only! When I mentioned this to Ken he laughed and said, 'Well if you want the people to listen to you preach, just tell them the story of Samson and Delilah!' There is no surer way of catching the people's attention than beginning a public speech or a sermon with a proverb.

Kawama Mission consisted of several acres of land originally given by the local chiefs, and was situated between two villages. There were three homes for the missionaries including a large two-storey building. The one I lived in was made of sun-dried brick with walls a foot thick and an 18-inch thick grass thatch roof. There was neither electricity nor plumbing. The toilet, or literally the *pikinini kaya* ('the little house') or *chimbusu* (a word which remains in the Harvey family vocabulary to this day), was situated on a small rise about 50 yards from the house. You could never be too careful when going outside to the toilet in the dark. There were leopards in the area and they hunt at night.

The rest of the mission buildings comprised of a small hospital staffed by a missionary nurse, a five-room primary school and a rather large church.

The local people, although Bemba-speaking, were of the Lunda tribe of the snake clan. Because of the beliefs of the tribe, they would never kill a snake, as it might be a relative. Three men were employed to cut the grass with long-handled instruments called *chikwekwe*—an onomatopoeia resembling the swish swish of the blade. These employees were from another tribe because if they came across snakes, they would not hesitate to kill them. During the wet season, when the grass would grow up to two metres tall, the workers would kill two or three snakes every day.

I had more than enough experiences with snakes at Kawama. One day I came out the front door of the house and three small boys were busy digging a hole in front of the step. 'What do you think you're doing?' I cried.

'*Ninsoka, ninsoka!*' ('It is snakes, it is snakes!') they yelled, pointing to the hole they had dug. Sure enough we dug a little more and uncovered several tiny bright green pencil-thin baby snakes. There are 138 species of snakes in Central Africa but only eight are venomous. Mention a green snake and people often say, 'Oh that's a green mamba, one of the deadliest.' The fact is that there are several types of green snakes that are quite harmless, but as far as snakes are concerned, it's always better to be safe than sorry.

One day I put the word out that I wanted a nice long snakeskin. Within days some fishermen brought me a 14 foot 6 inch (4.4m) water python that they had caught in their nets. It was tied up in a ball and I was assured it was dead. I wasn't sure about that, so I put it in a can of petrol for the night to finish it off. Next day I skinned it and one of the workers asked for the carcass. Some parts of the animal were quite valuable, including the brain and liver, used for curing such things as insanity and impotence. Although I had nailed the skin to a plank of wood, scraped it clean and applied salt, it didn't cure properly and smelt for years so much so that my wife wouldn't allow it in the house!

Travelling to and from the mission was an adventure. When the main road became impassable during the wet season, we had a 400-mile (643 Km) detour that passed through a tsetse fly area. Tsetse flies are not unlike common houseflies to look at, though they are a little longer in the body and are a greyish colour. When resting, the wings fold over one another like scissors. They fly silently and alight very gently. You are totally unaware of them until you are stabbed viciously with a sharp sting, which often draws blood. The thing that makes them so dreadful is that one species carries the deadly Trypanosomes that causes Trypanosomiasis—Sleeping Sickness. The Africans call this disease 'The Nodder'. If you become infected through the bite of a Tsetse fly, you grow increasingly drowsy, and begin to nod. This continues until you fall permanently asleep—a living death. The easiest thing to do when we drove through tsetse-infested areas was simply to close the windows of the car, even though we had no air conditioning. But if you got a puncture, or became stuck in the mud, you had a real problem. In these cases, it took two people to change a tyre—one to use the tools and the other to brush away the flies.

At the end of the dry season, the people have a practise of burning the grass so that the ash will fertilise the gardens. One morning we heard the cry of 'fire, fire' and discovered that the thatch roof of the church in the mission grounds had caught alight. After six months without rain it was tinder dry and the fire quickly consumed the entire roof. It was quite a large building that could seat several hundred people and the heat of the fire caused two of the mud brick walls to crumble. Around that time Ken had fallen ill, suffering from a mental and physical breakdown, and needed to be repatriated back to England. I was about to leave the mission with Ken when the fire broke out and, as we drove away, the church was ablaze. I felt so sorry for him—he believed his efforts, after many years at the mission, were going up in flames along with the church.

With Ken gone, I was the only white man left on the station, so I took over his role. There were four single women missionaries of far greater experience than I still on the station but, given the local situation, it was not fitting for a female to take over leadership. So I became the *bwana mukalamba*—'the big man—the one in charge'.

The Kawama Mission had been in existence since the beginning of the century, but the local elders were still not in charge of the assembly that met on the property – white men had governed it since the beginning. I decided that the colonial period was over and a few changes had to be made. First of all was the matter of ringing the large bell on the station that called the people to worship at 10.00 a.m. on a Sunday. Up until this point, it had always been rung by the senior missionary. I told the elders that I would no longer do that, and that it was now their responsibility. They gladly accepted, much to the consternation of the missionary ladies. 'They will never ring it on time' etc.

The communion wine was made of a local wild berry that, when crushed and mixed with water, resembled wine. This was prepared by the missionaries, but I informed the local elders that it would henceforth be their responsibility. Shock and horror from the sisters!

Then came the matter of arranging the preaching and Bible teaching every Sunday. This was also organised by the missionary-in-charge, so I suggested to the elders that they should take this over. They were delighted. The sisters were not.

What about rebuilding the burnt-out church? As I examined the problem with the elders I told them that I was not a builder and that it was best if they took responsibility for the repairs. They immediately decided not to have a thatched roof but what they called a 'tin roof'. I assured them of finding some monetary support for the new roof but it would be up to them to do the work. They commenced almost immediately and the walls were soon re-built. This included replacing two windows, and they arranged among themselves to build the wooden frames to be set into the wall. The walls had been completely finished with the two new windows installed when a missionary from a neighbouring mission came to visit. He had done a lot of building in the past and when he saw the new windows he almost howled with anger. 'You can't do that! Look these windows are not exactly the same, they are different sizes, they're not straight, take them out and redo them.'

'Hold on Jim,' I said, 'This is not your church, and it's not mine—it's theirs. If they're satisfied with the work, then that's fine by me. This assembly is 65 years old and if we can't let the elders run it themselves when are they going to learn? Times are changing and we have to let them run their own affairs.'

My colleague was very unhappy. But here was a church in an area many hours drive from a built-up town or city. It wasn't subject to building regulations of any description. The time to try and make Englishmen out of Africans was past.

Despite the changes I instituted, the mission still bore some very English hallmarks. Many of the traditions persisted, such as dressing for dinner. On Saturday afternoon we would meet for tea, and dress was formal—that is, a shirt and tie. Sunday night was another formal occasion—jacket and tie for the men, and the ladies in their latest long crimplene frocks. After dinner, the senior missionary would read a sermon from the latest Keswick Convention.

Thursday night, though, was fun night when we played *mah-jong* together. Many years later, when I visited Hong Kong, I discovered that Christians did not play *mah-jong* as it was considered a worldly practice contaminated by gambling.

My primary reason for being at Kawama was still language study. It was suggested that I prepare a sermon and have it carefully checked by my instructor. I would then visit all 14 assemblies related to the mission, preaching the same message at each one. By that time it would be part of me and I prepared a second sermon on a similar subject using many of the same words and phrases from the first. My teacher told me that when he was learning the language, no one had checked his sermons, and one day he discovered that he had inadvertently been going around the countryside telling people that they should run away from God!

I visited each of the 14 assemblies regularly. One day I set off on my bicycle to the congregation that was furthest away from the mission station. After a 90-minute ride I came across the new church building that I had heard about. It was made of mud brick with a grass thatch roof, barely high enough to stand up in. The pews were mud bricks and the communion table was a touch rickety, with legs made of tree branches of different sizes. A daughter of one of the elders had just returned from school in the city and proudly made her parents a ginger bread cake. Her father asked her to make another for the communion, so she carefully cooked it in a small tin box that served as an oven. She then coated it with chocolate icing and brought it along to church. This would serve as the 'bread'. The 'wine' consisted of sweet milky tea served from a very old and dented aluminium teapot. How proud the people were to welcome me to the Lord's Table with the very best food and drink they could offer. I didn't have the heart to try and explain that the original meaning of the communion was to use the local staple food and drink.

Each month the elders of all the churches would gather at the mission station and, at a meeting chaired by the senior missionary, they would tell about their problems and ask for guidance. When I attended this meeting for the first time, before Ken had left, he and I sat up the front facing the elders. He then said quite cynically, 'Look at them, there's not a man jack among them that hasn't been disciplined for either adultery or witchcraft!' That was the first inkling I had that Ken had become jaded and over-worked.

It was true, though, that most of the problems the elders reported related to adultery or witchcraft. Tangled stories of marriage breakups and remarriage, polygamy, incest and divorce were common. Having said that, there is a vast difference between the freedom they find in Christianity and the terrible system of witchcraft and superstition that once dominated their lives. The message of Jesus is overwhelmingly beautiful to them.

Tribal beliefs often placed an unbearable burden of fear on the people. Life is lived by omens and portents. For example, if you see the blood of your spouse you will die. If the hoot of an owl is heard by a family with a sick person in their house, then that person will surely die. If a baby's upper teeth appear first, then this is an evil omen. In fact, there was a time when such children were killed, as were twins, by being left in the bush to starve or be eaten by wild animals.

Sadly, for new Christians, the pressure of a non-Christian family was sometimes too much to resist. This was especially true for the women who were expected to obey not just their husbands, but also the elders of the tribe. Traditionally, a woman could only speak to her husband when kneeling. There was a multitude of harsh customs related to females.

One night when out camping, I was sitting outside writing my diary in the light of the full moon, and an older man approached me and began to talk about the stars. He said the star nearest the moon is called the wife of the moon and what we foreigners call the milky way is called *inshila ya mukaka*—the path of milk! To count the stars is 'to long for one's absent beloved'. Patting his chest he said, 'My name is *wa ntanda*'—'the father of a large family whose offspring cannot be counted', that is, like the stars. Some believe that the stars are the campfires of departed loved ones.

In the face of all these ancient traditions, white missionaries had not always modelled Christ in the best way. Once, when Ken and I were camping in a small fishing village beside Lake Mweru, the people spoke about the first white missionary who had come to the area. He would never allow an African to go near his house, let alone enter it. The tribes people were instructed to get off their bicycles and remove their hats when they walked past him. He would never eat with them and always sat on a chair at the front of a meeting or church service never on the ground or on the traditional mud brick seat.

On the same camping trip a fellow chopping wood for our campfire nearly cut off his big toe. Two men carried him to where I was seated and asked me to patch him up. 'He was cutting wood for your fire Bwana,' they said. The bone was only chipped so I bandaged him up. Several months later he arrived at the mission station and, grinning from ear to ear after politely greeting me by clapping his hands softly and bending low, said, 'Does bwana remember me—he of the cut big toe?' He had come to report that he had made a full recovery without even a limp. I cautioned him about telling the people in the area, otherwise I might have them coming to me for medical attention instead of going to our clinic.

Travelling out into remote bush areas was always an adventure. One trip was to an isolated village and the entire journey of 80 miles was done in first gear because of the rough terrain! The roof rack holding our tent fell off. The villagers had heard that we were on our way (I don't know how, as they have neither telephone nor postal service), so they built us a new house with five rooms. Made of sun-dried mud bricks with no windows or a ceiling, by the time we arrived it was already occupied by scores of bats. But we had to sleep there because it would have brought shame on the village if we had used our tent instead. There were only a few mosquitoes around, but there were millions of ants! To one side of the village was a column of red ants that were moving to a new location. They looked like a long reddish-brown rope where they marched ten-aside. There was a continuous stream of them that took 48 hours to pass before disappearing into a hole in the ground. The soldier ants among them formed a thick ring around the new hole so that only their own could enter.

One night, when I was asleep in another place, I felt itchiness on my head. After scratching for a while, I woke up properly and switched on the torch, only to discover that I was lying in the path of an army of red ants on manoeuvres. They had crossed from the bush, through the house into my bedroom, across the floor, up and over my bed, across my head, up the wall, outside, and off into the bush. The only way to divert them was to lay some flour in their path or cover the area with kerosene.

Apart from red ants, white ants were a constant bother. There are about 2,800 termite species and we appeared to have a good number of them at Kawama. All buildings had to have a metal layer inserted between the lower courses of mud bricks to prevent these creatures from destroying the structure. In the main bedroom, there was a large hole about a foot across and about six feet deep where the ants had eaten out the floor and the ground beneath it. The countryside was dotted with immense anthills, some the size of houses. Termites are sneaky creatures in that they can enter a wall of a building or the leg of a chair and eat out the inside, leaving the outer skin intact.

I believe I was the only white man ever to live at Kawama and not be carried out a sick man, stricken by malaria. The mosquitoes were very bad.

At night the door and window screens would be black with them trying to find a way inside. Mission doctors puzzled about my good health. At that time the recommended preventative medicines for malaria were either a daily Niviquin or a weekly Daraprim. I decided to take both at the same time and told no one about this.

Many years later when visiting a British Air Health Clinic in London for Japanese encephalitis and cholera inoculations, I was asked about what malaria medications I was taking. After 25 years I had stopped taking any and a doctor present who was observing the work of the health nurse argued that I should be taking something. He said, 'We recommend you take Daraprim every week and a daily dose of Nivaquin.' I don't think he believed me when I told him my story from the notorious Luapula Valley.

During my time at the Kawama mission, I kept a record of the food that was offered to us in the villages we visited. Because missionaries are considered honoured guests, we were always given the best food available. *Bwali* was always a feature of the menu. It is the main starch staple made of cassava or manioc, as described earlier. We were also provided with crushed peanut sauce, pumpkin leaves, goat meat stew, bush meat stew (probably consisting of such things as porcupine) small bony fish, pumpkin soup, eggs and dried fish. The people have a custom of eating only one type of food per meal, and eating only after midday—or as they describe it, 'when the sun is on top of your head'. On one occasion, when we were packed up ready to leave for home, a woman came to us carrying a very large bowl filled to the brim with pumpkin soup. We had just finished our breakfast and there was no way we could take it with us. So we got out of the car and thanked her warmly, then explained that we couldn't carry it home so we would like to donate it back to the village. The bowl was so large it wouldn't even fit through the car door without tipping sideways.

In contrast to the Africans I met in East Africa, the Balunda of the Luapula had no handicrafts whatsoever. Very basic figurines were made for initiation rites, but these were seldom seen in public. As mentioned earlier, their traditional houses were simple structures of sun-dried mud bricks and rough thatch. The only thing they made was a coarse basket for carrying produce. But their singing and aural abilities were magnificent.

It was a great privilege to work among these people teaching the Bible. They were always eager to hear the Word of God. For Bible teaching conferences, a section of bush was cleared and temporary shelters were set up. People from miles around would walk for hours to attend. The first night would usually be spent singing, and then the Bible teaching would begin and continue non-stop for hours the next day.

The most significant thing that happened for me personally during my time at Kawama was that I got married! As I mentioned earlier, I had my mind set on a certain girl. Her name was Lorraine Scott, and I had met her the day before I left New Zealand. She was a schoolteacher and, like me, was planning to work in the Congo. Lorraine had been in touch with Esther Sinclair who was based at the Luanza Mission Station. This was an entirely different language area to the location I was planning to work in, so despite my interest in her, it didn't look like we would see much of each other in the future. However, when trouble broke out in Congo and threw everyone's plans into disarray, I spied my opportunity. I wrote to Lorraine suggesting that, as we were both now free agents – that is, not committed to any particular area – perhaps we should consider working together. This meant marriage and we were soon engaged! She arrived in April and, after her first language exam, we were married in November and Lorraine moved to Kawama. I will leave all the romantic details for Lorraine's book!

Despite enjoying my time at Kawama, my desire was to work on the Copperbelt, rather than staying on to run an ancient mission station. The Copperbelt was the fastest growing area in the country by population. But, of the 114 missionaries stationed in the country, only one had set up in the Copperbelt region. As planned, my time in Kawama had helped me gain experience in the language and culture of the Bemba-speaking people. Now that I had handed over the entire responsibility of the mission station church to the local elders, I felt that I was free to return to the Copperbelt and help with the work there.

It was time to make a move. But there was a problem. The rainy season had caused widespread flooding and the Luapula River, beside which we lived, had overflowed its banks. The water was right up to our house and the roads were blocked. There was no way out except by boat. We were stranded. Food ran out. Someone came to the door and offered to sell us a huge bunch of bananas. For several weeks they were our only food—bananas for breakfast lunch and dinner. How many ways can you serve bananas?

When the flood receded we moved to Ndola. My main interest was in distributing literature (mainly the Scriptures) and Bible teaching. I became a foundation member of the teaching staff of what later developed into the Bible Institute of Central Africa. After Northern Rhodesia gained independence and became Zambia, this institution became the nation's first degree-issuing college. In the literature field I joined Ken Kruse, who had returned from furlough and was living in the area, in beginning a publishing organisation, which we called Copperbelt Christian Publications (CCP).

I needed an official organisation to purchase books from wholesalers, so I began a company called African Christian Books (ACB) that, after the Bible Society, has become the largest book distribution company in the country. Thirty years later, when I visited the Copperbelt, and saw the huge warehouse of books, I asked how the organisation had begun. 'Oh, Jean Reid started all this.' No it wasn't Jean, it was me. It was the same for CCP. An African fellow wrote a history of the mission, and not being around when I was there, omitted this information. It became apparent that my role as founder of ACB and CCP had been forgotten in the annals of history. Never mind, the work continues and that's the main thing!

Not long after we arrived in Ndola, I decided that I would spend the morning selling Scripture Portions and Bibles in the markets around the area. So I went to the Bible Society office in Kitwe and told the secretary Herb Casler what I would like to do, but said I didn't have enough money to buy stock. That wasn't a problem for Herb. He loaded up my car with Bibles and New Testaments in about 40 languages and asked me to pay for them once they had sold. As I drove home in my heavily laden car, I wondered how it would be possible to sell all those books. The Copperbelt was home to people from all over the country who had come to work in the mines. Northern Rhodesia is a country of about 78 indigenous languages.

Bibles sold for 6/6 (six shillings and six pence), New Testaments for three shillings, and New Testaments and Psalms for three shillings and six pence. I found that I could sell about five pounds worth of books every morning. That was about 20 Bibles and Testaments. A week later I returned to the Bible Society for more stock. Herb was very surprised, but overjoyed. There was a whole street of shops known as the 'second class trading area'. This was where the African people did their shopping, and all the shops were owned by Indian Gujarati. I soon found a ready market for Gujarati Bibles to these mostly Hindu people. When I showed the shopkeepers the Bibles and Testaments in the languages of their African staff, many were willing to allow their staff members to have what they wanted and take the money from their wages. I sold 66 Gujarati Bibles in a matter of a few weeks. According to Herb, this was unprecedented.

Within two months I had sold 358 Bibles and New Testaments, 1,750 Bible Portions and 700 other Christian books, in 40 different languages. The Scripture Gift Mission supplied me with large numbers of their publications in many languages and one of their reports states that I was their best customer in Africa.

The afternoons were spent in language study and preparing sermons and Bible studies in ChiBemba. Once a week, I would visit the hospital but I found this to be most difficult. The smells were awful.

When the time had come to move from Kawama, I met with strong criticism from nearly all my missionary colleagues. There was only one who encouraged me, and he himself had worked on the Copperbelt for a few years. He had to leave, though, and return to a bush station because he was unable to afford the higher cost of living in the town. He did warn me that I might find the costs prohibitive. Thankfully we can say we had no problems and were provided with all we needed.

One day I received a telephone call from Herb asking if he could come and see me. 'What could this be about?' I wondered. I had paid all my bills. He duly arrived and Lorraine and I were not a little astounded at the reason for his visit. He was due to go on furlough in the USA and was looking for someone to take over his work during his absence. The job would be Circulation Manager for the Bible Societies in Rhodesia

41

and Nyasaland—countries that are now Zambia, Zimbabwe and Malawi. The Bible Society would provide a house, car and regular salary but it would mean that we would have to move to Kitwe, another Copperbelt town. Our commending churches and colleagues in the field encouraged us to make the move and assured us of their full support if that was what we felt we should do. We accepted, and thus began my work with the Bible Society. Originally it was to be a twelve-month secondment, but it became 30 years!

A year with the Bible Society

The plan was that I take over some of Herb's work of running the Bible Society depot in Kitwe, and then cover all the mission stations in Central Africa. I began with Southern Rhodesia and, after securing the names and addresses of all the missions in that area, called on a Lutheran Mission situated out in the bush. The road was almost impassable, as recent rains had washed all the topsoil off, exposing the rocky foundation. It was first gear, and sometimes second gear, all the way. After meeting the missionary in charge, I had driven 20 miles all the way back to the main road, when I realised I had left my briefcase behind! Retracing my route, I vowed I would never make that mistake again.

A day later, I visited another Lutheran Mission but, just before reaching the station, I came to a river that was washing over the road. This ford was called an 'Irish bridge', with the river flowing over a concrete road foundation. There was a one-metre high waterfall just beside the crossing but I decided that, as this was the official road, it would be okay to cross. My Opel station wagon made it across with just a slight sideways movement, suggesting that it had floated a little. The missionaries were amazed to see me when I arrived and asked how I got there. 'Surely you didn't cross the river, it is in spate; the last vehicle to do that was swept away,' they said. Despite the risk of having to return the same way later that day to the main road, they waved me off and wished me luck and didn't bother to make sure I crossed safely. I put their apparent lack of concern down to them having confidence in my driving, as they watched me place all my luggage over the back axle to give the vehicle maximum traction.

It soon became clear that every missionary believed that his station was at the end of the worst road in the country. The main roads at that time were perfect and one could easily average a mile a minute, but not the side roads. They took a heavy toll on vehicles and once on my way home, as I made my way through an isolated area of bush country, the connecting shaft broke. After an hour or so, a passing motorist gave me a lift to the nearest town.

Visiting the mission stations was a great experience, but I was often saddened by the attitude of some missionaries regarding the need to make the Bible available to their people. One said, 'I'm a preacher, not a bookseller. If they want a Bible they can go to town and buy one.' Town was 200 miles away with no regular bus service and the people only had bicycles.

One missionary told me that all the people needed was a prayer book—that they had no need of the newly published, and first ever, Bible in their native Tonga language. I called upon all my selling skills that I had developed when working as a Rawleigh dealer. Eventually I succeeded in selling him not just a dozen copies, but a whole case of 200!

I travelled all over the three countries doing about 3,000 miles a month during my year with the Bible Society. The work went well, and I managed to sell the entire year's stock in just three months. Up to this time, the Bible Society had been publishing the Bible as translated by missionaries, and then leaving it to the missions and churches to distribute the new editions. My appointment was part of an experiment to use experienced salesmen to promote the distribution of the Scriptures. It was declared to be successful and, after a year, I was asked to go to West Africa to do the same thing.

Leaving Northern Rhodesia (which was very soon to become Zambia) was a difficult decision. After years of language study to assist in my work there, the concept of leaving was almost unthinkable. I felt as though I had invested so much time and effort. But after much prayer, Lorraine and I could see that relocating was the right thing to do, and so I moved on to other adventures.

Thirty four years after Lorraine and I had left Kawama, I returned for a visit. The 14 assemblies that had related to the Kawama mission when we were there had increased to 41. Pastor and evangelist Sims Mwansa, said that every three to five kilometres you will find a Brethren Assembly in this valley. The following month they were expecting 20 to 30 people to be baptised, along with about 3,000 to 4,000 people who would come to watch the ceremony. From time to time they have a district conference when at least 10,000 people come for a few days of solid Bible teaching.

The time I had spent in the Copperbelt region was rewarding and eye-opening for a young guy from New Zealand. I'm thankful that God allowed me to be part of that work for a few years. But he still had a lot more in store for that young guy, and a lot more unknown lands for me to visit!

3

NORTHERN RHODESIA TO NIGERIA—
sailing around Africa
1964

Lorraine, Rosanne and I arrived in Nigeria on 9th March 1964. Having relieved Herb Casler while he was on furlough, it was clear that there was a future for me in Bible Society work. Now I had been appointed to the full-time overseas staff of the British and Foreign Bible Society (BFBS), and was about to undertake new challenges in a totally different part of Africa. As always, mission work in remote places brings its share of difficulties—the process of getting to Nigeria was a challenge in itself.

After we had accepted the Bible Society's invitation to work full-time in Bible work, we waited in Northern Rhodesia for instructions. Time passed, but there was no word from BFBS headquarters in London as to what work they wanted us to do, or where they wanted us to do it. At the end of year, I contacted Norman Hunter, the Circulation Adviser for Africa, who told me not to worry, as he was sure word would come soon. He was of the opinion that I would be required in West Africa. The Caslers were due back just before Christmas, and we were still living in their house.

We were instructed to stay on there until further notice. We met the Caslers at the Ndola airport on 23rd December and they were astounded that we hadn't heard from Head Office. Graciously, they took a hotel, urging us to stay on in the house until we knew where we were going. That afternoon we began packing up knowing that we were going somewhere.

Next day a cable arrived from Frank Bedford, the Africa Secretary of BFBS, asking, in cryptic language, if we were willing to move to Lagos, Nigeria and take up a new position as Circulation Manager for the Bible Societies in West Africa. Later that day, a letter from Dr John Watson, General Secretary of the BFBS bore the same request. 'We are very short-staffed in Nigeria and we would like you to go there as soon as possible to help out'—or words to that effect.

On Christmas day, we took a break from packing to entertain my sister Edna and her family for Christmas dinner. Lorraine cooked a shoulder of lamb and laid out the feast on packing cases. After completing the packing a few days later, we moved to a mining company house that had been offered to us while the usual occupants were on holiday in South Africa.

The house was fully furnished—including a television, which was a brand new experience for us. I can still remember the very first film I saw on television. It was all about a small American boy who excelled as a young trumpeter. The only problem with the house was that the family who lived there had taken their dogs with them, but the dogs had left behind all their fleas. The house had been empty for a few weeks, giving the fleas a chance to multiply and become very hungry.

The political situation slowed down our plans because independence for Northern Rhodesia was rapidly approaching, and the country was soon to become Zambia. There were strict regulations as to how much money could be taken out of the country and clearance had to be given by the Central Bank. Many Europeans were beginning to move to other countries rather than live in independent black-ruled Zambia. Their sense of fear was fuelled when the leader of the United National Independence Party, Kenneth Kaunda, said that if his party were elected, his people would assume control of the police force within a month of taking office.

It took four weeks to obtain exit visas and I felt deeply embarrassed to be leaving the country, when many whites were literally fleeing. The timing of our departure had coincided with the exodus. We weren't leaving out of fear—but that's what it looked like. We had come here to serve the people. Unlike so many foreigners in Northern Rhodesia, we were not there to make money and have a comfortable life. I secured a booking for our luggage, including our little Morris Minor, on the *Straat Soenda*, a cargo vessel of the Royal Dutch Interocean Lines.

Just before leaving, I wrote the following letter to our friends:

We have greatly enjoyed the nine months that we have been in Kitwe when we have been engaged in circulating the Scriptures in the Federation of Rhodesia and Nyasaland. As far as numbers are concerned, it has been the best year ever and we are particularly thrilled that the little Bible depot that we have run as a sideline in Kitwe exceeded last year's sales of complete Bibles and New Testaments by over 10,000 copies.

A great joy has been training the African colporteurs, or itinerant Bible salesmen. In some parts of this area there are no evangelical missionaries, which means that the local people never hear the Gospel. Into these areas we send the colporteurs. Laden with their precious trunks of Books these men penetrate into areas where the Gospel has rarely been preached and thus give the people their only chance of procuring a copy of the Scriptures in which may be found the way of salvation.

The colporteurs have told us of many who have trusted Christ as their Saviour as a result of reading the Word of God. Some have come out of odd native churches. Many and varied have been the experiences of these Bible missionaries. One supervisor giving a report of his charge who works in one of those hot steamy valleys of Northern Rhodesia wrote,

'On the 2nd of this month he saw a lion in the bush path. Naturally he was frightened and hesitated to return to that remote part, however, I am sure that he will return there later on.'

It hasn't been easy for these men working in areas where political intimidation is rife. Colporteur James, working from an assembly mission station, cycled 300 miles on sandy bush paths and sold four books. The people refused to buy as they said they were only interested in one thing—politics. Therefore he was refused food and drink in many a village.

One of my tasks was to encourage missionaries to stock the Scriptures. You would be surprised if I told you of the number of mission stations that I have visited where I found not a single copy of the Scriptures available for sale to the people of the district. I recall visiting a mission station where 50,000 pounds had been spent on a modern hospital and 15,000 for the school—and not a penny towards the purchasing of Scriptures for the people.

I was told, 'We are too busy building up the hospital work and the schools to sell Bibles.' It is true to say that Africa has been thoroughly missionised but not necessarily evangelised.'

One of the last jobs I had before leaving Northern Rhodesia was to assist a Canadian Bible Society film maker, Manie Heuer, to make a film called *Freedom in their Souls* about the great changes going on all over the African continent. Manie usually worked alone and depended upon local people to assist him where necessary. I arranged for visits to the mines, where he secured shots of the great furnaces of molten copper and, during the night, scarlet and orange slag being poured from special railway trucks onto the huge mine dumps.

He was able to film one of the most exciting events in Bible Society work—when people receive the Bible in their language for the very first time. The Umbundu Bible had just been published, so we arranged for an Umbundu-speaking assembly to receive their first copies. This was a massive book because it was really two Bibles in one—Umbundu and Portuguese combined. Umbundu is a language spoken mostly in Angola, and the Portuguese colonial government required that any literature published in an African language should also have a Portuguese translation.

Manie needed some pictures of the independence movement and as there was a large political rally being held in Kitwe, we went along. Twenty thousand people sang and chanted slogans until the tension and fervour was tangible. The noise rose and fell and sometimes reached such a crescendo that it was a little frightening. Some of my friends thought that it was crazy for us to go, as no white person, except perhaps policemen, would ever dare to venture into such a rally.

Manie enjoyed himself immensely and captured great shots of the lively crowd. The trouble for me was that I could understand the language and could hear what was being said. One speaker came to the microphone and screamed insults at the government. He grossly insulted all people who did not support the United National Independence Party (UNIP) and urged the crowd 'to down' every one who was against them. In that context, 'to down' someone was to literally throw them down and kill them.

Being at the rally helped me understand that the country was going to change dramatically after we had left, and would never be the same again. I just hoped it would change for the better.

After a round of farewell meetings, meals and presentations from various groups we had worked with on the Copper Belt, we set our sights on Nigeria. One assembly presented us with a certificate of appreciation, which they thought we should put up on a wall in our next home. To be honest, I didn't really accept this in the spirit in which it was given, as I felt at the time that one didn't need certificates for doing God's work.

We left Kitwe on 17th January 1964, the day of the first general election, when the people would elect their own government. The journey to Lagos, Nigeria, would take 52 days—including a two-week holiday in South Africa on the way. Our Morris Mini was loaded to capacity. By now we had our first child, Rosanne. She was just six months old, and required a lot of space for her pushchair, folding plastic bath and a red bucket, which sat proudly on the roof rack.

We were one hundred miles into our journey when the motor over-heated and I just managed to get the car to a river for water. Service stations were few and far between. At the first repair garage along the way, the radiator thermostat was replaced. At the second, a mechanic who thought he knew about these things took it out. 'Thermostats don't work properly at this altitude of 5,000 (1,524 m) feet above sea level and in this heat.'

With the motor continuing to overheat, the radiator cap and the thermostat were replaced at the third garage. Five hundred miles along the way, the cooling system was blown out by a friendly mechanic. Still no good. I found that by keeping the speed to 40 mph (64 km) (the engine gave no more trouble for the remaining 1,500 miles (2,414 km) to Durban.

We had booked at the Swedish Mission Guest House, but when we arrived we discovered that there was no room for us—the new managers there said that they couldn't understand the booking methods of the previous ones. Thankfully we found accommodation at the Plaza Hotel where we had stayed whilst on holiday once before. We remembered this hotel for the almost perfect service of the Indian waiters and a manager who spoke to each of his guests every day.

We were in Durban in time to farewell Edna and Richard Lind and their family. They were returning to New Zealand after 14 years of missionary service in Africa. As we had lunch on board their ship, the *Northern Star*, we wondered whether conditions on our cargo ship to Nigeria would be as luxurious as this famous one class vessel of the Shaw Savill Company.

The Linds were leaving Africa and returning to New Zealand for the sake of their children's education. I owed them a great debt of gratitude for being instrumental in getting me to Africa in the first place, and for the numerous ways they helped us.

Lorraine, Rosanne and I were due to leave for West Africa the next day. The shipping agent asked me to have our car down at the wharf at 8.30 a.m. on 23rd February. The heavy luggage was on the wharf when I arrived. The little blue Mini was swung aboard the ship with such gusto that I wished I hadn't been watching. In the event, it reached Lagos without a scratch.

I went back for Lorraine and Rosanne, hiring a taxi driven by an Indian. On our return journey to the ship, a policeman stopped us and asked the driver why he was carrying white people—didn't he know that was against the law? As we pulled up for the policeman, the driver had hastily asked us to explain that we had asked him, not that he had asked us to use his taxi. The policeman was satisfied and let us go.

The Dutch first mate of the *Straat Soenda* gave us a warm welcome and showed us to our cabin. He told us that seeing as he was in charge of the cargo, his area of responsibility included the passengers too. He was very pleased to have a baby aboard. Our cabin was a large suite with single berths along two sides. At the end of one, there was a low steel cot for Rosanne. The other furnishings consisted of two armchairs, a table and a large dressing table. Our suite also included a dressing room with two wardrobes and a cupboard, and off that the bathroom with two hand basins. A smiling Chinese man followed us into the cabin and was introduced to us as our personal steward who attended to our every need. He brought us drinks, cleaned the cabin, and did the laundry to a standard we have never seen since. Our clothes came back clean and fresh and so soft that Lorraine tried to find out his secret. In the end, we decided that it was the sea air—being 2,000 miles (3,218 km) inland, the air in Northern Rhodesia had been totally different.

This was going to be a luxurious trip. We dined with the captain and his senior officers and were waited on at the table by other Chinese stewards. Although it wasn't a new ship, it was spotlessly clean and bright. There were only two passenger cabins—one double and a single. The single would be occupied from Capetown. We slept on board that night as the ship was due to leave at first light the next day.

A low rumble and vibration woke us at 6.30 a.m. and we were on our way. As soon as we cleared the heads of Durban harbour we hit what are known as the 'Durban dumpers'. The change was so sudden. One minute we were gliding smoothly down the harbour, the next, the ship was pitching and tossing alarmingly. Lorraine soon felt ill and decided against lunch. I ate well but lost it all by 4.30 p.m. We were all in bed an hour later and slept well all night.

The pitching and tossing continued the next day. We were sailing through the notorious waters around the Cape of Good Hope, where the Atlantic and Indian Oceans meet. The steward brought us a little lunch in bed. Rosanne sat in a highchair between our berths and smiled and gurgled at her wan-looking parents.

On the third day we arrived in Capetown. What blessed relief! It was so calm and smooth in the harbour. We had been there before and liked the city very much, especially the view at night, the beautiful shoreline and mountains by day. But it was never as attractive as the morning we escaped those rolling seas. Once we were in port, friends came to see us and took us out for the day. Ernest Salisbury—Bwana James of the Congo—came on board and we also met up with the Abernethys, friends who had been in Kitwe with us.

We sailed for Luanda at 9.00 p.m. that evening. A doctor and his wife now occupied the single cabin. Dr Tommy Graham had persuaded the company to allow him and his wife, Bunty, to occupy the single cabin. 'They have made up a bed in the bath,' said Tommy.

The Atlantic was friendlier than the Indian Ocean. The ship rolled a great deal but Lorraine and I had found our sea legs by now and the motion didn't worry us a bit. I spent the first day splicing 8-mm movie footage that I had shot just before leaving the Copperbelt. The Chinese cooks provided wonderful food. It was a mixture of Dutch, Malaysian, Chinese and Indonesian. Most of it was quite new to us and we enjoyed it all.

Rosanne in her highchair was given the place of honour at the Captain's right hand as she reminded him of his five-month-old daughter. He often used to hold her hand throughout the meal. The officers were Dutch, and the crew were from Hong Kong. When I found a group of them playing *mah-jong* they were amazed that I knew how to play. I bought a set from one of them for about US$5.

For five days, we sailed northwards towards the equator. The engineer told us we were doing 17 knots night and day. The sea smoothed out and the conditions became idyllic. Unfortunately Lorraine developed a painful boil in her ear. Our steward doted on Rosanne and couldn't do enough for us. One day we encountered a huge school of porpoises that leapt and danced around the ship for several minutes. Flying fish sped along beside us—some of them could skim along the top of the water for 50 yards (45 m).

We arrived at Luanda, Angola, at 10.00 p.m. The lights of the city looked beautiful on the water. There was no berth available for the ship, so we sat in the harbour all next morning. I tried my hand at fishing, and caught one fish, which I gave to the cook for lunch. From the ship we could see a number of armed Portuguese police patrolling the area, but very few Africans. Many of the buildings around the waterfront were quite modern and presented a fine view of a city built beside the sea. It looked quite a peaceful place, except for the four Portuguese frigates in the harbour. Agitation for independence had not yet begun in earnest. We berthed at 6.00 p.m. and scores of Africans came aboard to unload and load cargo while the captain went to a bullfight.

We crossed the equator on 4th March at 10.00 p.m. and arrived at Port Harcourt, Nigeria, the next day. The ship turned into the mouth of the great Niger River, which seemed like a gap along the shoreline. After a short distance we stopped to pick up the river pilot. It appeared to be an uninhabited part of the delta as there were only mangrove swamps to be seen.

The small white pilot boat was waiting for us in mid-river and the pilot climbed aboard. He would guide us the 31 miles (50 km) up river to the port. Suddenly a long canoe powered by an outboard motor emerged from the mangroves and sped toward us. Another twenty canoes soon appeared, raced to the ship and surrounded the stern. They had come to buy cigarettes and whisky from the Chinese crew.

The crewmembers would let down a basket on a rope and demand US$200 for a case of whisky. Up would come a bundle of money and down would go the whisky. They sold about 200 cases and lots of cigarettes, which they would have bought duty free in Hong Kong. It was all over in about 10 minutes. There was a strange subdued silence at supper that night. The captain was plainly embarrassed about the smuggling operation, but for whatever reason he had allowed it to occur.

By morning a great army of dockworkers had invaded the ship. There were six fine looking cranes on the wharf but the harbourmaster told us that none of them were in working order. 'They refused to maintain them.' He was the last surviving European on the harbour staff and he was looking forward to retirement. Our immediate impression was that West Africa was certainly quite different from the Africa we had known in the South.

The area around the wharf was very dirty, with rubbish lying all over the place. We crossed a small bridge on which the following notice was displayed: 'Don't urinate here.' There were several men standing on the bridge calmly ignoring the entreaty. I had just explained to Lorraine that the majority tribe in Eastern Nigeria was the Ibo tribe (pronounced eebows). 'Iboes,' she exclaimed, 'more like Peeboes!'

We left Port Harcourt at 10.30 p.m. and, once out in the river, again picked up the pilot. After waiting a while for him to appear, the captain sent a small boat ashore to wake the pilot up and bring him back to the ship. Later, when we dropped him off again at the area near the river mouth, there was no sign of the smugglers.

It only took a day to travel the 390 miles (627 km) to Lagos. As in Luanda, there was no berth available at the Apapa docks, so we anchored out at sea in a queue of three ships. There we bobbed about for three days, by which time nine ships were waiting for a place at the docks.

Our ship berthed at Apapa docks at 9.30 a.m. on Tuesday 9th March, and thus began our sojourn in Nigeria. It took all day to clear immigration and customs, although the kindly officer in charge decided that we ought not to pay any duty.

Ross Manning, an Australian, Business Manager, of the Bible Societies in West Africa, met us at the wharf. While we were still aboard, he shouted up to us, 'Boy, am I glad to see you. Now I can go home for furlough!' Fortunately he didn't go until July, which gave me time to settle in before he left.

It took one and a half hours to drive the 7 miles (11 km) from the wharf to the home of the Mannings. It was 92° F (33° C) and almost maximum humidity. Our first impression of Lagos, according to my diary entry, was, 'Crowds and crowds of people like Bombay when it comes to density. Hundreds of trucks, cars, and cycles—the roads jammed all the time. Everyone is trying to sell something.'

We spent the first night at the Bible Society's house in an enclave of about 50 houses called Palm Grove. It was an oasis of calm in a frenetic city, a real haven, with a high concrete wall around it to keep out the undesirables. When evening came, the night watchmen appeared—one for each house. I wondered about the general security in a country where each house needed a night watchman.

Our luggage was stored for the night in a seven-room flat that had been rented for us up the street from the Mannings. The next morning was spent obtaining a drivers licence. At face value, that seemed like a simple enough thing to do—but not in Lagos. It was a full day's work. First of all there was an hour and a half drive through the traffic. Then a run through a gauntlet of form-filling offers from young men whose work seemed to be helping illiterates obtain licences.

The office was crowded with men seated on low benches all around the room. There were long queues at each service window and much talking and shouting. Fortunately there was a special window for foreigners and we were dealt with quite quickly and efficiently. Then, there was a two-hour drive through the congested roads all the way home.

I had a local workshop clear the Mini through customs and register it for Nigeria. This process usually took three to five days and was best left to the locals. The insurance premium staggered me—the annual charge was the equivalent of one third of the car's value!

Later that afternoon, I went to our flat and discovered that it had been broken into. Mattresses, our typewriter, an 8mm-movie projector, a film editing machine, a notebook of sermons in English and Bemba, Lorraine's Oxford loose-leaf Bible and one suitcase were missing. We had two Rawleigh sample cases that were identical. One contained items of no real consequence—just dirty clothes and toilet gear. But the other was very precious. It contained most of our best slides of Northern Rhodesia, including 200 taken just before we left and complete reports of my work, including a newly written staff training course, and my special Bible.

After graduating from the Bible Training Institute (now Laidlaw College), I purchased the best quality Bible available. It was an Oxford wide margin to which I added many notes, maps and a concordance. Everything I had ever learned, I noted in that Bible. There was nothing more important or precious to me, apart from my family. I held my breath. I could hardly bear to open the remaining suitcase that had been left behind by the thieves, to see which of the two identical cases it was. I gingerly unlocked it and stared in disbelief at the dirty clothes. None of the night watchmen had heard or seen anything!

Though it took me many weeks to get over the loss of my precious Bible, a few months later I began to realise that it had been for the good. It meant that I had to restudy the Scriptures anew, and not depend upon previous studies. Just at this time the American Bible Society had published the Good News New Testament in Today's English Version. Because I had to use English as a second language in West Africa, the simpler English in this version suited my audience better.

My official Bible Society title was Circulation Manager for the Bible Societies in West Africa serving Nigeria, Dahomey (now Benin), Togo and consultant to Ghana. This was a new post so I had no one to follow. Apart from Ross Manning, the Business Manager, the other key person was the General Secretary, an Englishman named Rev. Leslie Taylor. Within six months I had taken over both positions because Taylor was on sick leave in England, and Manning had headed home as planned on a six-month furlough.

I had received no instruction from the BFBS Head Office in London regarding how the local Bible Society work would function while Manning and Taylor were absent, so I assumed responsibility for both their positions, plus my own. I wrote to head office and told them what I was doing. 'You're in charge,' said Ross before he left, 'here are the cheque books.'

Thus I became Acting General Secretary, Acting Business Manager and Circulation Manager. I know this situation sounds strange to us today, but at that time, when communication was so slow, the policy of the BFBS was to give their agents a free hand and full responsibility to run the work in the most appropriate way. We didn't even have budgets to work to—only something called 'estimates'.

The first task I set myself was to make a careful study of sales from the previous two years. I was puzzled that, although there was said to be such a hunger for the Scriptures, the Bible Society's sales were only 250,012 volumes of bound books of Scripture in the previous year. That didn't seem enough for a population of 55,000,000 (even with a 50 percent Muslim population). I asked to see the sales ledgers for the last two years and set about analysing them. Then I decided to test the market for myself.

One evening, on the way home from the office, I stopped at a small roadside market and produced a few Gospel Portions. When the people saw them they showed immediate interest and I sold all 105 copies in 30 minutes. This was very exciting, so I decided to do a real test. I collected 1,000 Gospels from the storeroom and drove to the nearest market in Ebuta Metta.

I folded down the rear door of the Holden station wagon I used for Bible work, and offered the books for sale. Market women crowded around to see what this white man was selling. The British and Foreign Bible Society had announced a new program for Africa called 'The Million Gospel Campaign'. Gospels were to be sold for one penny each. So I offered my 1,000 gospels at this price—the same price as one orange at that time.

The people pushed and shoved, and I sold them as fast as I could take the money. They knew what they were buying. 'These are parts of the Bible,' I shouted, 'English and Yoruba.' I sold 960 gospels in one and half-hours. The crowd had become so boisterous I stopped selling before the stock was exhausted because I feared trouble. People surrounded the vehicle, pressing in from every side. When I got into the driver's seat, I took the last 40 copies with me. As I prepared to drive away, I wound down the window, threw the booklets into the air, and shouted, 'These ones are free!' The people dived for them and not one copy hit the ground before it was snatched up. In the ensuing milieu around that side of the station wagon, a path opened up in the crowd for me to drive through and get away.

This was the first of many such experiences. So I wrote to the BFBS and told them that the Million Gospel Campaign for Africa could be a million just for Nigeria.

The first missionaries to Nigeria arrived from Jamaica in 1842, and Nigerians accepted the message of Christianity with great gusto. Within 120 years, half the population were Christian of some sort or other, divided into 860 denominations. (These have multiplied several times over the years since the 1960s.) They range from the ultra conservative to the blatantly unscriptural.

In a one mile (1.6 km) section of a road in Eastern Nigeria I counted 40 different denominations that were within sight of the road. We had to be very careful with the names of churches when sending mail. For example, 'Churches of Christ' was a different group to 'The Churches of Christ'. 'Church of the Christ' was not the same as 'The Church of The Christ.' Not a mile from our house in Lagos was a very large building emblazoned with 'IMMANUEL' in large white letters. I was intrigued, and went to visit. I was met at the door by some men who said they were apostles of Jesus Christ. They showed the way to their leader who, I was assured, was the Son of God. He was upstairs and as I climbed the stairs, the ceiling came down very low so that I had to bend over to fit. A large Yoruba man dressed in expensive traditional clothes met me and welcomed me into his presence. He introduced himself as Jesus Christ and quickly began to explain that he was indeed Emmanuel, which means 'God with us'. He had returned to earth to establish his kingdom. 'When you came up my stairs you had to bend down low and that was to fulfil my prophecy when the Bible says, "every knee will bow".'

To describe the room in which I met him as 'opulent' would be an understatement. It was furnished with the most expensive and luxurious furniture imaginable. Two huge chandeliers glittered like diamonds, a grandfather clock was gold plated, the floor covered with Persian carpets. The curtains and drapes were flecked with gold and the finest ornaments of every description completed the décor.

The man who would be Jesus Christ rambled on and on, sometimes speaking in a quiet soothing voice and then shouting and roaring like a mad man, his eyes filled with hostility and hatred. Then he would suddenly became calm and gentle again. 'You have seen my bread shops,' he said, referring to a chain of shops he owned around town. 'They are called the Son of God Bread of Life shops. That's because I am the Bread of Life.

When I came the first time, I had nowhere to lay my head, nowhere to sleep, but now I am enjoying all the fruits of my world.'

'I saw many women downstairs, do they belong to your group?' I asked.

'Of course they belong, they belong to me. They are my women. They cook and clean and comfort me. I need many women to do that.'

I have to admit that he knew the Bible well and quoted many passages as examples of the way he was fulfilling the prophesies of the return of Jesus Christ. He threw his arms about, fingers laden with gold and diamond rings, his powerful voice exclaiming that he was God's son returned to earth to claim his kingdom. But I felt I was in the presence of evil.

When I showed him a range of Yoruba Bibles, he chose a dozen of the most expensive gilt-edge leather ones. I had to listen to him for an hour before I could escape from his presence.

A few months later when travelling in Eastern Nigeria, I came across another man who also claimed to be Jesus Christ. He lived in a small village in an oil palm plantation. His 'apostles' took me to meet him in an upstairs room—this one was the opposite of the one in Lagos. His home was relatively poorly furnished and he was very quiet. He patiently explained in a soft voice that he was the fulfilment of the prophecy that the Son of God would return to earth and that he was the one. He also admitted that most of his followers were women but he had 12 male apostles.

In the other extreme, there were many fine evangelical churches that were faithful to the teachings of the Bible. Missions like the Qua Ibo Mission, Sudan Interior Mission and the Sudan United Mission. They had built many schools, hospitals and Bible schools in Nigeria. The Anglicans also had a number of schools, some of which conducted three school sessions a day—the equivalent of having three schools in one building, providing education to several thousand children.

One evening, before Ross Manning had left for furlough, we had dinner with him and his wife, Chris. They told us of an unusual problem with the local auxiliary of the Bible Society who had a tendency to organise meetings and speakers without informing the people concerned. Sure enough, a few months later, on a Monday morning, I was walking along the footpath near the Bible Society office when I noticed a pink poster on a lamppost with my name on it in large letters. It advertised a harvest festival service at a nearby evangelical church and stated that I was to be the preacher for the event. I looked at the date. It was for yesterday, and I had never heard a word about it!

As I analysed Scripture sales over the previous two years I noticed that bookshops, mostly owned by Muslims, sold more complete Bibles than all the Christian missions and churches sold of Bibles, New Testaments and Portions. True to form in the great West African market cash economy, the Muslim traders always paid cash.

So I decided to visit some of these shops. First of all I called upon Aladipo's Bookshop. He was not a regular customer and most of his stock was communist books mostly on sale at 6 pence each because that was a time when the communists had flooded Africa with their literature. Mr Aladipo bought a dozen Bibles from me. I called on many bookshops located along narrow streets with open drains of dirty water along each side. Drains should read sewers because they were filled to overflowing with liquid filth of all descriptions. I spent several days visiting these shops.

On Lagos Island, in one day, I sold 1,000 Bibles for cash. One shop, that was only as wide as two doors and about three metres deep was a long-standing customer of the Bible Society, selling many thousands of Bibles a year.

These traders gave us a lot of problems because they would never keep their prices consistent. When there was a plentiful supply available, they would sell their stock below the standard selling price of 6/6 (six shillings and six pence), but when the Bible Society ran out and stock became scarce, they would boost their prices to as much as three times the standard price. Because the Bible was a required textbook in the numerous Christian schools in Nigeria, it was always easy to sell to these bookshops that stood to make a tidy profit.

Everything was based on supply and demand. If a trader caught wind that a history textbook, for example, was likely to become scarce, he would unload his other stock at below cost price in order to buy up the textbook in question and then sell it at inflated prices. I heard of one fellow based in London who kept his eye on the publishing industry in the United Kingdom and telephoned his cousin in Lagos, alerting him of impending shortages.

Selling Bibles was hard work in the heat and humidity of Lagos. Because of the congested streets and lack of parking spaces, it was often necessary to walk long distances with a heavy sample case when visiting a bookshop or minister. The footpaths were always clogged with small stores and salespeople of all kinds.

Everyone was selling something. You could buy almost anything on the footpath—from a single aspirin tablet or single matchstick, to an empty cardboard box, coat hangers, or wooden clothes pegs. One day I found two fellows selling a small hand Platen printing press.

After a month in Nigeria, I wrote a missive that I called 'a first impressions letter' to supporters, friends and family at home:

Before leaving Northern Rhodesia we often wondered why we were asked to help in the work in Nigeria, as it seemed so far away and out of the ChiBemba language area. We have been here long enough to understand.

There is more scope for Scripture distribution here than we could possibly have imagined. Let us illustrate it in this way. When working as a missionary in Ndola, concentrating on literature work, in seven months I sold 600 Bibles and New Testaments and 12,000 Scripture Portions. We felt that this was a reasonable effort.

In Nigeria in four hours I sold 2,243 Gospel Portions out on a street and in a school. The first seven ministers I met that day bought a total of 3,125 Gospel Portions. That is a total of 5,368.

This paragraph will be difficult to write. We want to try and describe this great city of Lagos—but it is almost beyond our powers of description. It is quite different from East, South or Central Africa. The women wear the national costume, which appears to consist of many yards of material swathed around them. The majority of men wear outfits that look like a pair of pyjama trousers and a long robe with large sleeves plus a squashed looking fez hat.

Almost every woman is a trader selling everything from vegetables to used cardboard cartons. The narrow streets are jammed with tiny stalls and shops selling every commodity under the sun.

Nigeria has been an independent country for four years and so the Government, public administration and all public services are in the complete charge of Nigerians. The result is that everything is done their way, and that's fair enough since it is their country. The health department building is in one of the suburbs and is now a most unhealthy looking place.

The people are very friendly and helpful at all times. They are more straightforward than those of Southern Africa. We have met some very fine folk among them.

It was the traffic that intrigued us most of all. There are thousands of cars on the road and the streets are narrow. Buses and trucks hoot and roar their way through the traffic. They handle seven-ton trucks, as though were Minis. There appears to be one rule of the road that is more or less followed—keep to the left—but even so one cannot presume that everyone will do this. There are a large number of one-way streets but only very few are marked as such.

At a traffic light vehicles will form extra lanes even along the footpath and out on the wrong side of the road. When the lights turn green what was supposed to be two lanes of traffic facing each other would have become three or even four lanes. With this happening on both sides of the intersection there is an almighty mix up as four lanes approaching each other try to form two again each way as they all race to find a passage down the road.

It wasn't long before Lorraine decided that she didn't want to drive the Mini in Lagos traffic. I think what unnerved her the most was a large articulated lorry in front of us that tried to reverse around a roundabout and only by taking evasive action were we prevented from ending up under its tray. The traffic was constantly referred to in any conversation. My diary has many entries like the only entry for 15th June 1966: 'Large tanker overturned and was on it's back at Ikorodu Road roundabout this morning.'

Thirty years later the situation hadn't improved very much as the following excerpt from a New Zealand newspaper suggests:

The Levin Chronicle Autoline supplement of 18th December 1992 carried an article about Nigeria's infamous road conditions, which quoted the Nigerian Economist Weekly. It reminded readers that 'in addition to the dreadful killer AIDS that abounds in Africa these days, in Nigeria there is another one. It is called RAIDS i.e. Road Accidents Immune Delusion Syndrome. There are 240 road deaths a year to every 10,000 people in Nigeria. There are only three in Japan and slightly more in the USA. This means there are about 10,000 deaths a year.

'The aftermath of at least 30 recent accidents, from burning cars to upturned tanker lorries can be seen on the average day along the 600 km road between Lagos and the nation's new capital, Abuja,' concluded the article.

While on the subject of traffic, the mammy-wagons of Nigeria deserve a mention. A mammy-wagon is a lorry converted into a bus. A roof is built over the tray and a series of wooden planks set cross-wise. Passengers sit on these with their backs to the front, probably, as one writer put it, 'to prevent heart seizure when they see what the driver is up to'.

The driver usually sits half out of the door and steers with his left hand—or used to when we were there. In the years after we departed, Nigeria changed its road code and made everyone drive on the right hand side. Some missionaries told us that they stayed indoors for a week after the changeover for fear of drivers with short memories.

The mammy-wagons were usually painted in bright colours and to the first time visitor, appear to be driven by very spiritual people. As part of their decoration, many display saintly statements, such as, 'One with God is a Majority'. Or, 'God Forgave My Sin'. Plus there are a few others with meanings that may not be so apparent to the stranger: 'Man Must Whack', 'No Telephone to Heaven', 'Into Thy Hands'.

Only the most daring driver would try to overtake a mammy-wagon. It is said that some drivers purchase their licences rather than sit the appropriate tests. They keep themselves going by chewing stimulating kola nuts. I remember reading a criticism of them in a Lagos newspaper, which ran, 'The mammy-wagon is the cheapest means of transport in Nigeria—as a great many people on their way to heaven have found out.'

Lagos is only seven degrees north of the equator and, being at sea level, experiences extreme heat. Our first letter home states:

Our thermometer has not gone below 86 degrees F (30° C) since we have been here. It is just hot and humid all the time with a temperature drop of only five degrees during the night. Of course it's not the high temperature that makes it unpleasant but the continuous high humidity that enervates both body and mind. Office hours here are from 8.00 a.m. to 2.30 p.m. and that's long enough without air conditioning.

The morning that Chris Manning left for furlough, we prepared to go to the airport to see her off. I went to the garage behind our flat, unlocked the door, and behold there was no car. I reported the loss to the local police and they assiduously took all the details. I told them it would be easy to find, as this was only red and white Holden station wagon in the country.

'Have you a Bible for me?' asked the officer in charge.

'You recover my car and I'll give you a Bible.'

The police came and questioned our houseboy, or 'steward' as he preferred to be called, and charged him for disorderly behaviour. It appeared he was involved with the theft. The steward of the house next door told the police that our steward and a man called Thomas had taken the car. For over an hour, our steward strenuously denied knowing a man called Thomas. Then, as he was taken away, he quietly asked me, 'Has my friend Thomas been to see you with a letter?' He confessed to the police, after 24 hours in custody, that he and another steward named Thomas had taken the car out late one night the previous week. The night watch had slept through it all.

Two days later, a missionary friend phoned to say that he had seen my car on its side about 30 miles (48 km) to the north, beside the one and only road out of Lagos. It was missing two wheels. It must have been a spectacular accident because across the road from it was a truck loaded with timber upside down and a mammy-wagon also lay on its roof nearby.

After I identified that it was indeed my vehicle, I reported the find to the police. The officer's laconic response was, 'Our patrols must have passed it many times but they didn't see it.' That was his way of saying, 'Because you didn't dash me (give me something) we didn't see it.'

This 'dash' business takes some getting used to. It's best described as a service charge paid before the service is given—a kind of incentive. A patient in a government hospital is expected to dash the nurse when asking for a bedpan. It may never be taken away if he doesn't! A lot of foreigners consider it a bribe, but these same people wouldn't dream of not tipping their waiter back home.

Lorraine had a regular caller at the house—Rebecca, the vegetable vendor. Rebecca was a huge woman, probably close to 300lbs (136 kg) and about six feet (1.8 m) tall. She carried a large white enamel bowl on her head which, when filled with all manner of vegetables, must have weighed at least 100lbs (45 kg.). She could place it on the ground by herself but couldn't lift it up to her head without assistance.

When she first started coming to our back door, she brought a beautiful range of good veggies. As time went by though, the quality deteriorated because she came later in the day when the best had been sold. Then we discovered that Lorraine was no longer offered the best vegetables because she didn't encourage Rebecca with a tot of whisky or gin.

Another interesting character, who called at our house once a month, was the hairdresser. The first time he came, he presented his letter of credentials and testimonials from various important people such as magistrates and the Provincial Governor of the Colonial times. The hairdresser's official title was 'Mr Henry Aladipo Q.R.M.H.G. (Qualified Registered Member of Hair Dressers Guild.) having successfully completed a correspondence course'.

The other thing that took a lot of getting used to was the unrelenting noise in Lagos. In a letter home to New Zealand Lorraine wrote:

Just now these are all the noises I can hear. First of all we have a huge fan that hangs from the ceiling in our lounge. It is making a whirring noise. Somebody out side is laughing, a train whistles nearby, a truck has gone by at quite a speed, there is a radio playing, cars hooting away, somebody is doing the dishes in the flat below, even a dog with a bell around it neck goes by, there are crickets and other insects letting us know that they are truly alive, and always you can hear people talking, some in their houses, or walking on the street and the watchmen get together for a chat. One never spends a quiet evening here.

At sundown the night watchman came on duty. Called a 'watchnight' in local English, this old fellow was armed with a substantial wooden staff. At intervals throughout the night he would pound the staff on the concrete path to assure everyone that he was awake. Other watchnights along the street would pound their sticks in answer. This hourly commotion was supposed to be reassuring, not disturbing. Later, when living in Eastern Nigeria, our nightwatch was armed with a bow and poisoned arrows. Many are the stories that people told of their watchnights. One night, before retiring, I checked on a new man we had hired and found him asleep. I woke him up and told him that he wasn't paid to sleep. When he declared he wasn't sleeping I said, 'But I could hear you snoring.'

'Oh sir, I wasn't sleeping, only snoring.'

One night he came to me complaining of stomach pains and asked for a laxative. Many Nigerians believe that the best form of medicine is a good strong laxative—the more bitter the taste, the more efficacious the medicine is considered to be. I got out my bottle of Rawleighs liniment. This, taken internally with sugar, was my father's remedy for a tummy upset. So I prepared a good dose, a quarter of a teaspoon, with a lot of sugar in some warm water, and gave it to him. It nearly blew his head off. When he had regained his breath, he thanked me profusely for this wonderful medicine that he felt sure would have an immediate effect. It worked!

Nothing drove people round the bend faster than the Nigerian telephone system. One reporter wrote that a telephone in Nigeria is 'a gadget for recording silence', and that's certainly all we got much of the time.

People had all sorts of theories as to how to get a connection. I watched one Englishman in our house demonstrate his method. He would dial each number and a split second before it reached the completion of the dial, he'd let it go. His technique didn't work on ours. Perhaps it had something to do with the fact that the telephone cables along our street had been dug up. The cables needed to be repaired so often that the workmen decided it would be easiest to just leave them exposed, ready for the next time work had to be done.

With my combined roles of Acting General Secretary, Acting Business Manager and Circulation Manager, I was very busy. I decided I didn't have time to type my own letters as my managerial predecessors had done, so I hired a secretary. Just at the right moment, a young Yoruba lad named Godfrey came to the office looking for work. He was one of the six or seven that called every day in the hope of finding employment. He was a law student and was a brilliant typist with extremely fast and neat shorthand. It was possible for him to take dictation for two days straight. He would sit there in front of my desk, his face a picture of concentration as he peered through his dark horn-rimmed glasses at his shorthand pad. After a couple of days of catching up on this administrative work, I would leave him to type the notes up while I went on the road. On returning a few days later, all the letters would be done perfectly and ready for signing. I never had another secretary like him.

The Bible Societies have long advocated the translation of the Bible into as many languages as possible. Over the years, a great deal of knowledge and experience has been collected. A team of specialist consultants has been established and is available to churches and missions all over the world.

But in the 1960s this service was still in its infancy, which meant that many translators worked on their own without access to specialist help.

One day, a group of four men visited me in Lagos and placed on my desk the manuscripts of the four gospels in their mother tongue. They were from a small tribe in the east and proudly told me that they had worked on one gospel each. The first question to ask was concerning the translations and languages they had used as their sources. It turned out that they had each used only one English translation. Two had used the King James Version, one the Revised Version and another the Revised Standard Version. They hadn't collaborated on the spelling of proper nouns such as 'Jerusalem'. I made a quick check on how they spelt Jesus. They had transliterated his name in four different ways—'Yesu', 'Yesus', 'Jesus' and 'Jesu'. We had a translation consultant, Dr Bill Reyburn, based in Jos, Northern Nigeria, so I asked him to meet them.

A few days later, the six of us met together and the men discussed some of the problems they had. One of them said, 'Dis god he make sum ting, so he be woman.' With this logic in mind, he had translated the Lord's Prayer as 'Our mother in heaven'. So Bill had to correct that. They don't have bread in their culture, so that presented another problem. Also there were a number of instances where they had misunderstood the 17th century English from which they were translating. One of the men using the Authorised Version (KJV) came unstuck with the fourth word of the gospel that reads, 'The book of the *generation* of Jesus Christ.' He couldn't understand how Jesus Christ could make electricity!

The fourth largest ethnic group in Nigeria is the Tiv. At that time they numbered about two million and, as a result of the work of the Dutch Reformed Church Mission of South Africa, many had become Christians. This mission set about translating the Bible into the Tiv language and I received a message to pay them a visit in order to arrange the production of their first full Bible in Tiv. The family I stayed with had a strong evangelical faith and read a chapter of the Bible at the table after each meal. The translation committee presented me with the manuscript of the Tiv Bible with a request that we print 50,000 copies. I explained to them that as a rule, we do not print a large first edition of a new Bible. Despite well-intentioned proof reading, mistakes can slip through, so it's best to print, say, 10,000 the first time, then after attending to any corrections, do a large run. The Bible Society had a major say in this because we were offering to subsidise the Bible by about 50 percent. However the translation committee were insistent that the manuscript was perfect. It had been carefully checked and it was 100 percent pure. My response was, 'It's our experience that no manuscript is ever perfect.' They were insistent and told me that each of the five translators had checked and rechecked everything. They would not believe that proofreading is an entirely different skill to translating and writing.

'Please print us 50,000,' they said, 'It's on us.' I relented and duly placed the order.

When a new Bible is issued for the first time, the usual practice is to produce a few specially bound copies for the translators, plus a quantity of unsubsidised luxury leather bindings. The committee ordered 500 of these. I then had to explain that apart from the special ones for the translators, the luxury leather binding should be done in the second printing after any errors had been eradicated. Again they stuck to their guns and insisted on having the luxury ones done immediately.

Several months later, the Tiv Bible arrived from the printers in England and I had the privilege of attending the celebrations. A huge crowd gathered for this monumental occasion. It was a time of great rejoicing. That evening, my host read Luke chapter 15 from the new translation. He read the story of the lost sheep, which went like this: 'If any man has ninety-nine sheep and loses one of them, would he not leave the ninety-nine, go out and look for the one that is lost?' He paused and thought about it, then read it again. Something was wrong, that didn't sound right. He looked at it again. 'Oh my goodness,' he exclaimed, 'look at this!' It says here, 'If any man has ninety-nine sheep and loses one. That should be one hundred, not ninety-nine! He had one hundred!' The first print run sold out within 20 days, carrying 50,000 replications of that mistake.

Eventually Ross Manning was appointed General Secretary and that meant I could get on with my own job as Circulation Manager. After he returned from furlough, I was asked to move to Eastern Nigeria and concentrate on building up the work there. So that I could travel freely,

I was provided with a new Taunus Van that had been converted into a caravan, complete with bed, cupboards, cooking and washing facilities. It performed a dreadful bucking motion whenever we hit a bump in the road, but at least it gave me independence. Because of poor communications, it wasn't always possible to advise people that I planned to visit them. With my van, I could turn up at any time and not be an embarrassment to the hostess who didn't have the spare bed ready.

Now and again the police would find me sleeping in a quiet place in the forest and check up on me. One time they woke me at 5.30 a.m. and told me to report to the police station later that morning. When they found an Esso Oil Company road map in the vehicle they said that they were very suspicious of me.

'Why do you have a road map?'

'Because I do not know all the roads in your country.'

'Why do you want to know all the roads?'

'Well I don't need to know all the roads, but when I travel at least I can find my way.'

'Why do you come on this road?'

'Because I want to visit some Ogoni villages and sell the people some New Testaments in their language.'

'Ogoni! Ogoni! You have a book in Ogoni? Ogoni are stupid people, they don't read. I don't believe you. Show me an Ogoni book. It is a camera that you have not an Ogoni book.'

The police officer nearly threw the New Testament onto the ground in disgust. 'Ogonis! All you'll find there is smelly fish, dirty women and drunken men. Go.'

I went to the vehicle and produced a New Testament in his own language. 'Ah a Bible, a Bible for me! How wonderful. Now please you go to the Ogonis, maybe God speak Ogoni to them in their Bible.'

We moved to the city of Enugu in the southeast of Nigeria, and rented a house in Aria Road, which turned out to be a street where several missionary families lived. Our home was a brand new three-storey place with plenty of room for an office and storeroom. The problem was, there was no furniture available in the shops. I found a furniture maker who would build to order. The only wood he used was the local Sapeli mahogany. He made me a large double pedestal writing desk and then covered it with mahogany Formica! Two men carried it about four kilometres on their heads, all the way from the workshop to my house. I could hardly lift up one side. The furniture maker also made us beds of solid mahogany and covered the headboards with Formica as well. The final piece was a Formica covered mahogany dining room table.

I was having such success in selling the Scriptures in Nigeria that soon the BFBS head office was asking for photographs of the work, but I couldn't find a local photographer. The office asked so often that eventually I decided I'd better learn photography myself if I was to get any peace. Ashley Tuck, a New Zealander, had joined the SIM mission organisation as a photographer, and was currently employed as a printer at the Challenge Press in Lagos. He was only too willing to teach me black and white processing and the basics of photojournalism. He and his wife Daphne gave up some of their holidays and came to stay with us in Enugu. Through much trial and error, I learned to photograph everything that came my way. The kitchen became the film development laboratory and the bathroom was my darkroom. I bought a 400-foot (122 m) length of film from Kodak, cut it up into cassette lengths myself and set about becoming a serious photographer. I took my camera everywhere and photographed everything that moved. My Bible work took me all over the country. I always did my own driving and, as often as not, travelled alone. This meant I could stop anywhere, at any time, to take photographs.

I sent my first batch of pictures to London in 1966. In 1989, after becoming the United Bible Societies Photojournalist in the newly formed World Service Centre in Reading, England, I had a visitor from the BFBS. He had come looking for black and white photos of Africa. 'You're not going to believe this,' he said, pulling a folder from his bag, 'but the only decent pictures we have of African faces are these three and they are dated 1974.'

'The dates are wrong,' said I, 'They were taken in 1966.'

He looked at me curiously, 'How do you know, you don't mean to say that you took them?'

The travelling was always fun, although it was often a little dangerous. On one occasion in the north, travelling on a relatively good road, I came up a small rise at about 60 mph through a small village and down a hill that curved to the left. Ahead was a one-lane bridge with a truck in the middle of it, travelling towards me. The truck was heavily laden and moving slowly. There was no way I could stop and had to make the decision whether to try for the bridge, slipping in behind the truck as it cleared the crossing or going straight into the river. The two choices flashed through my mind and I had to decide what to do. Going into the river would be disastrous, no question. The alternative was to hope the truck cleared the bridge in time, but it was an enormous risk. I'd either hit the truck or the bridge or both which, at that speed, would be curtains for me, or just squeeze through provided I'd straighten up to cross the bridge safely. It was the gravest situation I have ever been in when driving.

I decided to have a go at the bridge. How I managed it I'll never know, except to believe that guardian angels were there to prevent me hitting the side of the bridge after missing the truck. In my mind to this day, I can still see the look on the truck driver's face as I came at him down that hill. I was so shaken that I pulled up and rested for a while until my heart slowed down and hands stopped quivering.

After some time, I became dissatisfied with the results of my black and white photography—the pictures didn't have the punch and sparkle I was after. Ash advised me to use a yellow lens filter. In black and white photography, the trick is in how the colours are translated onto the black and white film. A yellow filter helps to darken the effect of blue, making the sky look more vivid in black and white. I spent a few days holiday on the Miango plateau photographing everything I could find—the trees and rocks and the few people that were about. Someone told me of a village where the people were quite different from the other tribes in the area. They were the astonishing 'duck-billed' people.

The story goes that in the days when the tribe was troubled by slavers, the women tried to disfigure themselves by placing objects in the lower lips. The custom continued, giving the women their distinctive look. I was welcomed into the village quite happily, and I discovered them to be the most primitive people I had ever seen.

The women wore few clothes. Some had well-used monkey skins wrapped around them in which to carry babies. A tuft of grass fore and aft served as a skirt, while the men for the most part wore European shorts. The women also wore hats made of solid mud, caked onto the hair.

A girl of about eight years approached me and showed me her lower lip. I think she was proud to be on the way to becoming a woman. A small stick, about the size of a matchstick, was stuck through her lower lip. As she became older this would be replaced with one a little thicker until she was able to wear a three or four inch thick plate, or cross-section of a tree branch. Some of the teenage girls had graduated to a cross section of maize stalk.

These embellishments didn't stop the women talking, and they chatted away to me, demanding a shilling each for their photographs. Local missionaries said that a National Geographic Magazine team had paid them all a pound each and thus upped the going rate from what used to be a few pennies. They appeared to have no modern implements except an old knife. No pots, pans or spoons—truly still in the Stone Age.

One day, I received a letter from a Sunday school in a very small town in New Zealand called Pio Pio. They had sent me ten dollars to 'buy food for starving children'. At that time there weren't any starving children that I knew about so I decided to spend the money on some 'Bread of Life' for children who weren't getting any.

I had heard of a school for blind children in Lagos, called the Paceli School, that was run by Roman Catholic sisters. So I went along to see if they would be interested in some Braille Scriptures. This was before the days of Vatican Two (which allowed Roman Catholics to own a Bible of their own) and we were usually given a short shrift by Catholic institutions.

With a certain amount of apprehension, I knocked on the office door of the sister-in-charge. She welcomed me warmly and I showed her the Braille Gospel of Matthew that I had brought along. I explained that I would like to donate some Bible Portions to the school library as well as to individual children. She was delighted. 'An angel has sent you. This is a wonderful gift!'

'You misunderstand me Sister, I would like to give all the children a book each as well as a complete Bible for the library.'

'Wonderful, when can you bring them?'

Thinking that I'd better strike while the iron was hot, I suggested the next day. 'No that would be too soon. We must prepare ourselves and we'll have a little party and you can present them all one by one.'

'That would be very nice Sister, but don't you think we should check to see if the children can understand this book? It's the old Authorised Version of the English Bible in Grade 2 Braille.'

'That is no problem, these children speak English here and some have been here for many years.'

Just at that moment a boy was passing by her office and she called him in. He was quite tall, totally blind with one eye half-protruding from its socket. The eyeball was red and looked sore.

The sister handed him the Gospel of Matthew and said, 'Solomon what is this?'

He felt it carefully and said, 'It's a book.'

'Yes of course it's a book. Read it. Read it boy.'

Solomon turned the book over slowly found the front cover and opened to the title page and began reading. 'The Gospel of Matthew from the Bible, published by the British and . . .'

'Read the book boy,' said the sister, 'That's just the first page.'

Solomon turned over a few pages and put his fingers on the page and, without pausing, read aloud, 'The people which sat in darkness saw a great light; and to them that sat in the region and shadow of death light is sprung up.' He looked up his face beaming, 'Sister, this is a wonderful book.'

The sister was deeply moved, and so was I. 'You must come next Friday and we will receive you out on the lawn. Truly an angel has sent you. Thank you so much.'

I turned up on the Friday with my vehicle loaded to the roof with Braille Portions of Scripture. The ten dollars from New Zealand wasn't enough to pay for one book, but I was using the opportunity to donate all that we had in stock as a free gift. The whole school was assembled on the lawn, buzzing with excitement. The sister made a speech, mentioning angels several times and then, trying to be as angelic as possible, I presented each child with a book of the Bible in Braille. As soon as a book was received, the child would sit down and immediately begin to read. As is the usual custom, they read aloud. Soon there was a hum of voices reading from all parts of the Bible at once. I could hear bits of Isaiah and Jeremiah, Genesis chapter one and Revelation. A couple had books of the Psalms and one fellow had Matthew and was gamely having a go at the long genealogy with which that book begins. You know the one: 'And Adam begat Aminadab; and Aminadab begat Naason; and Naason begat Salmon . . .'

About a year later, I met an English lady who taught blind children. She was very excited and began to tell me that she had just come from the Paceli School for the Blind. 'I think all those children are Christians,' she said. 'They certainly are all reading the Bible and loving it.' She went on to explain that the sister in charge said that since the children began reading the Bible they had changed completely. The only fights they had now were boys squabbling over what books they were going to read next.

We, (and we were now four as Clive was born in February - Lorraine along with Rosanne had gone ahead for his birth in New Zealand) were due to leave Nigeria in a few weeks on transfer to the South Pacific, so I went along to the school to see for myself. The sister was overjoyed and could not express her gratitude fully enough at the way the Bible had changed the whole school. She insisted that I return on a particular date when the school would put on a farewell party for me.

It was some party! It consisted of a two-hour concert just for me. The kids sang songs and read poems about the Bible. The boys gave a dramatic and enthusiastic performance of the Good Samaritan parable—especially the part where the robbers attack the traveller. It was all a touching and eloquent way of saying thank you to the Bible Society and to that little Sunday School in Pio Pio.

Alas the Italian colour transparency film used to photograph on this occasion was so severely damaged by heat and humidity that the slides had a horrible green cast right through them, so I have no good photos of the event.

An occasion of great significance that occurred while we were living in Nigeria was the first ever assembly of National Bible Societies in Africa. This was held in a Teachers' Training Centre in Winneba, Ghana. Ghana's first president Nkumah had built this college for the purpose of teaching his particular ideology, which was very anti-God. An important guest was Father Walter Abbott from the Vatican. He had come to explain to us the meaning of the rulings of the Second Vatican Council (Vatican II) in regard to use of Scripture by Catholics. In short, they were now not only permitted to possess, but also encouraged to study, the Bible. For two hours, he was closely questioned by everyone present because there wasn't a man-jack there that hadn't been turned away from a Roman Catholic Institution of some sort at some time or the other while trying to distribute Scriptures. Absolute assurances were given that, from now on, things had changed. Some of us were sceptical—surely there would be at least a few traditional bishops who would stand up against this new ruling. Father

Abbott was adamant, 'Just let us know in Rome if you ever have trouble with a bishop over this matter and we'll take it up with him.'

After the conference was over, I had the pleasure of driving Father Abbot to Benin, Togo and Nigeria where I had the unusual task of introducing him to the bishops of these countries.

Everything stated at the conference by this emissary of the Vatican, although almost unbelievable and wildly controversial for many Catholics at the time, turned out to be true. A few years later, the Bible Society was able to report that in many countries, Roman Catholics were buying more Bibles than Protestants.

On one occasion, towards the end of a busy day, I called on a Roman Catholic school on the main road north of Enugu. This was prior to Vatican II, but the headmaster readily agreed to allow me to sell Scripture Portions to the children. He brought the students out one class at a time and they eagerly examined all the little books I had. There was a whole set of books of the New Testament and some from the Old Testament, such as Genesis, Psalms and Proverbs. Soon they were calling for copies of Saint Luke, Saint John and Saint Mark. Then someone cried, 'Can I have Saint Acts?' Another said, 'Saint Revelation please.' The children were adding 'saint' to the title of every book. So they wanted 'Saint Genesis', 'Saint Proverbs' and the like. 'Can I have Saint Joseph?' asked a little boy. I thought quickly, and gave him Genesis showing him where to find the story of Joseph. It wasn't until later that I realised he must have been thinking about Joseph, the husband of Mary.

The stock was almost gone; then I remembered I had one carton of Easter Selections. This was a small, bright blue book entitled 'He is Risen'. I let the children buy it for one penny. When all of the other books were sold, they began buying the Easter one, even though Easter was a long way off.

I felt a little hand on my leg. I was wearing shorts. It persisted in touching and tapping me until I looked behind me to see a very small girl. She looked up at me and said, 'Sir, can I have Saint Risen?'

4

VISIT TO WEST AFRICA—border struggles

1994

The journey to Central and West Africa began with my first ride on the *Euro Star*—the channel tunnel train from Waterloo Station, London, to Gare du Nord in Paris. It took only 20 minutes to pass under the English Channel and five hours for the complete trip. As we whisked along on the French side at 300 kph (186 mph), I couldn't help but think of the fact that, here I was travelling on one of the world's newest trains of sixteen coaches and two locomotives, the whole thing weighing 800 tonnes, moving so fast the lampposts were a blur, and that two days later, I would be in one of the world's poorest countries where finding a taxi with four wheels would be an achievement.

On board, the service was like Business Class on an airliner and the hostess, who before offering any assistance, stood by my seat and said, 'This might be a French train, but I am not French, I am Spanish, now would you like a drink?' There were only six passengers in our car so she had time to lavish her attention on each of us.

Once in Paris, I met up with my colleague, journalist Geoffrey Stamp, at the Air France check in counter for our flight to Bamako, the capital of

Mali. We were there the prescribed two hours before departure, but the place was already packed solid with Africans returning home.

Bamako, Mali

We planned to stay for one day in Mali but, upon arrival, the immigration officer declared that this was not possible as 24-hour visas were not available. We could be given a two-week visa provided we applied for it at the embassy in Paris. 'So you will return to Paris, apply for the visa, then come back to me, and *voila* you are welcome!' A more senior (and more helpful) officer noticed our dilemma and called us into his office. Within 20 seconds he had stamped our passports with a single day visa.

We didn't need to take our luggage with us, so it was doing endless circles on the carousel until a sympathetic French lady from another airline offered to store it in her office until our next flight.

We were then told to wait in the departure lounge while another senior officer 'double-checked our visas'. Several policemen and two women police officers came to greet us, shaking hands solemnly and greeting us in several languages—French, English, Spanish and Bambara. I had seen a few words in Bambara and the reply to a greeting is, *i nice*. The sounds of the words fascinated me so I had remembered them. They were a little startled when I gave that response.

It all seemed quite odd to us—why were we being greeted by this delegation? Who did they think we were? Then one asked, 'Are you policemen?'

I said, 'Well . . . we are . . .' trying to decide if we should say we were Bible Society people, or Christian workers, or just tourists—it's always difficult to know how to represent yourself in a new country.

Geoff interrupted and said quite slowly, 'Well, (pause) not really, (pause) we are . . .'

The policewoman didn't let him finish the sentence, she interrupted saying, 'You are welcome,' and walked away. The senior officer, with great respect, then escorted us to the front of the building and called over a taxi driver whom we hired for a couple of hours.

Our driver's name was Abdul and he drove what Geoff described as 'the remains of a Toyota'. It was a thirty-year-old model, missing all the dashboard instruments. The suspension was shot, the doors were held closed by pieces of wire, the wheel bearings complained and the diff fairly screamed at us.

We ground our way down the road to Bamako, the capital city, 15 km away. Many countries, no matter how poor they are, believe in first impressions. The road from the international airport was a splendid four-lane highway through the desert-like terrain to the city. It was probably the best bit of road in the country.

Everything was very dry and dusty, as it was *hamatan* season. The *hamatan* is the annual dust storm that comes down from the Sahara. It picks up tiny particles of desert dust and blows it down to the Gulf of Guinea. It is like a fog and, in a bad year, can almost block out the sun.

Mali means 'hippopotamus' and Bamako 'the place of the crocodile'. The Niger River runs through the centre of the city. At the beginning of last century, it was the capital of the French Sudan and now has a population of nearly two million. Mali gained its independence, along with so many other African countries, in 1960. The famous Timbuktu is within Mali's borders, and I had always wanted to go there. But I was in Mali on Bible Society business, so my time was not my own. At the market in Bamako, a tout offered us a two-week 'Timbuktour' for a special price of US$1,700! Timbuktu was once the centre of a great commercial power and traded in gold, ivory, slaves, salt, horses and kola nuts.

Mali is one of the poorest countries in the world and the life expectancy is only 44 years. The UNESCO description is grim. Literacy is about 32 percent. Fifteen percent of children die within the first year, but despite this high infant mortality rate, the population is increasing by about three percent per annum. In general, it is estimated that the people get only about 60 percent of the required minimum calorie intake.

This is the fifth largest country in Africa with about half extending into the Sahara desert. I should put that the other way—the Sahara is actually moving further and further into Mali in a process called 'desertification'.

The Bamako Cathedral stands out like a sore thumb, in the sense that it is a red stone Gothic-style building that looks as though it has been plucked right out of Europe. The Grand Mosque is close by and is a little taller than the church. Only one percent of the population is Christian.

The centre of the city is a huge market. Like all African markets, it was a fascinating place to visit. The craftsmanship on display was amazing—especially the fine silver filigree that is made with the most basic of tools.

The people there didn't like being photographed, so I had to be very careful and it was difficult to get anything worthwhile. A woman asked me for a coin for a bus fare and I agreed if she would let me take her photograph. She agreed but after pocketing the coin refused. A couple of young fellows came up and began to make trouble. Another man approached me and said, 'Go quickly else you will have problems.' Malians have a reputation for being friendly, but we felt a high degree of tension in the place.

Since independence from France, there have been several bloody coups, including one change of government that involved a couple of former leaders, including the minister of education, being burned alive.

The large General Hospital and the Presidential Palace are situated on hills at the edge of the city. Our taxi ground its way up to the top where we could get a view of the Niger River at sunset. We had stopped to change a tyre, when the president passed us going up the hill, not with the huge motorcade that is so common in Africa, but just a single humble police car. This suggested to me that he felt quite secure in his position—either that or he couldn't afford an extravagant motorcade on his way to work. The country survives on aid and the president's predecessors had been accused of siphoning off huge amounts of cash to foreign bank accounts. Back in town, the driver decided to refuel and have the suspension fixed. This was done at a speed that would have credited a motor racing pit crew!

After checking in for our next flight, and passing through the third security check, I noticed a fellow leaning casually against the wall. I was sure I had seen him several times during the day but to avoid alarming Geoff, didn't say anything. This wasn't the first time over the years that I had experienced this—I was certain the guy was a security man detailed to keep an eye on us. As I passed him I gave a half grin of acknowledgement and he responded with a sheepish smile.

Ethiopian Airlines decided to upgrade us to First Class for the overnight trip to N'djamena in Chad. We were the only passengers in the cabin and three beautiful stewardesses did their best to make us comfortable and made many attempts to empty their bottles of local wine and fine port! At all times, at least one stayed on high alert, waiting to respond to the slightest signal for service. They even let us remain stretched out on the large seats when landing and taking off at Niamey, capital of Niger. There was no need for safety belts to be fastened. Their attitude was, 'This is our home and tonight it is your home, so enjoy yourselves.'

Chad

Arrival at N'djamena was slowed up a little when the half dozen passengers who disembarked, found that the immigration staff were asleep in an adjoining room. It was about 5.00 a.m. It took a security guard a full five minutes of beating on their door to wake them up. The six of us stood quietly in a queue trying not to laugh or make rude comments. When the officials finally emerged, the look on their faces seemed to say, 'How dare you come at this unearthly hour!'

After settling into our hotel we slept until 9.00 a.m., then were taken to the police to register our arrival. This kind of practice is not uncommon in certain third world countries. Another immigration form was completed and a demand was made for two passport photographs to go with the paperwork. When Geoff remonstrated with them that this was most unusual the officer said, 'This is the normal thing to do around the world.' We didn't bother to enlighten him. Fortunately we had a couple of spare photos back at the hotel for situations like this. Over the course of the trip, visiting various countries, we used a total of 10 copies of our passport photos. I always carried 12 copies when visiting Africa and I reminded myself to always carry them in the travel wallet, rather than leaving them in the hotel room.

Our next port of call was another department called the 'immigration police', where I was presented with my photography permit—a two-page document that bore my name and also the name and photograph of the local Bible Society business manager. We joked that if I got into trouble, he would be the one to go to jail, not me. It was a very serious matter in Chad to take a photograph of any description without official permission. The permit cost US$50.

All this accomplished, the staff of the Bible Society in Chad proudly showed us their new office. Each member came forward to solemnly greet us. Several people had come to the office so that Geoff could interview them about how the Bible had changed their lives. Geoff conducted the interviews in French, while I talked to the staff.

The newly hired watchman came to greet me. He described his role and how important he felt it was. I asked him about his weapons. He proudly produced a thick wooden baton and a steel thing that is difficult to describe. It was like a sword with two knives protruding at right angles. It looked as though you could cut off someone's head by slicing at a person, getting his head between the knives. The handle end was sharply pointed and could be used as a spear. His colleague, the night watchman, also had a loaded gun. 'But he's only got one bullet.'

The office secretary had been employed for only four months. I asked her about her former job. She answered in English, 'No, after school I was on the bed.' I guessed that meant she had been ill. After telling me she had been married for four years, I asked about children. 'No, I have a malady. I am not in heat.'

'Ahem, well, yes, ah, how do you like this job?'

'It's very good, but I want to tell you about my malady. I am not in heat. I don't get hot, so no children.' Such is the frankness of most Africans, which can floor you if you are not prepared for it. She suddenly brightened, 'But my husband works at the university. I am very proud of him.'

Just over half the population of Chad is Muslim and 35 percent is Christian. The rest of the people are animists. During the past 20 years, when native believers have been the evangelists, the rate of growth of the churches has risen dramatically. One Brethren evangelist told us that they thought there were about 1,000 Brethren assemblies in the country, but he had just returned from a long tour and discovered many hundreds of assemblies they didn't know existed. Because they do not have any formal registration process it is very difficult to keep track of all the congregations. An evangelist would go to a village, preach and teach the gospel, form a church of those who converted from an animistic belief or Islam, stay a time to teach them the basics of their new faith, leave a Bible for the literate ones, move on, and not tell anyone about them until many months later.

Literacy is still a great problem, probably less than 15 percent, and the standard of education in primary schools is not high. At the last count there were 680,909 primary school pupils who were taught by 10,151 teachers—an average class size of 67. The standard of literacy among those who attend evangelical churches is much higher than the general public because people are encouraged to read the Bible.

After visiting church leaders in the city, we asked to be taken to a typical village in the countryside. We set off for a staff member's cousin's place that was well off the beaten track. The 'road' was really just a sandy track. When we arrived, all the villagers turned out to welcome us. The cousin was out in the fields so the local schoolteacher gave us a guided tour of the village. He was free to do this as he was currently on strike. The village consisted of mud huts with thatched roofs and a few with sheets of iron placed over the thatch.

The village well was lined with concrete and was about 30 metres (70 ft) deep. Women were drawing water out in large buckets made from goatskins. The complete skin of the goat was sewn up so the 'bucket' looked like a hairless goat with short legs and a neck, no but no head. It took two women to pull up a full bucket. The teacher said, 'It's ok for women drawing water to be topless but otherwise they must cover up at all times.' When he caught the puzzled look I gave him he said, 'It's hot work pulling up the water, so ok no dress.'

The children were happy to show us their empty classrooms as they had a free day. The rooms had no furniture of any kind, not even a table for the teacher—not even mats for the children to sit on. The headmaster's office had a small table and a cupboard in which he stored the children's books. We were not permitted to see the books, but the teacher said, 'Don't worry, every child has a book.' What he meant was that they all had writing books, but there were no textbooks of any description.

Despite the basic resources, this school was far superior to the traditional village Muslim school where the children are taught from the Koran. They learn long passages in Arabic by rote and finish up still not being able to read or write their own language or the official language of the country, French.

The Republic of Chad is a country of six million people. They were not treated well by their French colonizers. Twenty years ago, it was one of the world's poorest countries but with the discovery of large reserves of oil, and lots of gold, plus increased cotton production, the potential is very good if, as a colleague put it, the government handles things properly. Unfortunately, the one business that made the country infamous from the 1800s, slave trading, has not disappeared.

The U.S. State Department *Trafficking in Persons Report* of June 2009 stated:

Chadian children are also trafficked to Cameroon, the Central African Republic, and Nigeria for cattle herding . . . and for sexual exploitation.

We met a newly arrived UBS Translation Consultant who was still excited about discovering the meaning of the word used for the Biblical term 'salvation' in some of the local languages. The local usage literally meant 'having the chain removed from the neck'—which was, of course, a reference to slave trading.

One evening we drove along the Shari River to watch the sun set. The *hamatan* dust usually caused dusk to be quite spectacular. A drunken man who was being helped home by a relative, saw my long lens and ran towards me shouting, 'Don't kill me with that gun!' His relative, quite a large man, had difficulty in restraining him. If he got too close I would have had to poke him with the long lens.

One of the local villagers insisted on carrying my camera bag. He grabbed it from me and out spilled a lens—smashing its new $100 filter. It just so happened I was carrying a spare filter for this lens—something I had never done before.

The political situation in Chad was unstable. The president did not feel confident in his position. The previous week, the wife of the American ambassador had been driving past the presidential palace when her car broke down. Palace guards opened fire because it was illegal to stop outside the palace. Fortunately she jumped out of the vehicle very quickly and ran for her life. After dark, no one was allowed to walk down the road near the palace without the risk of being shot.

En route to our next destination, Cameroon, we took an MAF plane, flying south from the capital to Bongor. This one-hour flight would have taken many hours by the dusty potholed road plagued with numerous army roadblocks. The pilot flew at 2,000 feet in order to give us a good view. We flew over a desert with a few stubby trees and shrubs and, incredibly, there were many small villages of people living in these harsh conditions. There were no roads anywhere near them, only narrow tracks. Most of the villages consisted of a ring of small mud huts with thatched roofs. The mud is mixed with straw in a fashion that dates back thousands of years to the time of Moses. It is known as 'cob' and is scientifically proven to be cooler than cement and keeps the inside temperature almost constant.

On arrival at Bongor, the pilot buzzed the dirt runway before landing to scare off the goats, sheep and dogs that were loitering in the area. The nation-wide teachers strike was being observed here as well, so we were greeted by hundreds of school children who gathered in a large circle around the plane. They edged closer and closer until a man armed with a long branch attacked them and sent them scurrying away in a cloud of dust, only to gradually creep back again.

The local inspector of police came to greet us. He said he was a church elder and invited us to meet the mayor who, calling for a very large exercise book, noted our arrival in his town. Then began the official process of leaving Chad. The immigration office was a straw shelter where three officers studiously recorded our departure in three different logs. The police noted our departure in their own massive exercise books. Then they drove us to the border crossing with the Cameroon. By the time we left, we had been well and truly checked out of Chad!

Cameroon

The river that forms the border between Chad and Cameroon is only about 50 metres wide, and was serviced by a fairly new and efficient vehicle ferry. Like their colleagues in Chad, the Cameroon immigration officers were housed in a simple straw shelter. Two officers took down our details in their ubiquitous large exercise books. We were then escorted to another straw shelter where another officer administered the all-important rubber stamp. A fourth officer seated behind a rickety desk, probably the boss, did not disturb himself from a game of cards he was having with the driver of a 30 tonne lorry waiting to cross the border.

We were soon at the Louis Charpenet Centre, Yagoua, where the UBS was holding a weeklong workshop for Bible translators of eleven languages of Chad and northern Cameroon. Translations Consultant, Dr Paul Bitjick, had met me in Reading several months before and told me of this workshop. I indicated my interest in attending and he offered a warm welcome, not believing we would actually come. Great was his surprise and pleasure when we turned up. He immediately cancelled lectures and extended a special welcome 'to this outlandish place, where no one visits'.

Some of the stories these translators told us were quite incredible. It is one thing to read about the history of a country but to hear first hand the stories of bravery is a deeply humbling experience. One man, who lived in a small isolated Muslim village, was told that if he didn't desist from translating the Bible, he would be killed in the traditional way by being buried alive. So he moved to another place. He explained that killing a person in this way was very simple, effective and clean in that there is no blood spilt. Once the hole is covered over in the sandy terrain, there is very little evidence of any misdemeanour at all.

We travelled in a 30-year-old Peugeot 504 taxi. The odometer had stopped at 320,000 km several years before, but happily the vehicle was in comparatively good condition. Truth be told, it had probably done close to half a million kilometres. The lock on the rear door was broken so a long piece of rubber held it closed. I winced as the driver slammed the door on my laptop computer. It survived.

We stopped at a Guidar village and met the translator of the Guidar New Testament. He was now retired and lived in his traditional home. As soon as we arrived, he rushed inside his hut and put on his best clothes—a crumpled dark blue safari suit with a gaping hole under the left armpit. By doing so he was showing us great respect. The village consisted of a score of mud huts with no electricity. The single village well was very deep and primitive, lined at the top with an old car tyre. A loose metal cover was the only thing preventing small children falling in. He was very proud to receive us, albeit for just a few minutes, and to express his pleasure that 2,000 copies of his New Testament had been sold.

In the next, and only, town in the 240 km journey was Figuil, where we met the deputy mayor. Over a drink of non-alcoholic Guinness known here as 'pastor's beer', he told us how he had assisted in the research of the Guidar translation. He was a big fellow and I had to stand on a step to photograph him in his colourful cap.

We only just made it to the airport to catch our flight to Yaoundé, the capital of Cameroon. Our host was concerned because, although we had confirmed our tickets, this did not necessarily mean we would get a seat. Sure enough there were a number of disgruntled people catching our flight who had been bumped off the previous day's flight to make room for the local football team.

'I've seen a sign for a restaurant,' said our host, 'So go and eat.'

'Signs don't mean anything here,' I said. 'There's one for the men's toilet but it's closed, so I used the women's.' There were no doors to the toilets and the two young women cleaners were intrigued by my use of it. They stood at the door to watch my every move. When I waved them away, they just stood there and giggled.

The terminal building was an impressive modern design. It included all the facilities expected at an international terminal—but nothing was open. The international section took up most of the space, but there were only three flights per week. This was the hometown of the minister in charge of aviation.

Our flight came in an hour late and the boarding procedure was quite novel. As soon as the engines were turned off, the ground hostess approached the boarding gate to allow the disembarking passengers to enter the terminal. The embarking passengers rushed at her. She struggled to open the door, such was the crush around her. As soon as the door cracked open, the new passengers ran out onto the tarmac pushing aside the disembarkers and ran for the plane. We had been tipped off that this would happen so we were up the front of the crowd. After everyone was seated there were several unhappy people who couldn't find seats, so they had to get off.

The month-long Ramadan fast was under way and there were half a dozen Muslim men seated near me. Between Doula and Yaoundé, the sun had set and a drink was served. Three of the men took a soft drink but the others behind them refused. The would be drinkers checked and rechecked their watches, looked at the last remains of the setting sun and tried to decide if the day had ended. Sunset at ground level was never a problem but it was another matter at 20,000 feet above sea level. Behind them, their friends remonstrated with them and tried to discourage them from drinking. More checks of watches and observations of the sun and a great deal of talking followed. One of them hungrily fingered a tub of yogurt. The steward came along to collect the used glasses but they weren't going to give up their drinks. Just before landing the three finally agreed the day was over so they threw back their heads and downed their drinks.

The cabin announcements were made by a stewardess in garbled English. She didn't use the local Pidgin English, known as Wes Cos (West Coast), but the standard announcement sounded like this: 'Ash we are shoon to land in Yaoundé pasheners should fashen their sheetbels, raish the backsh of their sheets in an upritsh poshishion and musht shop shokking.'

Equatorial Guinea

Before we left Cameroon, we decided to spend a day in Equatorial Guinea.

The history of this country on the West Coast of Africa makes for dreadful reading. Despite its name it is not on the equator, but situated just below Cameroon and north of Angola. The tiny nation became independent from Spain in 1968. Many writers have tried to describe the horrors of a history that began when the Portuguese took over the area in the 16th century. At one stage the British leased the land in order to have a base to fight the slave trade.

The first elected president, Macías Nguema, quickly became a tyrant. He executed thousands of people who didn't vote for him and many thousands died of hard labour. Intellectuals were forced to leave the country and, by the time his regime was toppled in 1979, only one third of the populace at the time of independence remained alive—a mere 300,000. There were 28,000 political prisoners in Nguema's jails and they were treated brutally. The infamous Black Beach prison is only 200 metres from the president's palace.

Nguema cut off contact with the outside world, banned fishing and destroyed all fishing boats. He executed or tortured to death all his political rivals. All missionaries were expelled and he closed down all of the churches. Freedom of speech was annihilated and being a journalist or writer of any kind was a capital crime. Some estimates suggest that about 50,000 people died during his eleven years in power. It was the president's nephew who organized the coup and had him executed. He became president and rejoices in the name of Teodoro Obiang Nguema Mbasogo.

Wikipedia makes this statement about the first president: 'On Christmas 1975, Macías had 150 alleged coup plotters executed to the sound of a band playing Mary Hopkin's tune "Those Were the Days" in a national stadium.'

Equatorial Guinea has one of the worst human rights records in the world, consistently ranking among the 'worst of the worst' in Freedom House's annual survey of political and civil rights, and Reporters Without Borders ranks President Obiang among its 'predators' of press freedom.

The capital of Equatorial Guinea is Malobo, which is situated on a small island just off the coast of mainland Africa. This used to be called Fernando Po. Several years ago, when based in Nigeria, I had tried to visit but was refused entry. It was once quite a beautiful city in the sense that there are many fine Old Spanish tropical buildings, but the general condition of the city was now very poor. From my seat in a car, I couldn't see the bottom of the largest pothole I had ever seen in a city street.

We chartered an SIL Cessna 206. The performance of the officials in charge of the airport and immigration suggested that the government was inept and corrupt. The immigration police first of all asked that we fill in an immigration arrival form, then demanded a passport photo.

It took 20 minutes to check our two passports. Each of the three officers on duty read every page carefully, arguing over the meaning of some of the visa stamps. Then another long period elapsed while they argued about the validity of our visas in that they did not carry a date stamp. So they charged us for another visa. Fortunately they had no record of my earlier attempt to visit.

Then came a bill for 10,000 francs for 'baggage handling' and 'airport parking'. We had no baggage at all and the parking fee appeared to be for the man who waved the pilot to his parking position—this wasn't the 'airport-landing fee'—that was a different matter. Ours was the only plane that day. The Guinean man who met us told the officials not to be so stupid and refused to allow us to pay. The one customs officer on duty was woken up and she came out of her office to shake our hands, asked us no questions, then returned to her sleeping position in her office.

The immigration cards of the past few years were stacked up on shelves and were discoloured with age and dust. The one filing cabinet showed signs of being broken into so many times that the locks no longer worked.

The reputation of the violent nature of the police was confirmed in my mind when I noticed a baton bound in leather. I surreptitiously touched it when no one was looking and found that it was quite flexible. You could a beat a person with this and not leave any bruises.

Later in the day, when we left the country, the immigration officer demanded payment for our exit visas. A receipt was requested and he sat down at a 40-year-old manual typewriter and laboriously typed out a receipt. An air force captain appeared and in an officious manner, demanded payment for a report that he had to make regarding our arrival and departure. He said, 'I have to make a report of your visit to say that you came and went. This will cost money.' Our host quietly took him aside and asked him about this nonsense. The response was very simple, 'Only 2,000 francs ($4.50) is enough.'

Then there was the airport departure tax to pay. This cost 5,000 francs each. A hand written receipt was written out in a childish hand in pencil but no amount was specified. It just stated that we had paid the tax—writing that took another five minutes. Finally all was finished and our host said, 'Now go quickly before they think of something else.'

The pilot was ready for take off and an officer from the control tower came running over to speak to him. He didn't seem to have anything special to say but 'ummed' and 'aahed' a few times as though he was trying to see if there was a reason to delay us. He eventually left and went back to the tower without uttering a single sentence. We were about to take off when the tower called to say that we should wait. The controller said that there was a message coming through from the airport authorities, there were some 'irregularities' he said. The pilot answered saying that he did not understand what the man was talking about. A nonsense conversation followed until the pilot said, 'Let's get out of here, all they are trying to do is to find a way of extracting more money from us. I'll never come back here again.' He switched off his radio and we flew away.

On the streets of Equatorial Guinea I had to be very careful with my cameras as photography was strictly forbidden without the express permission of the president himself. Our host was the only missionary in the country and he had permission to use a camera so I worked under his authority, sometimes asking him to take the photograph if we were in a public place. It wasn't permissable to take a photograph of most buildings in the town, and if a camera was pointed even vaguely in the direction of the palace, a government building or a policeman, we risked instant imprisonment and confiscation of the camera.

The main objective of our visit was to see the team working on a translation of the Bubi New Testament for the Bube people. For some reason, the president didn't like the Bube so they tended to keep a low profile. A relatively small tribe they held most government positions under the colonists. They are now regarded as a minority. The translators were conversant in all three official languages of Equatorial Guinea—Spanish, French and Portuguese—as well as their own mother tongue. They were very pleased to see us when we found them hard at work at the Bible School.

We had lunch at a restaurant that was owned by descendents of freed slaves. They had become quite rich and important over the years and the owner was happy to tell us of their good fortune in being owners of a business. Down near the waterfront were a couple of caves about 10 metres (33 ft) deep in which slaves had been held. The slaves were jam-packed into them for safekeeping and we were told that of the many thousands of people who were treated like this, many died of suffocation.

My heart was heavy for the people of Equatorial Guinea as we flew over the dense tropical rainforests back to Yaoundé. Below us were, as one writer put it, 'the best coconut palms in the world', rich deposits of oil and the most unfortunate people in Africa.

Back in Cameroon

The daughter of the mayor of Yaoundé owned a restaurant that was situated, of all places, on the ground floor of the town hall below her father's office. She invited us to dinner and asked us beforehand what we would like to eat, suggesting porcupine or bush pig. We chose porcupine. At that time, we didn't realise that the trade in bush meat threatened a number of endangered species such as porcupine. It was quite pleasant with a nice herbal sauce, but I know people who wouldn't have enjoyed seeing the tiny claw on their plate.

Later, at our hotel, we met up with a film crew from the UK who were doing a BBC documentary on the bush meat problem and the deforestation of the country. One of their team was an enthusiastic young woman who, in a loud voice, described the bush meat problem. 'You know, they kill porcupines and eat them.' We gravely nodded our heads in agreement and wished them well. We kept quiet about our dinner.

On our way to church on Sunday morning, we stopped to buy some batteries. I took a shot down the road and noticed some policemen. They were some distance away and were not included in the photo. I could see them having a heated discussion and looking towards me, so I moved quickly into a nearby shop. Within minutes a couple of angry policemen stormed into the shop and hauled me out onto the road. In the usual mixture of French and English they accused me of taking their photo. I denied this. We were taken to the police station where the officer in charge declared that the only way to prove I hadn't taken their photo was to have the film developed. This they would do and we were told to report back next morning when, if I was cleared, we could recover our passports. This worried me as it was a professional film that required special processing. No one had explained whether it was illegal or not to photograph a policeman.

Next morning my film was returned *sans* policemen. They were all smiles and told us to be on our way, congratulating me for being honest. I resisted the crazy temptation to ask if I could photograph them in their station.

Togo

We took the 9.00 p.m. flight to Lomé, capital of Togo, but this wasn't without drama. The security men in charge of the x-ray machine spoke to me very quietly in a mixture of English and French and explained that their machine was unsafe for film. But if I showed some 'consideration' for not x-raying my film they would be very happy. In my 'emergency' pack were a couple of small blue Gideon French New Testament and Psalms. They hastily grabbed them and quickly stuffed them into their pockets and, all smiles, waved me through.

We visited the *Grande Marche* in Lomé. This is one of the great markets of West Africa. Here everything under the sun is on sale. The cloth market is quite exceptional. These are the famous Nana Benz women (the better off probably own a Mercedes Benz) who, along with their sisters in other West African countries, form an important part of the commercial life of the country.

Three times I had asked about the need for obtaining a visa and was assured that my New Zealand passport meant it was not required. I made many visits to this country when I was based in Nigeria but things change and it always pays to ask. The immigration officer, however, did not agree with the advice I had been given and spoke to me sternly about trying to enter the country without a visa. After much discussion between two senior officers it was decided that they would allow me to enter but impounded my passport. I was told that I should report to the police next morning and apply for a visa. I filled in a long form in quadruplet and handed over four passport photos. It would take four days to issue the visa. So four days later, on our way to the airport to depart from the country, I picked up my passport stamped with the visa. Togo seemed to follow the principle that the smaller the country the larger the visa stamp—a whole page!

Ghana

The next country we visited was Ghana, and I had waited an hour in the Ghanaian embassy in Togo while my application was considered. Had the papers come through from Accra as arranged? No one knew. I studied the customs and excise regulations on the wall and under motor vehicles it read, 'Motor vehicles for travelling in snow, golf carts and similar vehicles—25 percent duty.' Snow in Ghana! One of the world's hottest countries with no mountains! Amusing myself as I waited, I wished I hadn't left my snow boots back in England.

On arrival in Ghana Geoff went along to a special programme that was arranged at the Accra general hospital, so I lent him a camera while I spent time on the visas. He reported that the meeting with the staff and patients went very well until they decided to move from a small room to the corridor where there was more space. There was a moment of drama when someone moving a chair got it caught in an overhead fan, splintered wood flying all about the room. A local TV crew recorded the meeting but that incident was cut out of the piece they ran that night on the 7.00 p.m. news.

After a dinner of guinea fowl, which tasted like a good duck, we took a stroll down to the beach. We had hardly set foot on the sand when there was a chorus of protests from people who were standing on the other side of the road. 'Don't go down there.' They then warned us that there was real danger on the beach as there were men waiting in the dark, as they put it, 'to nobble ignorant and stupid tourists who think that it is safe to enjoy the sand, surf and stars'.

Nigeria

Our British travel agent had sent our passports for Nigerian visas and they inadvertently stamped mine with a visa that said I had a UK passport. They realized their mistake and cancelled it, but didn't issue another one because that would require another form to be filled out. When I saw what they had done, I knew that this could cause me trouble but there was no time to apply for another as we were leaving the next day. I informed our office in Lagos and they sent their Operations Manager to assist. It took him four full days of work to obtain the visa. He flew from Lagos to Abuja, back to Lagos then to Lomé (Togo). Finally, as a last resort he brought me to the consul in Lomé and told him in no uncertain terms how ashamed he was of the behaviour of the Nigerian officials. After 35 minutes of argument, the consul finally relented and stamped my passport.

On arrival in Lagos, we found that there was a double immigration barrier. Senior inspectors stood in front of the desks checking passports. When mine was checked he quickly found the cancelled visa and the one issued in Lomé. 'Why didn't you get a visa in London? Why did they cancel this? Why Lomé? I am very suspicious of you. This is very strange.' It was a bit difficult to explain the bungling of the London embassy and that there was no time to sort out the problem there.

The officer had his arms folded across his name badge. I asked him his name and this enraged him. He shouted in full voice, 'Why do you want to know my name? Who do you think you are?' His name badge became uncovered as he waved his arms about and I noticed that it was an Igbo name. I stared at it, then brightened and said, 'Oh I see you are from the East. I used to live in Enugu,' being careful to pronounce the word correctly not in the way most foreigners do. 'Sir Francis Ibiam, the former Governor of Eastern Nigeria, was the president of the Bible Society in Nigeria. I regard him as a personal friend and we are to stay with him in his home when we go to Enugu' (with careful pronunciation) next week. He will be very interested in my experience here.'

He stared at me intently and gradually the expression on his face slowly changed from rage to amazement. Finally, after asking the purpose of my visit, he let me pass. But he glowered, 'Only because you are visiting the Bible Society.' As I stepped past him he called with a broad smile and said, 'Please greet Sir Francis for me'.

The luggage carousel was under repair and we waited an hour for it to be restarted. A couple of Americans joked saying, 'All they need is a can of WD40.' There were many hundreds of pieces of luggage stacked in huge piles all over the room. Much of it was badly damaged, with personal items scattered about. Some of the items were under the label of two well-known international courier companies that would now be left to explain to their customers what had happened to their precious deliveries. The air conditioning in the terminal was also under repair.

The customs people waved us through and we were soon on the expressway to Bible House in Apapa, the wharf area of the city. The streets were lined with broken down wharf vehicles of every description. There were small tractors, front-end loaders, cranes and trolleys, large and small. I gave up trying to count them as there must have been many hundreds. It was quite unbelievable. Later, a harbour official told me that there was no budget for repairs and maintenance but soon, maybe next year, there would be money to fix them all.

It was exactly 30 years to the day since I had first walked into Apapa Bible House when I was appointed Circulation Manager for the Bible Societies in West Africa. There were two people still on the staff from my time there. One was Jacob, the cleaner, and I joked with him about how many brooms he must have worn out. 'O massa, too much, too much, da broom he get finished like me.'

'Ah Jacob, you still get too much for more brooms.' (You still have strength to use more brooms.) He always was a likeable fellow.

But despite Jacob's long-service history, the place was very dirty. The office was littered with dust-covered files; cupboards were bursting with old newspapers, files and stationery. Walls were covered with mildew and peeling paint. We found that the entire country was like this. Apart from hotels, the only clean and tidy place we visited was the home of Sir Francis Ibiam. It was spotless.

It was time to go to the Society's house in Palm Grove—in the same compound where Lorraine and I had lived when we first came to Nigeria in the 1960s. The fancy concrete arched gateway in the two-metre-high fence was still there and three security guards were on duty. There were a few hawkers and a young woman seated beside a huge enamel bowl that was filled with soapsuds. She was washing and scrubbing carrots with a small brush. 'Maybe she's going to make soapy carrot soup,' joked Geoff.

The Bible Society's house was built by a British builder in the 1950s and had an ornamental fireplace in the lounge. It was for show—just the surround with no grate. It was designed to make English people feel at home in this place six and a half degrees above the equator.

The house used to be surrounded by a large lawn that was always kept immaculate—the pride and joy of a fulltime gardener. But the lawn had gone and in its place was dry earth with neither a blade of grass nor a flower. The large backyard had gone as well and in its place was a block of 20 flats that was for official visitors. There was always a constant flow of visitors as there was a Bible Society office in each of the country's 16 states.

We were shown to our room with profuse apologies that there was neither water nor electricity. The phone in the office didn't work either. 'But we have some food,' said our host.

Only one other flat was occupied. A man and woman and a teenage girl were staying there. The woman said she was an evangelist and had just come from the north where she had held what she called 'successful evangelistic campaigns'. Geoff became quite excited and wanted to write a story about her. I cautioned him, saying I noticed a number of discrepancies in her tale, so we had better check her out first. That evening she knocked on our door and invited me to her room for a discussion with her and the family.

I entered the room and was surprised to find that the others of her party weren't there. I decided that I should leave at once and invited her to our room to speak with Geoff and me together. Before I could move, she closed the door and locked it, slipping the key into her pocket. This alarmed me. What was she up to?

'I want to talk to you personally and tell you about myself because I think you will be able to help.' Oh dear, she is going to ask me for money. She gave a long story of her activities in the north and dropped many names of church and government leaders. All the time she inched closer and closer to me finally placing her hand on my leg and saying, 'I think we could have nice evening together. My husband and daughter are not coming back tonight.'

Her story was all lies. She was a con woman. True she was an attractive 40 year old with clear smooth skin, not very dark. Her tight fitting top reminded me of the song 'June is busting out all over', and she occasionally stroked herself. The power was off and a couple of small hurricane lamps emitted an eerie glow in the stifling hot room. She talked on and on until I was at a loss to know how to get away. She finally came out straight and asked for money. She would pay me back in the morning, she said, after she had seen the president of the Bible Society who owed her money. He was her second cousin.

Attempting to force her to hand over the room key didn't seem to be an option. As always, I had my camera bag with me as I never went anywhere without it, so I suggested I take her photo. She quickly responded and said, 'How shall we do it? Shall I take my clothes off?' Ah this proved it—she was a con. There was nothing Christian about her. She'd do anything for money.

I pretended to search my bag for the right lens then said, 'I need to get another lens from my room. We need a special one for portraits and also a special film and a filter that will make your skin look so smooth and beautiful.' She stared at me trying to assess whether I was kidding or not. Two can play this game so I stood up, camera bag on my shoulder, and stroked her cheek saying, 'You have lovely skin and it will look wonderful in the special photo I will make. Open the door and I will get them.'

'Leave your bag here so I know you will come back.'

'I always carry my bag everywhere I go, even when I go to the toilet, it's part of me, without I cannot do my work. Don't worry we will see each other again.' I couldn't leave the bag with her because there was money in it, albeit in two cleverly concealed secret pockets.

What to do? 'Ok, you come with me,' and I moved to take her hand, gently caressing it. 'This is so soft and smooth, not like the market women.' She liked that and said, 'I can show you that all of me is smooth.'

'Come, let's get the other stuff,' pulling her gently toward the door. She took out the key and walked with me to my room. I knocked on the door. Geoff let me in and I whispered, 'Con. Close it and lock it.' He quickly closed the door.

'Tell her to go away and that I will see her in the morning. Say I can't come out as I have something urgent to do right now.' He quickly caught on and called, 'He can't come now—the president is on the phone and he has to talk to him.'

'That won't work, she knows there are no phones here.'

'We'll see you in the morning because now we have to prepare to see the president.

'Thanks mate, you caught on very quickly.'

'Well I could see what type she was. You ok?'

We never saw them again as they left during the night, the staff saying they had gone without paying their bill.

We were invited to meet the King of Badagery. Situated on the coast close to the border with Benin, this was the place where Christian missionaries first preached the gospel in Nigeria. A few local Bible Society supporters came with us.

We assembled in the audience chamber of the palace and waited quietly for the king. Suddenly a voice called out, "Aweh, aweh, aweh, long life to his majesty.' Moving at a sedate pace he took his seat on a huge upholstered throne set about two feet above us. Although not a particularly big man, his flowing robes of gold and green filled the throne.

As distinguished guests, we were seated on the 'first dais'. We were described in quaint Nigerian English even more lavishly than just simply 'distinguished', we were 'greatly illustrious' and 'exceedingly and honourably treasured by the people'.

Formal introductions ensued, which included the greatest praise for my former work in the country. The king spoke well of the Society and his people's need for the Bible. Geoff left me to reply, suggesting that I would know the protocol in addressing royalty. I drew on the best adjectives I knew to describe the important example the king made for his people, not just to his subjects, but all the people of the country. This pleased him greatly.

He excused himself for a minute and returned with two certificates. He explained that he had created a title for distinguished guests who visited his kingdom and wished to bestow it upon us both. It was the title of 'Badagery Pilgrim'.

A closing prayer was offered and I was intrigued to watch one of the chiefs remove his hat only to reveal he had a second one underneath it—this was a small white skullcap that a chief may never remove in public. The following day when we were at a meeting held in our honour, I asked a friendly chief about the second cap. He explained that seeing he himself was not a very high chief he only wore one hat. The next level meant a second hat and he himself was a retired Commissioner of Police but only a one-hat chief.

We assembled outside for an official photo with Geoff and I seated each side of the king. A large group of local people then put on a special programme of singing and short plays. After that, we were escorted through town to see the important historic sights.

Close by was the first mission station in the country. We were shown what they called the 'First Storey House in Nigeria'—that is, the first two-storey house. It was built by the first missionaries. Badagery was another important centre for the slave trade. We examined the heavy chains the slaves were forced to wear, along with iron collars and other instruments of torture—such as an awful looking device that was placed in the mouth of someone who talked or cried too much.

It has been estimated that, during the years of the slave trade, as many as 50,000,000 people were transported from West Africa to the Caribbean and North America with 2,000,000 moved through this port alone.

Nothing seems to go smoothly in Nigeria. We were to fly from the capital Abuja to Lagos. We were told that we could buy our tickets at the airport. On arrival at the parking place, our car was surrounded by about 20 young men and women all shouting at the top of their voices that they could sell us tickets. There was a chorus of, 'Where are you going? Are you going to Lagos? Our tickets are the best. Our ticket is the cheapest. Don't buy from him. Please buy from me. Their plane's delayed. It's broken.' A deafening chorus of shouting, pushing touts. We struggled through them to the terminal building. Various local airline offices were staffed with equally voluble people. 'Buy from me, their plane has been grounded. They are cheats. They are always late. They are not going.'

A young man raced by, knocking people over as he ran. Two rather large women followed calling people to stop him. 'He's a thief, a thief, stop him, stop him.'

We chose what we hoped was the most reliable agent and purchased our tickets. Planes of three other local airlines were lined up ready for Lagos. Never in my life had I seen such chaos at an airport. In the event, our plane left on time and delivered us safely to Lagos.

The check in for London went smoothly, but at the customs bench, an officer in a quiet voice said, 'Give me ten dollars.' No, I said in a loud voice, 'I am not giving you ten dollars.' Embarrassed she turned away. Geoff was next and was asked for money. 'No, Geoff,' (in a loud voice) 'you don't have to pay money here.' I was becoming tired of the constant graft. But he had a problem. A male customs officer examined Geoff's camera and found that it was switched on. He accused Geoff of taking photos in the airport—something that was strictly forbidden. I intervened and said, 'How can that be? It's so dark here he could not have taken a photo with that camera and film without a flash, and you can see that that camera doesn't have a flash. See this little window here, it shows the kind of film he has—it's a slow film and wouldn't work here. I'm a photographer and I know about these things. That camera does not have an automatic switch off function, he hasn't used it for hours.' All this came out on a loud volley that bewildered the officer, so he shrugged his shoulders and turned away. Lagos is a place where you can shout at people, so they let Geoff go.

Our upgraded Business Class seat on the British Airways felt so good. We didn't have to bribe the stewardess to bring us food and drink. She even offered us a blanket and pillow, and required no payment! I think we call that 'civilization'.

5

VISITS TO CENTRAL AFRICA—
no protocol for me
1980s & 1990s

The Air France flight arrived at Kinshasa in Zaire (now the Democratic Republic of the Congo) on time at 8.00 p.m. I was first off the plane and as I descended the steps to the tarmac could see a crowd of about 50 men shouting and waving, offering to carry my hand luggage or calling for my passport. Absolute bedlam. A policeman pushing back eager porters and immigration officials, offered to escort me through the formalities of immigration and customs. A second one joined him explaining that it would take two to manage the crowd. They tut-tutted all the way to the terminal building saying something about there being no 'protocol' for me. Not to be met by a local person automatically put a person in danger of unscrupulous officials. Several times I was asked who was meeting me.

The path to the immigration office was blocked by several aircraft, between which we had to weave our way, dodging propellers and fuel hoses.

At the terminal door, a very short man wearing a type of uniform asked for my passport. The police guard encouraged me to surrender it to him, assuring me that he was an immigration officer and thus would save me having to line up at the counter. I hesitated, this was out of order. Where was his office? He told me to ignore the other officials and go straight to collect my luggage. He assured me that he would bring it to me at the baggage carousel.

As I hesitated, he did the same for a second European visitor and a couple of local people, so I decided that it was legal and hoped for the best.

I stood at the baggage carousel for about 20 minutes and not another passenger appeared. There were about 20 men—not necessarily official porters for they wore neither uniforms nor badges—hanging about waiting to carry luggage. Every now and again an immigration officer would ask me if anyone was meeting me. I began to wonder if I'd done the right thing. Then my Zairian host, Nlandu, appeared. He'd managed to get into the security area along with his assistant.

It would take too long to describe in detail all the goings on for the next 30 minutes. Suffice to say that another senior immigration officer appeared and seemed to be angry at not being the one to handle my passport. Soon after joining me, Nlandu handed out a small pocket-sized French New Testament to the men who had been hanging around trying to 'help' me. Within minutes there were others coming to ask for a copy. This was one of the 'unofficial' uses we used to make of the Gideons French New Testament and Psalms. We imported and warehoused them for the Gideons.

The immigration official who had taken my passport suddenly appeared, waving my passport in the air as if to say, 'Here it is, sorry to keep you waiting.' He handed it to me saying in English, 'Have you anything for us?' I pretended not to understand and appealed to Nlandu. He opened his small bag and produced two more French New Testaments and Psalms saying, 'This is what we have for you, now please don't bother this man again and let him proceed.' The books were accepted and they all turned away, disappointed at the loss of potential income, but nevertheless pleased to have something of value. They would know that these beautiful little blue books would sell easily.

Nlandu handed me a special photography permit secured from the Ministry of Information at great cost. This gave me permission to take photographs in the country, but of course, not of government buildings, and certainly not the president's palace. Another international photographer had told me that if you so much as point the camera in the direction of the palace, even if it isn't in sight, there would be trouble. There were security police everywhere. They originally asked for US$500 for the permit, but later reduced the fee to $300 because we were not a commercial operation.

This letter got me through the rest of the tortuous procedure of various security men and customs. There were five men lined up at a bench all ready to examine my luggage. Two were heavily armed soldiers in uniform and they seemed to have the most say. The letter was carefully read and reread by all of them, which took about ten minutes. After some discussion, they decided to let me in without even asking for a statement or opening my bags. The queue of four people behind me was becoming restless.

That's usually the last hurdle, but not this time. Outside the door were two soldiers in white helmets armed with revolvers and rifles. They looked like military police. They wanted to know who I was, so out came the permit. One read it and with a disgusted tone said, 'Who is this that he should want to come here and photograph?'

'He's international press,' said Nlandu's assistant.

The soldiers motioned my host to step aside so that they could discuss the matter with him privately. After a few minutes the soldiers returned and waved us on our way. I don't know how much Nlandu paid, or if he paid anything, it was best not to know. On reflection I believe that at the airport, no less than 50 men offered assistance or dealt with me in one way or another. Some acted courteously and possibly in good faith, but there were not a few who were scoundrels ready to steal anything they could lay their hands on. Everyone was desperately looking for a way to earn a small sum of money, such was the unemployment and low wage problem here.

Once in the car, Nlandu discovered that the radio cassette deck had been stolen. Some clever fellow had prised open the door and taken the set but never left a mark. They had simply relocked the car and gone on their way.

In 1995, a section of the army revolted and took to the streets of Kinshasa, destroying cars, buses and shops. As many as half of the shops were destroyed, including many bookshops. Since that time, the Bible Society had employed colporteurs to sell Bibles on the streets, in the buses and trains and on the ferries that ply the great river Zaire. We called on a number of these colporteurs who work in the crowded markets, and then decided to see if there were any active on the waterfront.

Just in case it was a sensitive area, I left my camera bag in the car, which was being guarded by a staff member who was brought along for the purpose. I took one small camera, which I asked my colleague to carry, and walked through the market area to the waterfront. Scores of small boats and ferries were lined up nose in to the bank. The waterfront was busy with all manner of shipping, from dugout canoes to small tankers. We decided that, before looking for a mobile Bible seller, we would see if there were any police in the area and ask permission to photograph. There were none but an immigration officer approached us and asked what we were looking for.

He said that in order to photograph in this 'sensitive' area we needed another special permit from the Immigration Department. We immediately decided that there was no need for this, and said we would leave straight away. He said that we should report to his office. We tried to get away but he insisted that we follow him.

He led us to a decrepit little building made of two extensively damaged shipping containers that only had three walls, and told us to sit down. There were four men seated at a table. They were all in civilian clothes except for a soldier with a big rifle. I'm not a soldier and don't know guns but it looked a pretty impressive thing to me. It wasn't an AK47 or the like, I'd seen plenty of those. The men held pieces of rope or rubber that seemed to be their symbol of authority. They constantly wound them around their wrists and then unwound them. I knew what they were for and had seen people beaten about the head with such weapons.

Thirty minutes of discussion followed in a mixture of French, Swahili and KiKongo. I knew enough of two of these languages to realise that we were in big trouble. They declared that we had no right to photograph in that area, as it was a border area—despite the fact that the border with the Congo Republic was about 20 miles (32 km) away. Apparently, asking for permission was as bad as actually taking illegal photographs. Standing in the corner was a young man wearing only underclothes and white socks. He looked decidedly unhappy. His trouser belt was tied around his neck and his shoes and clothes were on the floor beside him. There were red marks all around his neck and I could imagine him being cruelly pulled along by a soldier after the belt had been fastened around his neck.

I was sent back to the car for my passport, with an immigration man shadowing me all the way. He even had the nerve to ask me for money to buy himself a drink. They took my passport and precious letter of authority to photocopy, tucked them away in a register book and sat my camera on top. The senior officer wrote out all the details of my passport and visa and my host's ID card. He asked for my hotel and room number. Room number? I pretended to forget. My host thought it was Number 18 but I didn't want to enlighten them. I had visions of an illegal and unwelcome night visitor.

The armed guard declared that he thought I was a soldier who had come to spy on Zaire and take back photos for my government. He wanted me to be aware of his authority and power by saying, 'I have a gun, and I could seize you and tie your hands together like this,' holding out his hands together and rubbing his wrists together.

Another 30 minutes of earnest discussion took place until finally the senior official went outside, beckoning my colleague to follow. A strange bit of reverse bargaining commenced. He demanded US$10. My host refused. Because he refused to pay, the price went up to $12. The official came back to ask me for the money. I refused. Outside again and the price went up to $15. No way, we were not paying anything—we were Christian workers. There was another discussion outside and when it finally reached $18 we gave in.

It was a case of the longer this went on the more expensive it would become so I was asked if I would agree to pay up. They wanted US dollars because the exchange rate had risen to over a million francs to the dollar.

They returned to the office and the official sat quietly saying or doing nothing. The 'office' had only three walls so I could look at the constant stream of people passing by. People averted their eyes not wanting to have anything to do with the officials. The official took out the documents, looked at them once more, then returned them to the register. For several minutes no one spoke. It was an eerie silence. I sat there wondering if I should be more worried than I felt. He took them out once more, fiddled with them and returned them to their hiding place. After five more minutes of complete silence, he took them out and without a word, handed them to my colleague. We said a hurried thank you and goodbye, and left as smartly as we could. My money was still in the vehicle, so we were escorted back to it and I paid up. This wasn't the time or place to maintain my belief that bribery should never be encouraged.

I would have loved to spend time looking around that market. There were items of all description on sale, especially dried fish and forest animals. But the small monkeys, split open and cooked whole, looked particularly gruesome with their little white teeth left to grin at the customer. They looked disturbingly like human babies.

The following evening I met up with a former colleague from Côte d'Ivoire. He was in the country to conduct a computer course at an important mission hospital in the countryside. He arrived at 2.00 a.m. and was confronted by a difficult immigration official at the airport. His first question was whether he had anyone to meet him. No he didn't, so he was taken away to a small office for questioning.

Although he had an entry visa, he was told that it wasn't valid as he didn't have a special letter of authority to visit the country. He was also told that he needed to have a copy of the letter with which he applied for his visa and a copy of his visa application forms. What nonsense! Luckily he had an email copy with him, but it was refused because it didn't bear the authorization stamp of approval from the appropriate ministry. He would have to purchase a new visa for his 10-day visit and this would cost US$1,500.

It took him an hour to argue his way out of that problem and was only released when the senior official on duty called in to see what the problem was. He knew the hospital and said that, because they do much to help the people, the man should let him go without further hassle. The 'charge' was then reduced to US$350. Of course, the fact is, he shouldn't have had to pay anything.

Outside the building, my friend also came across a pair of policemen who asked for money for coffee because they were there to keep him safe. As the taxi moved away another fellow hopped in while it was moving and said that he was also a policeman and asked for some money. But that wasn't the end of my friend's troubles.

On arrival at the guesthouse, the driver demanded a fare of US$150. The correct fare was about US$5. The receptionist on duty was able to scrape up $18 and he himself had about $6, but it took two hours of argument before the taxi driver would go. I was woken up by the yelling taxi driver, but I dared not show my face!

My Sunday was spent visiting seven churches. We would arrive at each church and send word to the pastor that we were there and thus receive permission to photograph the proceedings. All of the churches were packed out, with some having hundreds of people seated outside. One had a large canvas shelter over the road, leaving just a single lane for traffic. The local council is quite happy about this, so long as the shelter is removed as soon as the morning-long service is over. The smallest church we visited had about 800 people in the congregation and the largest 3,000. This particularly large church was started by a Christian doctor who always prayed with his patients. When he realised that more and more people were coming, not for medical treatment, but for prayer, he started a church service.

The economic situation in Zaire was very bad indeed. The banking system had all but collapsed. For the past three years, the Bible Society office had not used cheques but handled every financial transaction in cash. While the official exchange rate was quite reasonable and quite close to the condoned black market rate, people were not using the banks. If money was paid into an account there was no guarantee that it would ever come out. The excuse was always that there is no cash available, come back tomorrow. There was no point in writing out a cheque because even though the money may be shown as in the account the bank would never pay out on the cheque.

Our office used a private banking system set up by the Roman Catholic Church. When one of the seven depots around the country had an excess of cash, they simply passed it over to the local Catholics who credited the society's account in Kinshasa. All Zairian currency was immediately converted into hard currency so it didn't lose its value.

There was a camp for Rwandan refugees in Kinshasa provided by the Roman Catholic Archdiocese. Although it was within the city limits, the road had been cut by a storm earlier in the week. This meant having to take a circuitous route along a primitive path of several kilometres through some suburban villages. The terrain was so bad in places that the four-wheel drive was needed.

We found about 70 refugees who had somehow made the journey from Goma on the far side of the country to the capital. After spending a year in camps in the Goma area, these people had come by bus to Kisangani on the Zaire River and taken the boat to Kinshasa. This was a journey of two weeks, travelling as deck passengers. This meant that they cooked, slept and lived on the deck, often without any shelter from either the tropical sun or rainstorms.

The centre was luxurious compared to the camps I had seen in Goma. There they had only the meagrest of shelter made of straw and a piece of United Nations blue plastic sheeting. Here in the centre, they slept 20 to a room with plenty of space between beds.

Even the most important roads through Kinshasa had huge potholes and the majority of secondary roads had no paving left at all. The city is reputed to have about 4 million people—although no one really knows the exact number. In general, the infrastructure is very poor. Nlandu told me that his house phone works well because every week a technician calls to check it—with the help of a little financial encouragement. He also said that he didn't know of anyone who actually paid any income tax, because it was just easier to pay off the tax inspector.

Congo Brazzaville

Directly opposite Kinshasa, capital of the Democratic Republic of the Congo across the River Zaire, is Brazzaville, the capital city of the Congo Republic. Fast ferries take only 20 minutes to cross the swiftly flowing river, so I went across to the Congo for a couple of days.

Of course, it wasn't just a simple matter of catching the ferry and passing through a passport control. On arrival at the port on the Kinshasa side, a man dressed in a long bright blue gown demanded our passports. He was not inside an office, but outside, standing in the sun.

After some hesitation, we handed our passports over and followed the man to a dirty little office labelled 'Immigration Control'. The senior official, dressed in a fine white shirt and black tie, received us courteously, recording the details of the passport assisted by three other officers who treble checked all the details.

The blue gown then escorted us to another office where a departure form was completed. No less than seven men and women immigration officers handled the passport with various ones applying rubber stamps to the departure form and passport.

The blue gown hung around asking for a tip. He argued his case: he was our guide—did we not understand—without his help we would never be able to leave the country. He had shown us the offices we had to go to and see the right people. I left my colleague to deal with him.

Once aboard the double-decked ferry, we were soon on our way. I gave up counting the number of derelict boats, barges and ships of various sizes that littered the area along the bank of the river near the port. There were about one hundred of them. There were floating tangles of water hyacinth everywhere. This stuff has become a big problem in Central Africa. It was originally brought over from South America by someone who thought the powder blue and purple flowers would be lovely in his fishpond. The plant's roots are so strong that even floodwaters will not wash them away.

The great Central African river has two names, depending on what bank you are on. It's the Zaire River one side and the Congo on the other.

On arrival at the port of Brazzaville, the immigration people received us courteously, and quickly dealt with the formalities. When I filled out my arrival card, I inadvertently overlooked listing my passport number. No one noticed but waved me through. This reminded me of a Swiss United Nations officer I met once who travelled a great deal in Africa, and said his 'hobby' was to fill in his forms incorrectly by altering the passport numbers slightly. He likes to think of little clerks in crowded dingy government offices checking immigration arrival and departure forms and trying to reconcile them.

Congo Brazzaville, as it is commonly known, became independent from France in 1960 and chose the name of The Marxist-Leninist Peoples' Republic of the Congo. The French called it the Middle Congo. It has more oil than most African countries. I heard one traveller say that this is not a city where the people you meet tell you of places to eat and things to see. But that was even truer of Kinshasa. There is a mistrust of foreigners.

There I stood in Congo Brazzaville, trying to draw as little attention to myself as possible, thinking of all the people who had said that I would never be allowed in. I hadn't applied for a visa and these were 'never issued at the border' like mine had just been. Here I was with a three day visit approved in what has been called the most difficult equatorial African country to enter—the least visited, the least known and the most interesting.

It was immediately apparent that this capital city was in far better shape than Kinshasa. The roads were in a good state of repair and the place had an air of peace and quietness. It was much cleaner and there was more traffic. A Zaire man from our office, whose job it was to 'protect' me, observed, 'In this place there are many chemist shops and no sick people. In my country we have many sick people and no chemist shops.'

The country hides many dark secrets. It is one of the few countries where slavery is still tolerated. There are several Pygmy tribes who are enslaved by the Bantu people. The Pygmy number about seven percent of the population and have been subjected to periods of genocide.

The Bible Society executive secretary, who was to be my host, was a few minutes late meeting us. But he had a good reason. He had just that hour taken delivery of a brand new Mitsubishi four-wheel drive double-cab utility truck—a gift from the German Bible Society. I photographed him with his new truck so that the office in Germany could use the picture. They had asked me to do this, and I made a mental note to write and tell them how lucky they were that the truck had been released in time for my visit.

After seven weeks of haggling with customs to have the vehicle cleared, the executive secretary was a very happy man – grinning from ear to ear. He was still grinning when we left him a few days later. His prestige had shot up! He never referred to the vehicle simply as his 'car' or 'truck', but always with the full description, 'my Mitsubishi four-wheel drive double cab utility truck'.

Sadly, in the years since I visited, Congo Brazzaville has suffered a great deal through civil war. During that conflict, nearly a third of the population had to flee their homes. As of 2005, UNICEF reports that only 35 percent of health centres are open and 82 percent of the country's educational structures have vanished. Some schools have been closed for seven years. There were an estimated 5,000 child soldiers active in the conflict in 2005.

Then began a busy day of visiting various church leaders. Our schedule included a reception held by the leaders of the Kimbanguist church. This is an independent church founded by Simon Kimbangu in what was then the Belgian Congo (now the Democratic Republic of Congo). Although the church is commonly referred to by the simple name the 'Kimbanguist Church', its full name is actually the *'Église de Jésus Christ sur la Terre par son envoyé spécial Simon Kimbangu'* or, in English, 'The Church of Christ on Earth by His Special Envoy Simon Kimbangu'. It has a total membership throughout Africa of about 5.5 million.

In April 1921, Simon Kimbangu, a Baptist mission catechist, inaugurated a mass movement through his supposed miraculous healings and Biblical teaching. The Belgian authorities treated the faith with suspicion and imprisoned Kimbangu for most of his life (he died while in prison). The church was formally recognised by the Belgian colonial authorities in 1959.

Kimbangu had some different ideas about interpreting the Bible. For instance he felt that Jesus was a black man, so the church took a dim view of white missionaries. They had no place in Africa.

In 1982, I had visited the headquarters of this church in Zaire and saw the newly completed temple that had been built at Kamba. They had cleared an area of bush and erected this huge place of worship many miles from any town or city. It was 100 metres long and 50 metres wide. The son of the founder, who was the current leader, received me which, in light of church policy regarding white Christian workers, was considered a very rare thing.

Here in Congo Brazzaville, it was a great privilege to be received by the leader, and to be given a formal reception. We waited in a large room and, after a few minutes, the leaders of the church solemnly filed in and sat down opposite us.

When I told them I had been to Kamba and pointed out the founder's son in a painting on the wall as the one who had received me, the local leadership was greatly pleased – not to say astounded. Kimbangu had three sons, and the fact that I was able to point out the correct one in power at that time, proved my story. They could hardly believe that this foreigner had been to their most sacred place, and knew all about them. My stature greatly improved with these revelations, and later they asked my host why he hadn't explained to them more fully the importance of my visit!

They expressed their delight that the Bible Society was well established in the country and assured us of their support. It was a solemn meeting and I didn't feel free to photograph them.

Outside the reception hall, a choir was practicing. After photographing the singers, the leader then asked us to wait while they sang a special song for me. It was beautifully performed and I regretted that I didn't have a tape recorder with me.

As we drove away, the Secretary kept shaking his head in wonder at this visit. He fully expected to be refused entry with me, being a white man. I felt like saying, I'm not just a photojournalist you know!

We then called on the Salvation Army. The workers there use the Bible Society New Reader Portions in their literacy classes. Illiteracy is a great problem in the country because, since independence, the government has put more money into the military than education.

The local Bible Society representative had a problem. He took me to an old warehouse where he showed me a huge pile of very dusty cartons. They contained many thousands of French New Testaments & Psalms imported and warehoused by the Bible Society for the Gideons. 'What can we do with these? They have been here for eight years. We have paid the rent for them and now we want to be rid of them.' When I was assured that the local Gideon camp had no interest in them, I suggested he dump them. They were unreadable due to damage caused by the damp, dust and insects.

I promised to inform the Gideons head office about the situation. They ignored my letter probably because they did not know what to say. Later, when I suggested to the next Gideon leader that I met that I would send him the warehouse bill, he did not know what to do. It hurt to think that these books had been all but destroyed by the heat, humidity and white ants. He hated the idea of us wanting to dump them, after all they were the Word of God. Yet they couldn't be presented as sacred books.

Next day we called on a special school for disabled children run by the Roman Catholic Church. A nun of uncertain age was the headmistress. She was delighted to see us. She was a short wiry woman, very tough, but with a tender heart.

She smiled continually as we talked to her about her work with several hundred disabled children and was delighted to show us how they could read the Bible Society New Reader books.

The day after that, we called on the Roman Catholic Archbishop. He hadn't been cooperating well with the Bible Society and we were a little surprised that he was willing to see me. I seemed to have a knack for negotiating such situations, and it was part of my unofficial role to help deal with bishops! The result of the meeting was that he agreed to work with us. When we emerged from his office, the wiry little nun from the disabled school was also there to see him and had doubtless talked his ear off about the way we were helping his children.

The long day finished at 9.30 p.m. when we went to the home of the General Manager of the Congolese Hydrocarbon Company for dinner. His wife, who looked a picture in her national costume, carefully guided the servants as they served a delicious meal of mostly imported French food and drink. I counted eight house servants, cooks and drivers. My host was one of the most important men in the country, apart from Government leaders. There are significant oil deposits as well as extensive offshore holdings. He lived in a palatial house and talked incessantly about his work with the government. Every item in the house was of the best possible quality. He promised to give the new Bible Society all the help he could. A few years later, when civil war enveloped the country, I wondered what happened to him. Although security didn't seem to be a problem, he ordered his driver to accompany us back to my hotel—or should I say, *one* of his drivers!

Poto-Poto is known as the poor quarter of Brazzaville, although a good deal of the city is not exactly 'affluent'. Many houses are made of concrete breezeblock with corrugated iron roofs. We visited a Christian family who could be considered 'wealthy' as they had a fridge and an electric cooking stove. Their one-room house also contained a double bed with a very thin mattress, two rickety wooden chairs, a red plastic bath full of dirty clothes and a wooden cupboard. My colleague nudged me and whispered, 'See that,' pointing to the mosquito net hanging above the bed, 'that's the most important thing in this place.' That was a follow-up to an earlier conversation about the problem of malaria in the city. Malaria is still one of the worst killers in the world.

But this is a city of contrast because we were soon in another part that consisted of two-storeyed colonial houses, with shuttered windows—nice looking places set in what would have been beautiful gardens. The French were long gone, but we could see where they had been. The entire area was shaded by palms of various sorts and was aflame with masses of multicoloured bougainvillaea.

Next day we took the 2.00 p.m. ferry back to Kinshasa, which left at 4.00 p.m. The delay was caused by a severe tropical electrical storm across the river. The sky was black with storm clouds that were punctured by savage flashes of lightning. Several tonnes of rice from India and Pakistan were being loaded from hand trolleys. The coolies brought one trolley loaded with 20 fifty-kilogram bags of rice down a steep bank to the ferry. I was astonished at the way they could control such a heavily loaded trolley and not lose its contents over the side. The steel wheels narrowly missing unshod toes by millimetres.

Photography was permitted on the Congo side but not Zaire. As we approached the customs and immigration on the Zaire side I tried to conceal the limited camera equipment I had taken—only three cameras and five lenses. Apart from the laborious procedures of all the clerks and officers examining my passport and filling out all those forms and wielding their rubber stamps, re-entry into Zaire was comparatively uneventful.

Kinshasa

Transportation within the city of Kinshasa was a problem for the Bible Society staff. A number of them travelled for at least two hours every morning and night – that meant leaving home at about 5.00 a.m. to be in time for work at 8.00 a.m. They have breakfast together on arrival at Bible House. The office closes at 4.00 p.m., but some of the staff would not be home until 6.00 p.m. at the earliest, and even sometimes as late as 8.00 p.m. when the traffic is bad.

The staff there included about 40 colporteurs who came to the Bible House every day and sell Scriptures in the markets and around the city. They sold by commission—25 percent. The total distribution of Scriptures per month in the country was about 10,000 and these colporteurs in Kinshasa accounted for about 8,000 of the total sales. There was no shortage of people to buy the stock—one estimate put the population of the city at 5 to 6 million people.

In addition to the work being done in Kinshasa, the new Bible House in Goma (about 3,000 km from Kinshasa) was now selling about 4,000 Bibles a month.

During the previous ten years, there had been something of a spiritual revival in Kinshasa, with the creation of many independent denominations. Because these congregations are usually independent, there was no head office of any kind. Therefore the use of colporteurs was the only way that these individual groups could be contacted.

Inflation was rampant in the country and it was necessary to reconsider the Bible selling prices nearly every week.

The largest church in the city was the Lobonne Assemblies of God with 6,000 members. They hold two services on a Sunday morning, and we visited to have a look. I walked around the packed out 3,000-seat building and noticed a woman in a multicoloured dress standing near a window, with tears streaming down her face, pouring out her heart to God. I took a photo of her with a long lens. This image has appeared in numerous publications around the world totalling many millions of copies. As far as I know, she never knew that her photo had been taken.

Around the city, there were many weird and wonderful sites to be seen. In one day I saw: a fully loaded taxi being pushed down the hill minus one wheel, with its brake drum scraping along the ground; three women dressed in normal clothes but with fine negligee nightdresses over the top; a man dressed in a pair of pants and a bright red training bra; a couple of men filling the radiator of a 25-tonne lorry with a carton of beer bottles.

Another Experience

This, of course, had not been my first visit to the Congo—I had been there on a number of occasions. A few years before, I flew on KLM from Johannesburg to Kinshasa. There were only four passengers disembarking—always a bad sign when people don't want to visit a country! It was 5.00 a.m. We walked across the tarmac, no bus, but the walk was enjoyable and a chance to stretch the legs after a long flight. The early morning air was fresh.

We entered the Immigration Hall but there was no one in attendance. Then to the Customs area but there was not a soul in sight there either. Then on to the public area. I suggested to my fellow travellers that we had better go back and try and find someone. I had a feeling there would be big trouble when we tried to leave the country if our arrival hadn't been recorded. One fellow just swore, said he would get his office to deal with it, and wandered off. The rest of us returned to the Immigration hall.

After searching around for a few minutes we discovered a security guard asleep behind a stack of chairs. We woke him up and told him to find an Immigration officer. About ten minutes later, a small window in a hexagonal shaped cubicle in the middle of the hall opened a few inches a hand extended and a voice saying, '*Passporte, passporte.*'

In the customs area there wasn't a person in sight, it was completely empty. I left the airport not a little uneasy about not having filled out a customs form. Sure enough on leaving the country a few days later, the customs officer gave me trouble. Luckily my Congolese colleague anticipating problems was able to explain what had happened when I arrived. He led me to the door of the departure lounge and assured me that from here on everything would be all right.

There was a security guard just inside the door and he wanted to examine my hand luggage. He was amazed to find a whole bag containing about 120 rolls of film. He said, 'Does the customs man know you have all this film?' He then led me to the inner office of the senior officer. There were three men sitting on the floor, their backs against the wall and legs stretched out, looking like they had been through a lot. When a normally dark-faced African has a face that has turned grey, you know that something is wrong—very wrong. They looked as though they had been there for several days and were in very bad condition. They obviously had not bathed for some time and their gaunt faces told of hunger and dehydration. The detainees glanced up at me, then quickly looked downwards.

The security guard explained to the officer that I had a lot of things *'photographic'*. The officer sternly ordered him back to his post saying that he would deal with it.

I placed my camera bag on his desk and opened the flap saying, 'These are just cameras.' I kept the brown leather film bag on my shoulder pushed back behind me.

'Huh, *photographique,* that's ok now go, go, go,' he said.

I went—very quickly. Then I discovered the probable reason for the officer being so uptight. A Hercules plane was just landing, bearing the president of another African country who was on a state visit. A long red carpet had been laid out for him, and stretched from the terminal across the tarmac to where the plane would stop.

The plane taxied in and missed the carpet by about 100 metres. It did another circle, and this time stopped about 50 metres short. Round the plane went again, and this time stopped fairly close to the end of the carpet. The guard of honour quickly broke up and tried to drag the carpet to line up with the door of the plane. It folded awkwardly. There were three other European men waiting for my plane and one of them kept making derogatory remarks out the side of his mouth about presidential African pilots. The rest of us tried desperately to keep a straight face. As the short pompous man strutted along the carpet he would say things like, 'Now watch the little fellow trip over the crease in the carpet.'

Once aboard our flight I was a seated in the front row of First Class. Lorraine was a bit worried about me making this particular trip to the Congo, so I assured her that I would be all right and that I would book First Class for this sector. The chances of being treated well were better than in 'cattle class'. This reassured her. It was the only time I ever actually booked a First Class seat.

The front part of our utility Boeing 737 was blocked off for cargo. After takeoff, the stewardess disappeared into the cargo area and changed into her First Class service outfit. The door into this area was right in front of my seat was locked open so I could see what was going on in there. Her special uniform consisted of a grimy crumpled frilly white apron, which she wore over her regular uniform.

There was only one row of First Class seats and I was the sole passenger in this section. The stewardess loaded up her tray from the food containers scattered around the floor in the cargo area. A dozen bread rolls, uncovered, sat on a piece of paper at her feet. Most of them rolled off during takeoff. She spilled some black caviar onto the floor but she quickly scooped it up, placed it on her tray and presented it with aplomb. I served myself, carefully taking the food from the side of the plate that hadn't been spilled on the floor. The rest of the food consisted of three bread rolls, no butter, and two legs from an athletic chicken. The coffee, which was actually very nice, was served from a two gallon container that was filled to the brim, and it was all for me! It just sat on the floor unsecured and I kept my eye on it during takeoff, ready to lift my legs should it tip over and flow through the open door into my cabin.

Before landing in Cameroon, the hostess brought me my immigration and customs forms. Her speech was a quaint mixture of French and English, and I gathered that she was offering to fill them in for me. I gave her my passport and she sat beside me laboriously filling in the blank spaces with child-like writing. After this she took out a small notebook and wrote down my name and the hotel address where I would be staying in Douala.

'Why are you doing that?'

'Oh, me see you there. Me Salina.'

I took that to mean that it was the same hotel where the flight crew would be staying. The truth was that I actually didn't know where I was staying—that was up to my hosts to arrange. But long experience taught me to always put something down like the name of a well-known hotel, as that would surely satisfy the immigration people.

Late that night there was a knock on my door, and there was Salina. We were in the same hotel. She stood there with a large bottle of beer in one hand and three glasses in the other, grinning from ear to ear. Behind her stood another girl, maybe a hostess from economy class. I was in my pyjamas but had hastily grabbed a towel to wrap around me. They barged into my room and sat down on my bed and pointed to the one chair and said, 'Let's have a drink.'

'Why have you come? It's so late, I was sleeping,' I asked stupidly. 'Thank you very much but I don't drink beer.'

'You are very nice, we want to have a party with you.'

What to do? Calling hotel security wouldn't help because I knew there wasn't any. In the bathroom there was a notice informing guests that, due to some labour dispute, there was no hotel security but, in case of trouble, the police should be called. I decided that this was hardly a police matter, so better to let them have their drink and see them off. They were both quite solidly built so they were too big to literally push out of the room. I found some water and had a drink with them. We didn't have enough English and French between us to have a decent conversation so when the glasses were empty they politely thanked me and left for their own rooms. As Salina passed me on the way out she brushed her hand across my bottom and said, 'Later, if you get lonely call me, room 216.' Thank goodness they were gone. I never saw them again.

Zimbabwe

When Zimbabwe was still Southern Rhodesia and Harare was Salisbury, I always liked the way this city would appear out of the plain as you drove towards it. Away in the distance was a cluster of tall buildings that looked as though they appeared out of nowhere. It was a difficult city to photograph from the distance, but that's what I needed to do for my latest assignment.

I hired a taxi to take me out into the surrounding countryside. As we came into the city I stopped the car in order to take a photo that showed a main road and the railway line leading into downtown. As I was taking the photograph, a plain-clothes policeman approached and told me that it was illegal to take such photographs. He told me to accompany him to the police station. He ordered the taxi to take us to the CID headquarters.

He sat beside me in the back seat clutching my camera. I reached out for the camera saying, 'It's still switched on, let me switch it off.'

He angrily pulled it away saying, 'Don't touch it. This is my evidence.'

The car was driven up to the high steel gates of the CID and, after a brief discussion with the guards, the gates were opened for us. The taxi was driven into the courtyard and the gates closed behind us with a rattle and a bang. They didn't swing easily on their hinges and I had the stupid thought that if the gates were that creaky, what must the rest of the police system be like?

We entered the building with my guard holding tightly to my upper arm, grimly nodding to his colleagues as if to say, 'Look at this terrible white man I have here.'

I was taken to a senior CID officer and my guard explained why he had brought me in. The officer just grunted and ordered me to be taken to the next higher official. He too listened to my guard and without comment sent me higher up. This was the senior commander on duty and he asked me what was the trouble. Thankfully he allowed me to do the talking.

I explained the work of the Bible Society of Zimbabwe and the way it was linked to the worldwide fellowship of national Bible Societies called the United Bible Societies. Fortunately, I had in my camera bag a copy of the annual report of the Zimbabwe Society. This publication carried on the front cover a photo of the President of the country paying an official visit to the Society's offices.

My camera sat on the table and I continued to clutch my camera bag on my lap. No one asked to examine the bag. I was asked for my passport, but I wasn't going to surrender that if at all possible so, without telling a direct lie, I mumbled something like, 'Oh dear, where is it? I was planning to fly to Kenya this afternoon and everything is packed in my room.' It was actually in my camera bag in a semi-secret compartment. I could recite the number and date so those were recorded.

'But why were you taking photographs?' asked the commander. I explained that I considered Harare a beautiful city and wanted to photograph it. And, I explained carefully, a copy of all my photos would be given to the Bible Society in Zimbabwe, and one day they might need such a photo.

I was then taken to a room nearby and told to sit down. There was another white man in the room looking a little dejected. I couldn't help but notice that he looked a little like me with similar build and colouring. I asked him what he was doing here. 'I'd rather not say,' he replied.

'Don't talk,' barked the guard standing in the doorway.

I was then taken down several flights of steps to a lower basement where I was fingerprinted and photographed. At the same time the taxi driver, who had been waiting in this room, was told to go. I asked him to go to the Bible Society and tell them what had happened. He gave me his cigarette pack and asked me to write down the address. He was visibly shaking. He knew too much about this place. I thanked him and apologized for getting him into trouble. I had the feeling I was sinking deeper and deeper into trouble myself, yet at the same time, I felt a calm assurance that everything would turn out all right.

The finger printing was a messy business and I was given a very dirty rag to clean my hands afterwards. It made them worse so I used my handkerchief. As I put my hand in my pocket to pull it out, a policeman shouted, 'Don't put your hand in your pocket.' This was strange because at no time had I been searched or frisked, or had my camera bag examined.

It took five men to take my photograph. One set up a number board for me to hold. The photographer was using Polaroid film. After the photo developed they found it had been badly over exposed and my image was hardly discernible. This provoked a furious argument among them. Apparently each Polaroid film was numbered to coincide with the prison numbering system.

Over and above all the shouting a voice was heard, 'Take this man upstairs.' He was a huge, tall officer whose word must be obeyed. I held out my dirty hands, 'How about something to clean these?'

More shouting and a clean cloth was produced. 'Thank you very much,' said I as cheerfully as I could, and followed the officer up about five flights of stairs to the commander's room. There sat Mr Kumbarami, the General Secretary of the Bible Society in Zimbabwe. I blessed the taxi driver.

My true identity and situation had been verified and I was free to go. My camera was handed back, the film still intact. Sitting just inside the door of the CID building was my UBS colleague Ted Hope who had come along to give moral support. As we walked out and the main gate clanged behind us, Ted said, 'You are very lucky, not many people walk out of this place.'

I was a due to fly out to Nairobi, so I returned to my hotel in the company of a CID officer, collected my luggage and was driven to the airport. We arrived at the time the plane was due to leave. My plain-clothed CID man escorted me through the system and, looking like a *persona non grata*, I was put on the delayed flight. They had obviously called the airport and told them to delay departure.

It later transpired that the CID had confused me with a South African who was looking into African National Congress activities. It so happened that I had been standing outside an ANC safe house when I was accosted. No wonder the other gentleman I had seen inside the CID building hadn't wanted to talk.

South Sudan

As I write this, the southern part of Sudan is celebrating its independence from The Republic of Sudan. The northern part is largely Muslim while the south is Christian. Juba, the southern capital, is well over 1,000 kilometres from the national capital Khartoum and there has long been a communication problem between the two cities. In 1996, the German Bible Society responded to an appeal for a Bible House to be built in Juba. This was done in record time due to the help of ACROSS (Africa Committee for the Relief of Southern Sudan), who handled the building job. The Germans asked me to visit Juba and photograph the Bible House so that they could show their supporters what their donations had achieved.

Three times the Sudanese Embassy in London refused me a visa, but on the fourth application they relented. On arrival in Nairobi, Kenya, our office told me in no uncertain terms that it was impossible to visit Juba. In fact one colleague who had tried many times, came very close to insulting me by saying that it was impossible to get a visa and it was no longer possible to fly from Nairobi. There were no commercial flights available. The only airline that flew there, Air Sudan, was grounded because it had not paid its fuel bills. There was no overland route as the borders were closed to all traffic. I phoned MAF and they told me not to bother them, so that left the only other missionary airline, Methodist Aviation. Their response was simple, 'Sure we can fly you there, but you will have to get the all-important flight permission and that's not possible.' This permit could only be obtained from the Sudanese embassy.

The waiting room of the Sudanese Embassy in Nairobi was packed. As soon as I appeared a staff member asked me what I wanted. This is one of the occasions when it pays to be a white man in Africa. He took a newspaper and tore off the edge and told me write down what I wanted. I wrote, 'Flight permission to Juba to photograph the new Bible House.' I knew that if the Ambassador was a Muslim I had no hope, but if he was a Christian then maybe. Either way, I knew it was best to be up front.

Within a couple of minutes I was escorted into the presence of the Ambassador. He greeted me warmly and called for tea. This was a case when one must only speak when spoken to, so I waited for him to ask me what I wanted. He was dressed in Muslim garb and I feared the worst. He slowly stood up and walked around his desk and took from the corner a large roll of building plans. Spreading them out on his desk, he said that he was building a house and asked if I could help him to understand the nomenclature of the architect. After 45 minutes of discussing dwangs, rafters and joists, he declared himself satisfied with my explanations. He rolled up the plans and said, 'So you want a visa. Okay no problem,' and rang a bell for his secretary.

It took a few minutes to explain that London had already granted a visa, all I needed was flight permission for a one-day visit to Juba. He was mystified by the fact that I already had a visa, and he sat with his head in his hands and mumbled something, then declared that my request would create some difficulty. It would be necessary to contact Khartoum. 'I will telegraph them immediately,' and called for a secretary. He then asked me why I wanted to go to Juba, so I explained the work of the Bible Society and how the Germans had provided the money for the building that ACROSS had built. The Bible society supporters, I told him, would like to see photographs of the building.

He invited me to wait in his office for Khartoum's response while he made several telephone calls. The response from the north was quick and positive, and as he handed me the paperwork he said, 'I have a favour to ask. Please would you take a young lady with you? There is only you and your colleague isn't it, so there is room in the plane for another?' How could I refuse?

Next morning at 6.00 a.m. I met up with Ted Hope, a UBS translations consultant, who was taking the opportunity to fly with me and spend a few hours with a translation team. We were about to board the Cessna when a car pulled up and out hopped a woman of about 30 who was probably twice my weight. Her driver then produced her luggage, which consisted of several large packages. The pilot took one look and said that he could only take half the parcels. The woman then turned to Ted and said, 'Sorry, there is no room for you, I have to take all my things.'

'Sorry madam,' I said, 'he's going—I'm paying for this flight not you.' Fortunately she didn't argue.

The pilot then offered a front seat to one of us, pointing to Ted and me, and to the woman he said, 'Sorry you're too big.'

She shrugged her shoulders and said, 'Ok-k, I sit with him,' pointing her chin at me.

Soon after taking off from the Wilson Nairobi airport, we hit some turbulence. My fellow passenger didn't like it one bit, and grabbed hold of me for security. I pretended to retch, and she soon let go.

On arrival in Juba, we were met at the plane's door by two heavily armed soldiers—two pistols and an AK47 each. They motioned us to follow them and led us to the duty free shop. An airport duty free shop is usually a good indication of the type of country you're entering, so when I saw that the only things on sale were a couple of bottles of perfume and a tube of Colgate toothpaste, I knew what to expect downtown. Sure enough, later in the day when it was time for lunch, we were directed to the 'best place in town'. This was an outdoor bar and café that had only two items on the menu: tinned orange juice from Kenya, and samosas. No essentials for a bar or café, such as beer, tea, water, bread or rice.

My Bible Society host was very troubled about the fact that I had made the journey in order to photograph his new building. 'But photography without a permit is strictly forbidden here.' Photographing inside was no problem, but outdoors would be a different story. I noticed that over the road from the building was a market with a toilet block. By standing on a toilet seat using a long lens I was able to get good photos of the building through the open slots of the breezeblocks at the top of the wall. A nice discrete place to photograph from. It was an even better shot from the women's toilet. The Germans were very pleased.

The Bible House was considered by the mayor, when he opened it, to be the best building in the city. Built of brick in the local style, with an arched entrance way and windows, it did look very impressive.

I sensed a tense atmosphere about the town and when talking with English-speaking strangers it wasn't long before they began to complain about the government in the north. The fact that a new Bible House had been successfully built was a source of wonder to many. I had a brief meeting with the Minister of Education and he welcomed the initiative of the Bible Society to develop its work in the area. In guarded terms, he suggested that we were 'very lucky'. In what could almost be regarded as treason he said, 'We southerners have little or no affinity with the northerners.' The civil war between the north and south broke out shortly after my visit.

The Society's Landrover was out of fuel, so I was invited to fill the tank at about $5 per litre. We visited a Dinka village in the countryside. The Dinka are perhaps Africa's tallest people, and many of the men were about six feet tall. They are all quite thin and have a very dark skin. It is a real photographic challenge to create good skin tones and obtain the correct colour of their bright clothing. A class of high school girls dressed in white blouses were having a Bible study under a tree. White blouses, dark faces, white books and dark hands pushed the limits of colour transparency photography. The Dinkas have distinctive tribal markings on their faces, so it was important to portray these clearly.

There was an adult literacy class going on under another tree. A group of about 20 men sat in a circle and watched the teacher write on a blackboard. They were then each given a small textbook, and the letters from the first page were written up on the blackboard. The teacher had the class repeat the words after him. One man of about 40 sat with his book upside down and faithfully repeated all that the teacher said as he stared at his book.

'How can he learn?' I asked my colleague.

'That man, he will never learn,' was the response.

Sempiak Villas, Lombok

Lorraine, Ida and
Clive, Laut Biru Cafe,
Lombok

Lebaran train rush,
Jakarta

Child Rwandan
refugees

Lioness and cubs, Kenya

man worshipping, Taiwan

funeral of Balimo Five,
Jakarta

Muslim women at prayer,
Jakarta

Philippina woman

Duck-billed woman,
Nigeria

Lone bull elephant, Kenya

Author's passports

Brazilian starlet

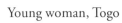

Young woman, Togo

6

VISIT TO ROMANIA, MOLDAVA, UKRAINE AND POLAND—living history

1992

A visit to three countries of Eastern Europe had been arranged by our Service Centre for the Middle East and Europe for Bible Society staff engaged in raising funds for the work in this area. The plan was that we would meet up in Frankfurt Airport.

The security check at Frankfurt was puzzling. These were the early days of modern airport security. After readily agreeing not to x-ray my film, one of the officers asked me to accompany him to a special inspection room. I didn't like the sound of that. 'It's the computer,' he said, and so I switched on my Texas Travelmate 3000 notebook. He carefully wiped it inside and out with a piece of paper then put the paper under a sheet of glass. He took a machine that emitted a very strong light and sounded like a vacuum cleaner, and passed it over the glass.

The computer was taken and the officer went over it carefully with his machine, covering every inch of it inside and out, then placed his machine into a slot of a large grey cabinet-like device. He checked a video screen connected to this contraption and after a minute said, 'Ok, you may go'. But

I was curious about this treatment of my precious notebook and asked what he was doing. The burly security officer looked me straight in the eye and grunted, 'We are looking for gunpowder. There is no gunpowder in it'.

In the waiting area for the flight to Bucharest, I found Dominique from France. There were four sleepy looking fellows who looked as though they might be the Canadians we were expecting. Soon Martin Eberhart from Switzerland joined us and Terje Hartberg, the group leader who was the coordinator of the Bible Society work in FEESU (Former Eastern Europe and the Soviet Union).

Arriving in Bucharest airport we were treated like VIP guests because we were sponsored by the Patriarch of the Romanian Orthodox Church—the highest church official in the land. His representative ushered us through immigration and customs control, and took us to a set of apartments. Before the fall of Communism, President Ceausescu had built many buildings, some say thousands, after razing about a third of historic Bucharest in an attempt to modernise his capital city. It is said that the demolition included 19 Orthodox Christian churches, six Jewish synagogues, three Protestant churches, and 30,000 residences. Our apartments were in one of the new buildings, and had been given to the Romanian Orthodox Church in part-reimbursement for property confiscated by the former government. We were a party of ten men and had the use of three flats. They were much better than hotel accommodation, at least the kind we could afford, because they were designed for communist party officials. One of the surprises in the newly fallen communist regimes was to discover the luxury in which some of their leaders had lived. My luxurious bedroom on the sixth floor looked over a magnificent open plaza within sight of the infamous Palace of the People. Two pretty young Orthodox nuns served us good home grown food supervised by a gentleman who was clearly proud of the service they all provided. He didn't do any work himself, he just stood over the young women, directing their every move.

The Palace of the People was the grand centrepiece of Ceausescu's modernization. This grandiose building is said to be the largest in the world after the Pentagon in USA. It is certainly the world's largest and most expensive 'civilian' building. It is 86m high from the ground up, and is 92m deep underground. It has 1,100 rooms. According to the literature

I found in my apartment room, this magnificent building includes one million cubic metres of marble, 3,500 tonnes of crystal for its 480 chandeliers, 1,409 ceiling lights, 700,000 tonnes of steel and bronze for monumental doors and windows, and 200,000 m² of woollen carpets of various sizes. Some of these carpets were so large and heavy that the carpet-making machines had to be moved inside the building to weave them on site.

After a breakfast of cheese, salami and bread, we set off for the ancient town of Curtea de Arges about 140 kilometres from Bucharest. The capital city was a sombre dull grey under a heavy overcast sky. The autumn leaves had deserted the trees that lined the streets. Pollution haze obliterated the distant views down the long straight streets; it was not a pretty sight at eight in the morning. Even the Palace of the People lacked its usual yellow glow in the dirty grey morning.

The countryside south of Bucharest was quite featureless, with most of the agricultural fields left fallow for the winter. An oil refinery about 100 km along the road was almost hidden under its own smoke and vapours, which poured from the numerous chimneys and cooling towers.

The town of Curtea de Arges is, as a government brochure put it, 'loaded with history and legend, blending together the memory of the past and the shining present'. It was founded in the 13th Century. The Fagaras Mountains are not far away and we could see the snow down to low levels. This town began its life as a crossing point of ancient trade routes along the Arges Valley.

There were two places that our hosts wanted us to see. One was a very old church and the other a monastery. The church, known as 'The Royal Church', was built in the same century as the town was founded, and is the oldest church building in Romania. It is open to the public, but is not used for worship services because the interior is decorated with paintings and icons from floor to ceiling. Some of these date back to the time when it was built and because incense is an important part of Orthodox worship, the modern day church leaders believe that it would damage the historic works of art.

While the group was being given a lecture on each of the paintings and icons, I slipped outside to meet some of the local people. There were two groups of small boys playing in the churchyard and they clearly came from different sides of the tracks. One lot was clean and tidy and very polite. The others were scruffy and dirty, and two brothers had deformed feet that caused them to walk on their ankles with the soles of their feet turned inwards. One took his gumboot off to show me. The foot was wrapped in a small towel with a rather dirty sock on over the top. The boys all posed beautifully for photos.

Back with the tour group, we were taken to the Monastery of Curtea de Arges—first to view the magnificent church, then to eat at the bishop's table. This building dates back to 1514 and is regarded as one of the most important examples of religious art and architecture in the world. The church is constructed from Albesti stone that glows a dull yellow in the sun. The guide delighted in telling us a local legend to the effect that after the church was dedicated, but not yet completely finished, the king decided that, in gratitude to God, he would sacrifice the first person he saw the following morning after he had worshipped there. This turned out to be his beloved wife and he had her 'buried in the church'. The guide did not explain exactly how he did this.

According to another legend, when the church was finished, the king had the architect climb to the top and then had the scaffolding removed so that the architect couldn't go off and design an even more beautiful structure elsewhere. The poor chap, being unable to climb down, made himself a pair of wings and floated down. The spot where he landed became a spring of water.

One of our number was an Orthodox Archdeacon named Michael Roshak, who had assisted the Bible Societies in establishing the work in former Soviet countries, especially the USSR. He was an American citizen but fluent in Russian and at the conclusion of our visit, he sang the Lord's Prayer. His strong rich tenor voice reverberated around the building and bounced down off the roof in a most spectacular way. A few local people who had come to the church for private worship stood back in amazement uttering words of astonishment at this 250 lb English-speaking priest singing his heart out so beautifully.

Next to the church was a monastery. It had been a palace of the king and was now home to the bishop. We were served a lavish luncheon of six courses. First of all, a special drink was served by two young men. They poured from an ordinary-looking teapot a hot drink that looked a bit like Chinese tea. Served in delicate china cups and saucers, it turned out to be hot plum brandy sweetened and spiced. It was delicious and is designed to warm up a person who has just come in from the cold. That suited us as it was so cold outside that there was ice on the puddles.

There was an open fire and one young fellow was assigned to keep it going. He sat beside it for the two hours we were there and watched the flames constantly, adding a little wood from time to time. The bishop was out of town, so we dined in comparative informality. We wondered when the food was going to stop coming. The first course was a plate of salami, red peppers, cheese, and tiny spiced meatballs. Then came soup, a beef dish, roast pork and a Romanian delicacy of meat and rice wrapped in cabbage leaves served with corn meal. Finally we were served a range of cakes, apples and coffee. Following another round of hot plum brandy was a home brewed white wine, and water from the monastery well.

The first ever national Bible Society in Romania had been inaugurated the day before, and the new General Secretary was our host for the day. He performed his first task in this new role by presenting a box of Bibles to the bishop's palace staff.

We were just about to leave, when an old lady, dressed in black with a scarf over her head, asked to speak to us. She had heard of our visit and had prepared a poem about the Bible. The poem was in Romanian and was quickly translated for us. Her name was Anna, and she assured us of her prayers as we tried to provide the Bible for her people. Despite having lived almost her entire life under communist rule, she had a strong unshakeable Christian faith.

After lunch, the sun came out for the first time that day and the glory of the special stone of the church became apparent—so I photographed it again.

It began to rain on the way home, but I was able to photograph a farmer and his two sons with an ox cart. He was simply delighted that we had stopped to take their photos. Then we came across two cartloads of hay, each drawn by two horses. This time the drivers were most unhappy about my cameras, and hid themselves in the hay as we converged. The wife of one of them completely submerged herself, reappearing only after we had passed, shaking her fist at me.

Next day was Sunday, and most of it was spent at a Romanian Orthodox Monastery a few kilometres outside Bucharest. It was situated beside a lake on a small island linked by a causeway. Our first duty was to visit the grave of a famous Bible translator, Gala Galactia (1688), who is buried in a cemetery on the island. We then attended the service at the church, which was already halfway through. Some of our party were led to the front of the congregation and, in the usual Orthodox custom, stood for the remaining hour and a half until the service was over.

I held back from the main group in order to be free to take photographs in and around the church. Of all the various Orthodox churches, the Romanian is the most tolerant of photographers. There were strong beams of sunlight shining through the windows near the back of the congregation, providing beautiful lighting. Some of the people stood while others knelt on the floor for long periods of time. I noticed one young woman praying her heart out for nearly an hour as she knelt close to the floor near the back door. One elderly man sitting in a very dark corner tearfully moaned in prayer for the time I was there. I wondered about the reason for his distress.

While I waited for the service to finish, a lady approached me rather hesitatingly and spoke to me in French, then German, then Romanian and then, as a last resort, in English. She showed me a letter that outlined her difficulties in getting an exit visa to emigrate from Romania to the United States. I was at pains to make her understand that, not being a citizen of that country, I had no influence to help her get a visa.

A young woman spent her time at the steel cabinet in which candles were burned outside the church. I asked her if she could speak English, to which she replied in Romanian that she could not. She then proceeded to chatter away to me in Romanian until I interrupted her, saying that I couldn't speak her language. Undaunted, she continued to chatter away without a pause. I asked her if I could take her photo but she refused. She pointed to a bleeding cold sore on her lip and then, passing her hand over her clothes, made it clear that she wasn't dressed for a photo. Her job was to relight candles that were blown out by the wind. Whenever someone came to place a candle, she stood aside and then returned to her task when they left.

After the service, the priest in charge, Father Jerome, stood on the steps outside the front of the church and explained many of the traditions of the monastery. He had studied in the USA and spoke English well. He had been our host two and half years previously, when Terje Hartberg, Steven Downey and I had visited the monastery. The thing that had impressed us then was his enthusiasm and joy in his monkhood. He hadn't changed a bit—he still spoke excitedly about life at the monastery. He was the latest in a long line of Orthodox priests from his family, going back five generations. He presented me with an unlabelled bottle of clear liquid. It was either homemade wine or plum brandy, so I asked him what I should tell customs. He smiled impishly and said, 'Just tell them it's holy water.'

It was now lunchtime, and a messenger came over from the dining room to invite us to eat with the monks. Two long lines of tables had been set up with all the monks on one side and we were shown our places on the other side. The rest of the places on our side were taken up by parishioners who were invited to eat.

This was a fast day, so instead of the usual fish being served we had vegetable soup and a plate of vegetables, served with delicious crusty brown bread from the monastery ovens. Two young novice monks served the food. A monk who had been selling candles and religious books in the church suddenly appeared at my elbow with a large jug of homemade wine. He was introduced as the 'wine specialist' and he took great pride in serving us his latest vintage, which was a very mild form of fermented grape juice. At a special small table on his own, sat the Abbott of the monastery, and two other tables were reserved for the father confessors.

The room was lined with paintings of the history of the monastery.

The food in Romanian monasteries is always good. It is usually grown on the premises and is completely unprocessed, unlike much of our modern food. Some of our number were concerned about putting on weight, but I assured them that the wholesome unprocessed food of monasteries was not the least bit fattening. The monastery was completely self-supporting, following the instruction given by St Benedict (d. AD535) who said that monasteries 'ought to be built so as to contain all necessities within [them] . . . so that monks shall have no need to wander abroad, as this is not helpful to their souls'.

Father Jerome took us to visit a very old church that was not usually used for public worship. While we were there a Romanian family came into the church just as Father Michael Roshak, Father Sabin and Father Jerome sang what is called 'the light liturgy'. They harmonised beautifully. I spoke to the family and, with assistance from a French speaker and a German speaker, was able to have a conversation with them. They were Mr and Mrs Gregorian, and they told us how they had kept the faith during the years of communism, despite having no Bible. Their 15-year-old son, George, and 10-year-old daughter, Halinee, had come to faith in Christ. Mr Gregorian told us of his delight when, one day in a church in Bucharest, they were at last able to buy a Romanian Bible. 'We read it together as a family every night,' said the mother. 'In fact our young daughter aged five years always reminds us to read as soon as we have finished eating'. There was a beautiful aura of peace around that family of five.

The local Pentecostal leader invited us to a service in his church from 5.00 to 7.00 p.m. About 400 people attended the meeting, which was very mild or subdued for Pentecostal type worship. Wilfred Wight from the Canadian Bible Society gave the greetings and the sermon on our behalf, and I was actually encouraged by the people to take photographs as the service proceeded.

We spent most of the next day on Patriarchal Mountain. First we went to the 310-year-old Patriarchal Printing Press where the first full Bible in Romanian was printed in 1687. In those days, each page was laboriously set and printed by hand one sheet at a time. Last year the Netherlands Bible Society, through the United Bible Societies, provided the church press with a brand new two colour Miller printing machine capable of producing an edition of 50,000 Bibles in a matter of weeks. It was an exciting time for the finance director, Pete van de Poppe, from that Society because he had handled the financing for the new press, and was now able to see it in person. The old Patriarchal Press still used ancient linotype machines that clattered away as the operators typed in the text and form the type from molten lead. There were still three such machines in full operational use at the Press.

It is well known nowadays that there were a great number of orphanages in Romania. This was a direct result of Dictator Ceausescu's policy of not permitting abortions and thereby encouraging the fastest possible population growth. The result was that unmarried women were encouraged to carry their children to full term and, if they could not care for them, the state took the children over. Our guide told us that the public were never told about these orphanages as most of them were regarded as state secrets. Thanks to massive amounts of aid from Western countries, the majority of these orphanages are now in much better condition than what they were under the former regime.

We visited the Queen Katherine Orphanage that used to house 800 children, but now has only 400 so is not as overcrowded as it once was. It was founded in 1897 and had a beautiful chapel in the grounds where young children were baptised when they were first brought to the home. The communists stopped that practice for many years.

This was a home for very young children up to the age of about three to four years. Not all were true orphans—some were kept at the home because they needed special care and treatment, especially those with motor neuron problems. The medical staff there seemed to know what they were doing. There was plenty of special equipment to assist children with walking difficulties and an American nurse was on-hand, sharing her knowledge with the staff.

We were then taken to Orphanage No 2, where 67 older children live. This was not as well provided for as the first one, but never the less in much better condition than the orphanages I had seen when I had visited the country two years previously. When the children were told that we had some presents of books for them, they squealed with delight. They were clean and tidy and well cared for, and immediately began to read the special Scripture booklets designed for young children.

The Patriarch of the Romanian Orthodox Church invited us to lunch at his palace (built in 1708). We received a call at 1.30 p.m. to the effect that he was ready and waiting for us. We hurried up the hill to his residence, where he received us in his reception room. While we waited a few minutes for him to appear, a young woman came through the door and, on seeing me, rushed over and hugged me tightly. All things considered, she held on for slightly longer than necessary—after all this was the Patriarchal Palace foyer, and we were standing in front of all those bishops, priests and Bible Society people. The woman was Carol Anaswara who, on our previous visit, had acted as our interpreter. She hadn't known of our visit this time and couldn't believe her eyes when she saw me. 'What are you doing here? Why didn't you send me my photo?' Actually I had sent her photographs, but apparently they hadn't arrived. Luckily I had brought one along with me just in case I saw her.

Patriarch Teofile received us most warmly and seated us around a large table in his magnificent reception room. To be received by him was tantamount to being received by a king, we were told. He epitomised what we would expect to see in such a leader—gracious and kindly in every word and action, pure white hair, and strong eyes that held their gaze carefully. He is regarded as the spiritual leader of a nation in which 99 percent of the population call themselves Christians, the majority being adherents to the Romanian Orthodox church. The room was decorated with paintings of former patriarchs, and glass cabinets containing the robes and paraphernalia of former holders of this high office. The woodwork was intricately carved and although quite dark in colour the room had a refined cultured elegance.

After the short reception, we passed though the magnificent room where the bishops sit in conference, and on to the patriarch's private chapel. This was lined with priceless icons and intricate woodcarvings. Then to the dining room, where two long tables in the form of an L had places for the patriarch and his staff and our group. It was another fast day, which meant that there would be no meat eaten until Christmas day. A sumptuous meal of many courses, fine dining at its best, was served by nuns whose standard of service would grace the best restaurants in the world.

I was seated next to Bishop Nifon, one of the two bishops who serve the patriarch—his 'right and left hands', as they are called. I'm not sure whether he was the right hand or the left hand. Bishop Nifon had been present at the meeting held in Sibiu two years previously, when we met all the church leaders of the country to discuss the possibility of founding a national Bible Society. That was a meeting of great tenseness and uncertainty, so to be in Romania at the time when the national Bible Society had been inaugurated was a great experience. Bishop Nifon said that he had to admit that contact with Western evangelical and protestant churches had taught the Orthodox a lesson in keeping the Bible to the fore and not just relying upon their traditions. He explained that the most important part of an orthodox service was the reading from the gospels.

While the luncheon was going on, Bishop Nifon and I had a lengthy conversation about the Bible and the way the UBS had helped to provide Bibles during the difficult years of the Ceausescu regime. 'How many times we have printed editions of the Psalms, the New Testament and the Bible,' he exclaimed. 'It's something incredible and wonderful for an Orthodox church to do this. And it was because the UBS was there to help us by sending in paper and binding materials so that we print these precious books.'

He explained how difficult it was to work under communism and how they had pleaded with God to give them wisdom. He said, 'At one time the UBS sent us a large quantity of Bible paper. This upset the government officials and they threatened to confiscate it and put it to government use. We explained that this was special paper for Bibles and is called 'Bible paper' and to use it for anything else would create great problems for the country. We told them that God might curse us if it was used for anything but Bibles. Even though they said they did not believe in God we played on their superstitions. When they realised it was a gift, they relented and allowed us to take delivery of it, and permitted the Patriarchal Press to print Bibles. We printed 300,000 copies and later on another 100,000. This was all due to the help given by the United Bible Societies. This is something that should never be forgotten.'

I asked him whether Romanian Christians study the Bible in their homes. He answered, 'We put 100,000 Bibles into the church shops, and they were all gone within two or three months. Yes, it is quite common now for Orthodox people to read and study the Bible in their homes.'

Towards the end of the meal, Patriarch Teocist rose to his feet to address us. He was not young and looked quite impressive in his pure white gown and purple sash. 'I am personally grateful to you and all of your staff for providing us with Bibles and New Testaments. There is a real need to do this and surely the people have great delight in receiving the Word of God.

'We are very happy to have this meeting with you. Some years have elapsed since the revolution, and still we do not have enough Bibles. We greatly appreciate your work.' He referred to the desire of some Western churches to promote church union under the ecumenical movement, but he said this was very difficult for them. But, 'working together with the Bible Society is the only way forward from an ecumenical point of view'.

Father Sabin Verzas, in his new role as the secretary of the Interconfessional Bible Society in Romania, then attempted to recount the number of Scriptures distributed in the country among the Orthodox and Protestant churches during the past few years. He couldn't quite remember the details and said, 'There were too many thousands. I think there were between 300,000 and 350,000 Bibles and 200,000 New Testaments distributed during the past three years,' he said. 'The essential thing is that most of these have been published through the entire help of the UBS. Here in Romania everyone knows that we have received these Bibles free of charge from the UBS'.

The patriarch interrupted, 'you should know that we need 1,500,000 Bibles for both the Orthodox and Protestant churches'.

'And we need them the sooner the better,' said Father Verzas. 'The selling price of a Bible is the same as two Coca-Colas. The cost of importing a Romanian Bible is about US$4 and is sold for about 90 cents.'

Terje Hartberg, the UBS Coordinator for Bible work in Central Europe and the Former Soviet Union (CEEFSU), made a few comments about the situation in Romania and suggested to the patriarch that seeing that 99 percent of the population considered themselves Christian, it follows that these people would all be open to receiving the Biblical message. He said, 'However, we don't need to be prophets to foresee how secularisation, capitalism and other non-Christian movements are going to begin to take over and dominate life in Romania.' Turning to the members of our group, who were all Bible Society fund raisers, he said, 'Let us remember to tell our friends back home what Bible work in Romania can do as an investment in the long-term future of Christianity in this country'.

Moldova

After Romania, we moved on to Moldova, a small landlocked state between Romania and Ukraine. A highlight of our time in Kishinev, the capital of Moldova, was a visit to a prison a few kilometres out of town. This was a medium to high security prison for first offenders of a serious nature. The vice-warden met us outside and welcomed us warmly, treating us as honoured guests. We were then taken into the jail.

Unlike most prisons, there was no need to register at the gate, give our names, submit passports, or have our bags searched. The vice-warden simply called out instructions to open the various gates until we were inside. It was a huge place, with many dark unlit crumbling stairways and a general feeling of cold dampness. As we passed by cells that were like dormitories, we could see that some of them were quite large rooms with two and three tier bunks standing close together. There were as many as fifty men to a room.

An announcement was made, inviting the inmates to come to a meeting with the Bible Society people. Soon there were about three hundred men assembled in the large prison auditorium. They listened with rapt attention as various members of our party spoke to them. Two of the young prisoners came up to the microphone and gave their testimonies, telling of the way the Lord had completely changed their lives.

The inmates were then invited to ask questions. There were several involving theological issues such as, why does God allow little children to suffer. We asked the theologians among us to answer these. Then one young man asked us how the conditions of their jail compared with other jails around the world. With one accord, everyone in our group turned to me because they knew I had visited more jails than any one else. My mind raced. What could I truthfully say with enough diplomacy to avoid inflaming any tensions that might already exist between the inmates and their wardens. It was likely that the question had been asked to further a campaign for better conditions and treatment.

I told them about the one in West Africa, where the boundary fence had a huge hole in it which everyone used as the entrance instead of the main gate. I described the worst prison I had seen, which was in South America. In May, I had visited a prison in Minsk, Belarus. That one, I was able to say, was by far the best in terms of good conditions and cleanliness. By this, I inferred that their prison, which had been under the same administration up until a year or so previously, would compare well. They seemed satisfied. We were amazed that the prison authorities would allow such a question to be asked and answered. Once outside the prison, Terje put his arm around my shoulders and called to the others 'Didn't I tell you? Maurice is our diplomat'.

There were many men in the prison who had been converted through the ministries of Christian groups. Some had come to faith in Christ simply by reading the Bible. After the meeting, many of the men were presented with New Testaments and we spent a few minutes mingling with them. We were then taken to the small chapel in another part of the jail. Brightly painted, decorated with flowers and well lit, it was like a beautiful oasis in the midst of a dark, damp and dirty unpainted place. About twenty of the men who had become Christians in the jail sang a hymn lustily, if not beautifully, and four told us that they had become Christians through reading the Bible. The warden said, 'We have had three baptismal services here and even a wedding'.

We stayed in a hotel that boasted hot running water in its advertising. But, in fact, the water was never even tepid. We took all our meals at the Baptist Church. Breakfast on the last morning was a feast that was more like lunch. Several huge fish, which had the appearance of being fried or baked, were set out on the table. They had made a pâté of the fish, moulded it into its original form and replaced the skin. A cook said, 'Go on, you can eat it from head to tail, there are no bones'. All in all, the meal would not have been out of place in a fine restaurant.

The lady cooks came in to say goodbye to us. We presented a Bible and a Children's Bible to each of them amid many tears of joy and thankfulness. They had worked like slaves for four days, and had slept the last night in the church, in order to provide this special breakfast. They would not accept payment for their services, as this was their way of expressing their gratefulness to the Bible Societies for the Bible, and for setting up a Bible Society office in their own church building. There were more tears and hugs as they said goodbye. Some of our group said they had never experienced such loving Christian hospitality before, or witnessed Christian women serving with such dedication and love. It was down to their gratefulness to God for the Bible.

On the way to the airport, we called to see the director of the Moldova Prison Service. This man made a remarkable speech. For eighteen years he had worked in the prison service. Two years previously, he had visited Germany and met a German evangelist who gave him a Bible. He read it and felt the truth beginning to grip him. Immediately his life began to change. As he spoke to us, he walked over to the shelf of books on the wall near his desk and took down a Bible saying, 'For many years this shelf contained books on humanity and communism, but now it has a Bible. I read this Bible every day and while I cannot say that I am a believer, I know that as I continue to read this book the time will come when I will become a real Christian'. He went on to say that from the time he began to permit Christian people to visit the prisons, he could see lives were being changed in the most dramatic way.

He explained that, under the old regime, people were locked up in jail and that was that. There was no interest taken in their well-being and they suffered greatly. As he spoke to us, we could sense his heart crying out imploring us to do something to help the prisoners morally and spiritually. Because of the positive effect they have had on the prison, he encourages Christian people to visit as much as possible. In fact the day before, there had been a leadership meeting of the prison service in his office when he was asked why there weren't more Christian visitors to the jails. He was asked to get on the phone and try to encourage more.

The prison director reminded us that for every prisoner, there are at least four other people suffering—a wife, mother, father and of course, in many cases, children. Here was a man who had developed a great concern for the welfare of the thousands of men under his care. This concern, he told us, had been created through reading the Bible, and we were deeply touched by his moving and passionate plea for help.

Ukraine

Next we flew to the 1,600-year-old city of Kiev, capital of the Ukraine. Ukraine has a population of over 52,000,000 and we were a little surprised at the complete lack of official formalities entering this new republic. Our international flight landed at the domestic airport and we simply walked through a small gate into the street. No immigration, no customs. Rev. Smadaal was there to meet us. He was a Norwegian working as a special consultant to the United Bible Societies and had played an important role in introducing the work of the Bible Societies into many of the communist countries of Eastern Europe. The General Secretary of the newly formed Ukraine Bible Society was also there to greet us.

Our plane was late, so it was necessary for four of us to go direct to the university where a dozen professors of the department of Oriental studies were waiting to receive us. A presentation was made of Hebrew Old Testaments and Greek New Testaments to these scholars of great renown. There were philologists of Chinese, Farsi, Ukraine, Arabic, Turkish and other related languages. They were interested in promoting and assisting in a new translation of the Bible into Ukraine, as well other languages spoken in their country.

One of the professors made a speech in which he said that a UBS translations consultant had visited them recently. He described translating the Bible into the languages of Papua New Guinea. 'We were astounded that he should think that we, students of great languages, would be interested in Stone Age people's languages. How he translated for them can't be compared with our languages that are from ancient times.' Piling on the insult, and omitting the visiting translator's true designation as 'doctor', he said, 'Mr Clark did not please us'. Once again, with one accord, my group turned to me for the response.

I knew Dr Clark very well so I was able to explain that he held several degrees up to doctorate level in three disciplines, could speak at least seven languages and could read several others, and advised on translation matters in languages ranging from ancient Thai to Tok Pisin. I explained that we needed people like him who could help translators who have no knowledge of the principles and practice of this work—unlike the learned group gathered here who had a Scriptural heritage going back many hundreds of years. I was sure, I said, that Dr Clark had been attempting to explain the need for all people to have the Bible in their own language. That seemed to satisfy everyone and at dinner later that night, Terje rose and said, 'I'd like to propose a toast to our diplomat'.

After leaving the university, we made a quick visit to a seminary at the Caves Monastery, which was the first one established in Russia by the Orthodox Church. This is part of the Kiev-Pechery-Lavra Monastery. It was a frustrating visit because we were late and the students had all gone home. Furthermore, we saw nothing of the huge complex of gold-domed churches, monastic buildings of all types, long castle-like walls or any of the myriad examples of ancient art. Underneath our feet was a great labyrinth of underground caves in which monks founded a monastery in 1051 We didn't even see even one metre of the unmeasured lengths of underground passages between the caves—some of which contain the mummified bodies of monks that have lain there for hundreds of years.

We were accommodated in the Hotel Rus, overlooking a 100,000-seat stadium. The key lady on our floor proved very helpful. A pair of silk stockings that would normally cost her couple of day's wages, if she could find them, helped this enthusiasm along nicely. When she delivered a bottle of mineral water to my room and spotted a pile of dirty washing, she offered to do it for me and return it next evening. She intended doing it herself rather than put it into the hotel system. In due course, it was returned to me beautifully washed and pressed, but she used the common old trick of getting good payment by saying, 'Pay me what you like, three or four dollars'. I paid four.

Next day we were taken to a government hospital where a Pentecostal group was to hold a service for the patients. Scores of walking wounded came along and, after the meeting, were very anxious to receive the free Bibles that we had brought along. It was a clean and tidy place, except for the toilets, which had the appearance of harbouring more diseases than the patients already had.

We were told that we would be visiting a home for disabled children, and then it was changed to a home for disabled orphan children. It was, in fact, State Orphanage No 21—a regular type orphanage for true orphans or abandoned children. All 247 were seated in the auditorium when we arrived. The Bible Society had brought along a new Children's Bible for each child and these were stacked up on a table on the stage. I watched the children sit and stare at all those books. Some were showing signs of excitement at the prospect of getting one. Others sat still and gazed quietly at the books, doubtless wondering if they would be lucky enough to get a copy.

When the time came to hand out the Bibles, members of our Canadian group were invited to help. Never had they seen as much eagerness for such a gift. It was soon time to go, but I really hated leaving those children. How good it would have been to spend some time playing and talking with them.

This was the Sabbath day and the Seventh Day Adventists were holding their evening service in a large public auditorium. Every seat was taken, and at the end of the service the minister asked all non-church members to leave the room as there would be a church meeting held for the new members of the church. About one hundred of us left the room, leaving about five hundred. All five hundred had been converted in the last evangelistic campaign held in the city a few months previously.

The following evening we were told of another Adventist campaign going on in a different place. We decided to attend for a few minutes on our way to catch the night train to Lvov in Western Ukraine. The meeting was held in the Palace of Culture—similar to a town hall, Soviet style. The first snow of winter was falling, and as we walked up the steps, I noticed that there were many people standing around in the cold. I was told that they were the Christians who had brought their friends to the church, but because there was no room for them, they waited outside while their unsaved friends attended the meeting.

We were told of a statement that had been made in that very place by former Soviet President Khrushchev. He had said at a meeting there, 'In twenty years time I will show you the last priest in Russia', or words to that effect, spelling out his clear intention to eradicate Christianity from the USSR. And yet here, in that same 3,000-seat auditorium, were more than 3,000 non-Christian people who had come to hear the gospel message.

The meeting was due to start at 5.00 p.m. and they locked the doors ten minutes later. The place was packed. People jammed the aisles and stood around the walls of the three balconies. There was a separate room where I found about three hundred children being taught the gospel story while their parents attended the main meeting. It was due to finish at 6.30 p.m. and a second one would start at 7.00 p.m. They expected a slightly smaller crowd at that, 'probably only 2,000 or a little more because it is now snowing', I was told.

The meetings were a very low-key affair. The first item on the program was a classical piece by a string quartet. The pastor came on and gave a few announcements and then handed over to the preacher. The Adventists expected to start a new church after the campaign, and the new pastor had already been selected. The campaigns would last for three or more weeks, and any person who attended the twenty meetings was given a free Bible. In the previous three campaigns, six hundred conversions had occurred in the first, four hundred in the second, and 1,200 in the third. The one we attended was expected to yield about 2,000. There were already about 30,000 members of the Adventist church throughout Ukraine, and that number was growing at the rate of about 5,000 each year.

My interpreter was a keen photographer and had taken me along so that he could borrow one of my cameras to photograph the meeting. As we worked together, I showed him how I would photograph a crowded auditorium without using a flash. My photographs turned out very well and I sent him a copy. I never did hear from him again.

One evening we attended a Pentecostal service. This was also held in a public hall because the church was not able to afford to build a big enough building. There were about eight hundred people present and about twenty responded to the invitation to accept Christ as their Saviour.

Kiev was an interesting city with a population of nearly three million. Apart from being the capital of the Republic of the Ukraine, it has an important place in the history of Russia. It is known as the mother city of Russia because it was from here that the state of modern Russia descended. Kiev had been sacked by invading armies several times, last of all by the Germans. They killed or captured half a million Soviet troops, killed 100,000 Jews and carted off another 100,000 people to slavery in Germany. Nearby is a huge ravine about 2.5 kilometres long and fifty metres deep. In September 1941, after the city was captured, the Nazis massacred 52,000 Kievans there in a meticulously planned operation designed to intimidate and demoralize the population. The victims were made to stand in front of the ravine and, as they were shot, the bodies fell in and were buried in this enormous mass grave.

The overnight train to Lvov was quite comfortable. We were accommodated in first-class cabins that cost as much as a short ride on a London bus. The warmth and comfort aboard the train was a good contrast to the long cold wait we had had on the open platform in slushy half-melted snow. There were several other long distance trains standing nearby. Smoke curled from small chimneys on each carriage as water was heated for tea. Soon after we started out at 8.05 p.m., a helpful stewardess on our carriage generously provided us two servings of tea each—double the regulation amount. The tea was served in glasses placed in chrome plated holders. Our Ukrainian host, who was travelling in a different coach, had given her these instructions and I presented her with a pair of stockings to ensure we did not lack for anything.

We arrived on time in Lvov and, after checking into our hotel, were taken to the first ever interconfessional church service held in the region. It was held in the 18th century Cathedral of St George. This is a magnificent building richly adorned with paintings and icons, and many gilded carvings and furnishings. It has a splendid sculpture of St George the slayer of dragons on the top. The leaders of all the denominations had been invited to this prayer service in honour of the visit of our Bible Society group. We all agreed that it was a singular miracle that all the church leaders could be found praising God together in the same place.

Light snow fell for most of the day as we moved from church to church. In the Ukrainian Greek Catholic Church Seminary of the Holy Spirit, we met over two hundred young men training for the priesthood. This seminary had been handed over to the church a year previously. There was a wonderful irony in the fact that the facility had been built twenty years ago as a holiday camp for the Young Pioneers, the communist youth organisation. In these meeting rooms, young people had been taught that there is no God. But today young men were learning to study and preach the Scriptures of Truth.

We ate lunch with the students, using the one main implement needed for food here—a spoon. We were told meat is only ever served minced, so that it can be eaten with this utensil. Each student was required to bring their own spoon to the school, and they carried them around in their pockets. As one of the lecturers put it, 'all they need is a Bible and a spoon.'

Another church we visited rejoiced in the name, 'the Autocephalous Ukraine Orthodox Church'. 'Autocephalous' means 'self-governing'. Here we met with the rector and staff of the seminary. The students were working in very poor conditions in a partly refurbished building next door to an infectious diseases hospital; which, in the opinion of the rector, was a very dangerous place to be. He talked for some minutes about this hospital. Later we found out that he had been in charge of the church for forty-two years and, despite his fears about communicable diseases escaping through the windows, as he put it, he appeared to be in excellent health! Some of the students attending the seminary had to rise at 4.30 a.m. in order to travel to the school and be on time for opening worship at 8.00 a.m. They went without food all day, as there was no provision of a place to cook or eat.

The nearby church was a grand building; the fourth to be built on the site in something like six centuries. We were interested to hear about an early edition of the four gospels in the old Slavonic language. This particular tome weighed thirty-two kilograms. It was usually displayed only two or three times a year, but was specially brought out for us to see. Printed in

1533, probably using non-moveable type, and bound in scarlet, it is one of the oldest books of its kind in the world. It was exquisitely decorated by hand with swirling initial letters painted in brilliant colours.

Lvov looked like a beautiful and interesting city, but with only a few hours of daylight and much time spent indoors there was little chance to do any sightseeing. There were many different types of buildings that represented western architecture through the centuries. Many of the streets were cobbled and rather uncomfortable to travel over in a car. Potholes were numerous and drivers had to contend with trams, trolleybuses, narrow roads, and a rather flexible road code.

The Poles had ruled the town for 450 years but the history of this place, like so many others in Europe, is long and complicated. The statistics from the Second World War were once again staggering: 136,000 Jews died here when the town was overrun by the Nazis, and a further 350,000 were sent to concentration camps.

As we passed by the Opera and Ballet Theatre our guide told us of the horror of the people when they pulled down the statue of Lenin and discovered that the foundation had been built up using old gravestones.

My last engagement in Lvov was a combined meeting of Pentecostal, Adventist and Baptist Christians in a Pentecostal church. This was held on Tuesday at 10.00 a.m. and the place was packed in honour of the United Bible Societies. Afterwards, the pastors provided us with a typical Ukrainian lunch.

After the meal there were speeches and one pastor spoke beautifully about how important the Word of God was to them. He said that President Brezhnev had tried to make the people hungry for communism. There had been many poems and slogans displayed around the towns of the Ukraine. One was, 'Please my sons, memorize my words, bread is the main thing in our lives'. 'He did his job well, in that we all had bread', said the pastor. 'The Ukraine has the richest soil on earth and it produced a golden harvest of grain every year. But you know that the Bread of Life is the one thing we need to feed our souls. But our souls were without bread.

Churches were closed, there was no possibility to bring Bibles here, and we were not allowed to teach our children the Bible.'

The pastor continued, 'Then Gorbachev came into the government and at one meeting of the communists he said these words, "Bread is not the only thing in our lives." Those were not his words; they were the words of Jesus Christ.

'How did Gorbachev, the main communist, know these words? It was Gorbachev who gave us bread in the sense that he has allowed new freedoms. The end result of his statement is your coming here today and the formation of our new Ukrainian Bible Society.

'We thank the Bible Societies who helped to send these Bibles to us and our main task is to see that all families have the Bible in their own homes. Now we are living in golden times. Such times in the Ukraine are set in gold. Our churches are open and people are searching for Bibles, the words of God. This land is yielding another golden harvest of souls.'

Bread is very significant to the people of the Ukraine. At one point, Stalin attempted to wipe the population out by demanding that all their wheat be given to the government. This edict resulted in a disastrous famine in which many people died. The event is recorded in history as the Holodomor famine. Starving families, attempting to conserve a little grain for themselves, were brutally murdered or sent to labour camps if they were caught. Ultimately it was Stalin's plan to destroy the Poles and the Jews. Huge numbers were sent to labour camps in Siberia and Far East Russia.

Stalin's actions were certainly not the only trauma that Ukrainians have suffered in their history. The most famous catastrophe in recent memory was, of course, the Chernobyl disaster.

On a subsequent visit to Ukraine, I was taken into the area that had been seriously affected by that event. The city of Chernobyl takes its name from the Ukrainian word for mugwort or wormwood—an utterly bitter herb. Many believe that the implications of this name are an apt description of the nuclear power plant catastrophe that occurred there in 1986.

On Saturday, April 26, 1986, a meltdown occurred in the main reactor of the power plant, causing what has been widely regarded as the worst accident in the history of nuclear power. Many people living near the nuclear plant died as a result of radiation sickness, and there has been an on-going legacy of children suffering from serious medical issues, such as brittle bones. In addition to mutations and severe radiation poisoning, many children suffer from a 'previously unknown cardiac degradation condition' so common in the area it is known as 'Chernobyl heart'.

The Bible Society in the Ukraine arranged for me to visit several groups affected by the Chernobyl disaster. I was taken to a small village where there were a large number of orphan children. They had all lost their parents during the disaster. This small village was specially created for these children and their carers, and was set in an isolated area surrounded by pretty woods. Medical people check them every week.

The children's wards in several hospitals had to be enlarged to cater for the numbers of child patients. Most distressing of all, for me, were visits to special hospitals created to care for children suffering mainly from various blood cancers.

One hospital I was told was 'top secret' and special permission had to be given for me to visit on the condition that it was never identified. We were required to dress in white overalls, wash our hands, remove our shoes and wear funny-looking protective white hats. One patient, a ten year old boy to whom I gave a children's Bible, had skin almost as white as his bed sheets and black lips. A pretty little golden-haired girl had no lip colour at all. The nursing sister in charge told us quietly that all the children we had seen that morning would soon die.

We spent three days travelling in the affected area. 'We are quite safe here,' assured my host, 'so long as we don't eat any of the vegetables or chickens they grow here.' The area has become a large wildlife sanctuary with many animals returning that haven't been seen for many years, such as bears, foxes and beavers. Herds of horses roam the area—the progeny of animals released after the explosion. The most obvious creatures are the storks that nest atop telegraph poles.

A special museum has been established and it had quite an eerie atmosphere. The entrance has a series of town signboards with pink slashes through their names, indicating that those places were not to be entered. Dramatic dioramas and exhibits tell the vivid story of the horrific event.

From 1986 to 2000, 350,400 people were evacuated and resettled from the most severely contaminated areas of Belarus, Russia, and Ukraine.

One day, when I was in Moscow with a party of Bible Society staff from various countries, we noticed a woman weeping bitterly beside a bus stop. A Canadian colleague asked us to stop and she talked to her. This grey-haired woman, who looked quite old but was probably only about fifty, had a tragic story to tell. Her entire family was destroyed in the Chernobyl disaster. She lost her husband, children, relatives home and job—everything. All the family died soon after the nuclear explosion.

A 2006 report predicted 30,000 to 60,000 cancer deaths as a result of Chernobyl fallout. A Greenpeace report puts this figure at 200,000 or more. However, a book authored by Russian scientists and published by the New York Academy of Sciences in 2009, concluded that 985,000 deaths occurred between 1986 and 2004 as a result of radioactive contamination.

In these Eastern European countries that have suffered so much over the years, nothing is so encouraging as hearing of the difference that Christianity can make in people's lives. One pastor told us the story of a former Ukrainian heavyweight-boxing champion. This man was known as 'Kostel', which means 'the crutch', because if anyone tangled with him they would finish up on crutches. He was in prison and the authorities could not change him in any way. He would use his great physical force against the prison officers and everyone lived in fear of him.

A group of Baptists came to the prison and held an evangelistic service. They gave Bibles to some of the men, including Kostel. He began to read the Bible and it wasn't long before his dominating unruly spirit began to flow away. He decided to accept Christ as his Saviour and was baptised. Overnight he became as quiet as a little child.

There were so many men converted in that jail that they had to build a chapel for them. The prison ran its own farm and they soon began to send vegetables and butter to people in the nearby town who were in need. When the authorities heard about this, they asked how this could be possible when there was usually a shortage of food in prisons. The Christian prisoners answered that their primary concern was for the local orphanages. They said that they wanted to feed the children first, then themselves.

'This is an example how the Bible changes human nature. Those prisoners did not live in luxury but were concerned for others. There is a great number of stories we can tell you like this one' said the pastor eyeing my tape recorder. 'Your tape won't be able to contain them all'

After an amazing visit to Ukraine, it was time for me to check out of my hotel and take a flight to Moscow. I had heard stories of Aeroflot having no fuel for some flights and, sure enough, after waiting all evening, mine was cancelled. I was told to be ready at 7.00 a.m. for the next flight to Moscow.

Then, at nearly midnight, a message came through saying that there would be no flight for me at all. The train journey to Moscow from Lvov was 24 hours, so I decided against it and aimed to return home via Warsaw the next day. The Polish airline LOT came in on time, and took our entire group to Warsaw. At Warsaw's new international terminal, we said our good byes to each other and headed for five different countries. Some confessed that they were a little sad at returning home, finding it difficult to leave the wonderful people of the three countries we had visited.

I needed to overnight in Warsaw and a friendly taxi driver offered to take me to a modestly priced hotel downtown. As we passed through the airport, several other drivers with labels proclaiming them to be 'personal taxi drivers' tried to stop him. 'Mafia, mafia,' one middle-aged fellow whispered to me with a concerned look on his face. I hesitated a moment and decided to carry on. I was led to a regular taxi and had no problems.

The driver took me to the only hotel available. It was slightly dilapidated, but all the other hotels were full I was told. Maybe this was the one that paid him a commission.

'There are no single rooms.'

'What about double rooms.'

'No.'

Things were getting desperate.

'A suite?'

'Yes there is a suite and it costs a million zlotys a night.'

That was over a third of the monthly wage in Poland, but it was better than the three million I would have had to pay for a single room at the five star hotels down the road. The room key was as long as my index finger, attached to a half-kilo brass nameplate.

My next problem was getting a seat on a plane home to England. I also needed to contact my office and let the Bible Society in Russia know that I wasn't coming—it had been impossible to call them from Lvov. After a few attempts, the telephone operator told me that I could make just one call. So I called my assistant Rachel in Reading. I asked her to fax Moscow, and call Lorraine to tell her the good news that I was coming home two days early. This has rarely happened before. The local British Airways office offered me a business class seat at a lower price than any economy seat available, provided that I pay for it immediately.

Once settled into my hotel room, I caught up with my reports and writing. There were a number of brochures and magazines about Poland, and some items were a little unusual. One article gave advice to foreigners planning to marry Polish women. It included such useful information as the price of a wedding dress (three to four million zlotys).

The last paragraph suggested a cheaper way of doing things. It read, 'You can lower your costs by organizing your wedding at a fire-station, or by going to your wedding on a tractor or a motorcycle or by serving fermented rye instead of noble drinks'.

7

SLOVENIA and CROATIA—beware of the Cetniks

1994

It was an exciting prospect to visit the former Yugoslavia. The plan was to meet up with the UBS Europe Regional Secretary in Zurich and fly on Swiss Air to Ljubljana, capital of Slovenia, in what used to be the northern-most part of Yugoslavia. I waited until the very last minute before deciding what to do, but he didn't show up. So I boarded the plane and hoped to meet up with another colleague in Slovenia who had been due to arrive a few days before me. I was a little apprehensive because we were going into a war zone.

The history of Yugoslavia is very complicated as it dates back to the Ancient Greeks and the Roman Empire, even to the Stone Age. Over the centuries, parts of the country belonged to all sorts of nations. Being a buffer between East and West, it has been used like a gateway, or a doormat, when plundering armies have passed through.

Yugoslavia as a nation came into existence just after the Second World War. The First World War started here, in Sarajevo, when a Serbian nationalist tossed a bomb at Archduke Ferdinand, the heir to the Austro-Hungarian Empire. It bounced off the car, but later in the day another Serbian shot the Archduke at point blank range. A month later, what began as a regional dispute, inflamed into the Great War in which eight million soldiers perished.

When I arrived, the Slovenian immigration officer made no comment and asked no questions, letting me in without a visa. Customs were equally cool and waved me through. I waited around the airport until I was the only passenger left. No one came to meet me, so I decided to change some money and take a taxi to a major hotel in the city. I was about to get into a taxi when a gentleman appeared who looked as though he was searching for someone. It was Michael Kuzmie, my Bible Society contact in Ljubljana.

The city is known as 'foggy Ljubljana' and it certainly lived up to its reputation as we headed into town. One piece of tourist literature rather breathlessly described Ljubljana as:

'The capital and heart of a new country, between the Alps and the Adriatic. It is both a small town and a big city: small because it is home to no more than 340,000 inhabitants, yet big because it has all the features of metropolis, and even more: archaeological finds from the times of the Roman Empire, an old town centre with Baroque, Renaissance and Art Nouveau facades crowned by a majestic castle, romantic bridges which criss-cross the river Ljubljana, and the mark left on the city by one of its native sons during the first half of this century—the world famous architect Joze Plecnik.'

The great problem this beautiful city has had over the centuries is that it lay on the crossroads of major routes to and from Europe and Asia, and invaders have passed through it in all directions.

The first opera house was built in 1660 and there are numerous theatres, galleries and museums. Beethoven, Haydn, Brahms and Paganini were, at different times, members of the city Philharmonic Orchestra that was founded in 1701.

The pride of the people in their newly independent republic was quite obvious. But the dreadful war, which was still going on in neighbouring Bosnia-Herzegovina, was a constant embarrassment to them. Unemployment was rife and the cost of living was high. Some young men were in the habit of going across the borders into the war zone, and joining in the fighting for the weekend.

The hotel where I stayed put on a good breakfast for guests—that is, if you like your coffee and eggs cold. While waiting for a colleague I read through the extensive menu. All the dishes were listed in six different languages—although the English had suffered quite a bit. Like 'Veal cutlet to wish' or 'Seved mushrooms'. Another item, which I sincerely hoped was misspelt, was 'Sausage in Hog's crease'. I didn't have the courage to try it.

A great deal of Bible printing had been done in the old Yugoslavia, and I visited a press that had worked for the Bible Societies for twenty years. It was housed in a modern dark blue skyscraper, and the managing director proudly showed me around the huge factory where over three hundred people operated a set of spotlessly clean and gleaming machines. They were in the process of printing a variety of jobs, including the local telephone book, a Dutch encyclopaedia, children's books in French, and a Slovenian novel.

Most important to me was the sight of a Serbian Bible being printed on a big grey press. This press was working rather slowly, and as each sheet was printed, it was carefully guided onto the stack by the two men operating the machine. Very thin 30 gram Bible paper was being used for this job, and the printing manager explained that the paper was difficult to use and had to be handled carefully. There are comparatively few presses in the world that can print with this particular paper. I was there to see the first sheet of an edition of 21,000 copies.

In the dispatch department were 10,000 Slovenian Bibles ready for shipment to Serbia. This was no longer as straightforward as it had been before the break-up of the country. These Bibles would be sent to Hungary and then into Serbia, because the United Nations had placed an embargo on all goods moving between Slovenia and Serbia. A permit was required for transhipment through Hungary, but it was not very difficult to obtain as all imports of Scripture were permitted.

My missing colleague, Gunnliek, finally caught up with me. The rest of the day was spent in a meeting with the church leaders of Slovenia to consider the proposed constitution for a Bible Society of Slovenia. Being the only native English speaker present, I was conscripted to write the corrections and alterations to the text, and proffered advice from time to time on Bible Society policies and practice.

The meeting touched on a number of interesting topics, the first being a question raised by a linguist regarding the Slovenian word for 'Bible'. Roman Catholics and Protestants used slightly different words. Another topic of discussion was whether the society might be called the Slovenian Bible Society. That sounded nice to the ears of these people who were still rejoicing over their newfound independence. However, it had to be pointed out that this would infer that it was the society for all Slovenians, wherever they lived, and there are many scattered around the world. The term Bible Society of Slovenia would tie it to a geographical location and indicate that it would serve all people living within the nation, whatever their language.

Being a Roman Catholic country where 99% of the people regarded themselves Catholic, it was a tricky business to ensure that the Protestant churches were adequately represented and that the RC church did not have an outright majority. But everyone was gracious and a happy conclusion was reached. A date was then set for a constituent assembly for the inauguration of the society. It was an historic days work.

Gunnliek and I took a train to Zagreb, capital of Croatia, having seen little of Ljubljana, despite the fact that the guidebook suggested that the city was the type 'one should linger on in'. The lady in the booking office sold us a ticket each and then said, 'If you want a reserved seat I can, but you must pay 325 Tolar.' We thought this would be a good idea and paid up. She issued the reserved seat coupons and then said, 'There is no special seat booked. The train is not full and there are plenty of seats. Just choose the one you want.'

'But why should we pay for a reservation if one is not necessary?' asked Gunnliek. No answer, just a sweet smile.

Our train was the Munich to Zagreb Eurocity express and it arrived on time and was spotlessly clean. There were only a handful of people who travelled through to Croatia. As we approached the border an announcement was made regarding the border crossing. We were requested to have our travel documents ready for inspection. The only official to put in an appearance was a Slovenian customs man who stood at the door of our compartment and said, 'Customs, you have nothing?' And, without waiting for a reply, walked away.

I bought an official guidebook that reminded us that Croatia has 'recently been swept by the storm of war and violence, leaving behind on its body deep scars'. Zagreb is no stranger to war. It has been occupied by the Tartars, Avars, Goths, Francs, Hapsburgers, Ungars, Turks, Serbs and, more recently, Germans.

The next day was spent with various church leaders, discussing the possibility of setting up a national Bible Society for Croatia. It was no longer possible to carry out the work from Belgrade as communications had been cut. Even telephone calls were now routed via Hungary into Belgrade. There were a number of Protestant churches but, once again, the Roman Catholics were the majority, with about 80% of the population claiming to be Catholic.

The meeting took place at the Information Centre, where important work was being carried out to provide aid to refugees. I left the meeting a few times to witness refugees from Bosnia come in for food and other necessities. The dreadful plight of these people struck me while I was photographing outside the building. Two ladies approached me, crying with distress. They wore threadbare coats and had faded scarves over their heads. I couldn't understand what they were saying but it was heart-rending to see how distressed they were. Their gaunt faces told a story of hunger. I directed them inside, and they were soon provided with plastic bags of food. The Information Centre housed good stocks of basic food of all kinds, as well as soap and cleaning materials. Much of this had been supplied by TEAR Fund and the Samaritan's Purse.

The UBS had been able to help the refugees as well by enabling the centre to publish Children's Bibles. An edition was printed by arrangement with the copywriter holders, and we had extra ones printed for the refugees. These books were placed on the shelves at the centre and people were free to take one if they wished. When I was there, the books were nearly all gone but I found a few copies, sitting on a shelf next to pork bellies and uncut bacon. 'There you are,' said Miriam, wife of the director of the centre, 'Food for the body and the soul'.

Later I was told that the centre had many visitors from England and America. 'They talk a lot and make photos and some of them write about us in their magazines but we never hear from them again. There are so many of them', Miriam said, 'I don't know why they come. But you don't have to worry. The Bible Society has been so good to us. They immediately responded to our need for Bibles, it was so quick and you didn't come to look first. You first of all sent the books. Not like these other people. They come, they look and write and study us and then do nothing'.

While we were talking, a lady came in with a little boy. I showed the Children's Bible to him and asked him to read something to me, while his mother collected food supplies. He managed quite well, so I asked if he could take the Bible home. There was a long explanation in Croatian, and it turned out that these were not refugees, but a poor local family who needed help. Therefore the Bible, which was given by the UBS for refugees, could not be given to this child. Fair enough, but I said, 'I am from the UBS, therefore I give you permission to give this boy a Children's Bible'. With a shrug of the shoulders the centre employee said, 'Ok, it's for you to say so'. But this was a problem I had seen in other places as well. Refugees are often supplied with goods and services that far out-class what the local people have.

I had set the morning aside to photograph the people of Zagreb, but unfortunately the rain drizzled down; not heavy, but just enough to be a nuisance and make photography difficult. St Stephen's Cathedral was just a short walk from the hotel, so I decided that this would be a good place to get photographs of Roman Catholic people worshipping. There would be large crowds at all services during Lent. This was not going to be easy. There was scaffolding covering the carved Gothic portal and it was dark and gloomy inside. It is an amazing structure and is considered the most famous building in the city. It was built in 1217 and has undergone renovations of various kinds due to the natural and human disasters wreaked upon it over the centuries. It has twin towers that are over one hundred metres metres high. Just inside the door was a display of some pieces of ancient stone carvings from the original building that had occupied the site. There was an appeal for funds to continue the repair and restoration work.

It was too dark for regular photography without flash, and would be too disruptive to set up for low light work, so I looked around for another photo opportunity. As I approached the door, a woman opened it and as the light from the outside lit her up against the old door, I could see that this would make an effective picture. Positioning myself just inside the door, I surprised a few people coming in to worship by taking their photograph when they least expected it. A whole school of children suddenly appeared. They were led into the cathedral and out again within a few minutes. Their teachers had quite a job trying to keep them quiet.

An outdoor vegetable market made a colourful scene even in the sombre light, but it was difficult to photograph in the rain. An old lady selling flowers was very much against the idea of having her picture taken when I asked her, so I found it better to surreptitiously photograph the scene from a distance. Soon my fingers were aching with cold, so I retreated to a coffee shop to warm up. The news was on and I could tell it was all about the war. The coffee lady constantly sighed and shook her head in disgust as the names of towns that had come under attack were mentioned. The bulletin was then given in English, so I knew I had guessed right.

The chance to get close to the war zone came unexpectedly. Daniel Berkovicn, who had been asked to take care of my arrangements, apologised that he had to be away from Zagreb for a couple of days. He had to give some lectures at a Bible College in Osijek. 'That's two hundred and eighty kilometres from here, close to the front line,' he said. 'Can I come with you?' I asked. 'I'd prefer to get away from the capital city and see something of the countryside.' And being at the front line sounded exciting! He readily agreed and we set off the next day. Another pastor travelled with us.

The countryside was flat all the way, except for a low range of hills that we crossed. All of it was beautiful agricultural land. As we approached Osijek, Daniel was unsure of the turn off from the motorway. We almost reached the Cetnik lines before realising we had better turn back. The Cetniks were the Serbian guerrillas, or irregulars, the ones that had been causing all the trouble and creating mayhem wherever they went. They were usually heavily armed.

At the Bible College, all the students were involved in lectures or swatting for an exam the next day. They came not only from Croatia, but also Slovenia, Macedonia, the Ukraine and Bulgaria. During the evening I could hear the whump and kerumpp of mortars in the not-too-distant front line. 'They fire off a few mortars every now and again just to remind us they are there', said an ex-Australian soccer player I met in a café late that night. I had taken an evening stroll while my guide and his colleagues had a meeting about the monthly magazine published from Osijek.

In the café were a number of men who warmly welcomed me into their midst. We talked a great deal about the war. All of them had done their share of fighting to defend their new nation. They told me that the Serbs were out to capture as much land as possible. About a year previously, the Serbs had shelled Osijek for about three months, and I saw the extent of the damage for myself the next morning. 'Are you safe now?' I asked the men in the café. 'Will they attempt to invade Croatia or will they be satisfied by taking most of Bosnia-Herzegovina?'

'We don't know. We just don't know,' said my new found friends. 'You cannot understand the way the Serbs are thinking. They might come. We shall see. But if they try, we shall repel them'.

The war in former Yugoslavia had shocked the world—especially the atrocities committed in Bosnia. I heard some stories that were so horrific that I can't repeat them here. They were just as shocking as the stories I had heard in Central Africa. It was as if all sense of moral responsibility disappeared. In war, it seems, nothing is too bad an action against your enemy. But the puzzling thing is that these people had lived together for centuries. Many families resorted to fighting each other—people who had lived in harmony all their lives. Not a few had intermarried, and suddenly they turned on each other. Many young children were killed as in-laws fought over them, and older ones were abused horribly. There were some who had killed their grandchildren because they had a parent from the other side. The thinking, as one man said to me, was, 'It is better these bastards die than live with my blood'.

Most of the people I met who had suffered did not readily talk about their experiences, and I certainly wasn't prepared to question them. But after a little time, details would emerge that left one dazed and ashamed of the human race.

Next morning, I had just a couple of hours before returning to Zagreb, so I set about trying to see something of the damage sustained by the city during the three-month bombardment. Again the weather was dismal. First of all I was taken to the hospital. It had received several direct hits—on purpose, so I was told. The Serbs aimed for the most densely populated parts of the town. Complete office buildings were demolished some left with just the brick walls standing. Many of the blocks of flats were covered in machine gun bullet holes. The Croatian army had blown up the main bridge over the river to prevent the enemy entering the town with heavy tanks. They made a proper job of it and, although repair work had started, it would take a long time to complete.

I walked down the road and around the corner, and spotted a relief centre. It was a sobering experience to speak with people who had suffered so much at the hands of people they considered uncivilised brutes. Hearing their stories firsthand was a lot different to watching a TV report. The relief centre was operated by a group called AGAPE—the humanitarian arm of the evangelical church in Croatia. I saw a woman with an old pram piled high with goods, including a sack of potatoes perched on top. She was leaving a dilapidated old building, in front of which a crowd of people waited. I went inside and discovered that it was an old auditorium—perhaps a theatre, as there was a balcony. The chairs had been cleared out and in their place were piles of food. In one corner, stacked to the roof, were tonnes of potatoes in open-weave sacks that had been sent from Germany. Most sacks included a number of rotten potatoes and were coated in black earth. They looked unappetizing, but hungry people were glad to have them.

There were commercial sized tins of baked beans, jam, fruit, sugar and all manner of food and drink. Someone had sent what looked like a couple of tonnes of toilet paper and large sized cartons of washing powder. There were sacks of flour and rice, and large quantities of second hand clothes.

171

Two large trucks from Germany had just delivered thirty more tonnes of humanitarian aid.

Apart from these supplies, there was also some Christian literature available; such as a local monthly magazine published by the Evangelical church, the Gospel of Mark from the Living Bible, and a well-known Scripture tract called 'Help from Above'. People were free to take these as they wanted but, alas, there were no New Testaments or Bibles. The supply that had been received from the UBS some months ago had long gone. Another large shipment was due. I asked the man in charge of receiving delivered goods if he had any Bibles.

'Bibles. Bibles. No Bibles. Sorry you can't have one.'

'No, no, I am from the Bible Society. We want to send some more to you.'

'Sorry, no Bibles. No, no.'

Carefully and slowly I explained that the Bible Society had sent the Bibles he had received last year. His English wasn't up to it. He spread his hands and shrugged his shoulders, 'You no can Bible.'

He allowed me to take photographs of the workers. The only ones who weren't too pleased were a couple of ladies dishing out flour. A big man handling the potatoes grinned from ear to ear when I took his photo and said something in German. He was obviously keen to get a message back to Germany about the poor quality of the potatoes. He held up a good potato and gestured to the people crowded round the door and said, 'They potato.' Which I assume meant, 'They need potatoes, good ones.'

After photographing the people receiving aid, I left feeling quite depressed. I felt that the Bible Society had somehow failed them. There should have been a good supply of Bibles or New Testaments for anyone who wanted one. It is a well-established fact that, in refugee situations, there is always a great demand for Bibles. It took a long time for me to stop thinking about those people. None could speak English, but their eyes said so much; the deepest sorrow and anguish could be seen there. Some seemed close to tears as they greeted one another. There were others who quite clearly were saying thank you for the help they had been given. One gentleman in fine clothing who had lost everything, gravely nodded a greeting to me with a dignified thank you.

Some of the women, who wouldn't normally want to have their photographs taken by a stranger, allowed me to do so with some reluctance, knowing that it was only right to show the donors that the aid had been gratefully received.

I found that the people still waiting for food were the most anxious to have their photos taken, as though this would speed up the process of getting the help they so desperately needed. Once they had been served, so to speak, they wanted to be off home as fast as possible.

Later, as I passed some of them on the street, they nodded and smiled their greetings once again.

Travelling back to Zagreb on a better and faster road meant passing through an area that had been held by Serbs and was now under the protection of the United Nations. The first checkpoint was manned by Argentine soldiers. They stopped us and asked our business, then let us proceed. Their roadblock was in a lonely place in the hills right next to a demolished house. As we left I asked if I could take a photograph of their post. One of the men said, 'Yes but be quick'.

Entire villages had been destroyed. Many houses had been burnt out; others had taken a mortar and were half demolished. Some had been mined and were now reduced to a heap of rubble. Apparently the procedure adopted by the Cetniks was to shell the place first, then mine the remaining buildings. Although I could see no sign of life in many of these villages, I was told that there were still a few people living in some of the now derelict houses.

I kept Saturday free to visit the Serbian Orthodox Church in Zagreb. When I found the church, which turned out to be very close to the hotel, it wasn't full of people worshipping. Instead, a bit of practical Christianity was going on. There were piles and piles of second hand clothing all over the church and people were sorting it out so it could be sent to displaced

Bosnians. It was the Serb armies that had driven people from Bosnia but here was the Serbian Orthodox Church demonstrating real Christian love. Unfortunately I couldn't find anyone who could speak English, so was unable to get the full story of what was going on.

As I thought about the photographs I had taken in the country, I realised that I had very few of the people. Nearby was a large market that the official guidebook rather picturesquely described as:

'The stomach of Zagreb—the oldest and largest platter, plate, bowl placed in front of the hungry mouths of the city. She is like an old aunt who awakes first in order to make the first meal of the day, breakfast, for the countless infants who shall, still sleepy and warm from their beds, storm in from all sides.'

The description went on to state that 81,000 tonnes of food is sold there per month, plus half a million eggs, all carted away in plastic shopping bags by the 70,000 people who visit it every day.

Here people from the countryside were selling fruit and vegetables. There was a bitingly cold wind, which caused many of the older women to wrap woollen scarves around their heads, leaving just their faces exposed. It was difficult to photograph them well as they would look away when they saw the camera. I resorted to a 300mm lens that enabled me to stand back quite a distance from the subject.

I was in Ban Josip Jelacic Square when the noonday gun was fired. I hadn't known that such a practice existed and, because it was fired nearby, it was a pretty loud boom. You can guess that my first reaction, after being in a war zone, was to take cover, and I quickly looked around, camera at the ready, for a place to shelter from the assault. I soon realised that no one had taken the slightest notice of the explosion, except for a young man and his girlfriend standing near me, who simply checked their watches. In that split second I thought that the war had come to Zagreb!

I read about the gun later and it was described thus:

'In the upper town of Zagreb there is a gun which has been killing time for the people of Zagreb. Everyday at noon the Zagreb artillery fires from the historical tower of Lotrscak. This gun is used to conserve the zenith of the day so it would last longer. The Zagreb noon gun is actually meant for the blind.'

Despite the fact that my run-in with the noonday gun had been a false alarm, people in the capital are taught basic procedures to escape trouble. On each floor of the hotel there was an information sheet listing possible calamities and what should be done in each eventuality. At the top of the list was a picture of soldiers crouching down as if engaged in house to house fighting. Next, there was a picture of planes dropping bombs. Then there was a yellow cloud representing a nuclear, biological or gas bomb, and finally pictures of fire and flooding.

Zagreb is 'about to meet its nine hundredth birthday,' said the mayor in the tourist handbook of the city. He wrote that Zagreb is one of Europe's youngest cities and now capital of one of the world's youngest countries. Apparently we all owe a lot to this city because the fountain pen was invented here and was named after one of its citizens, a Mr Penkala. This clever man also invented the propelling pencil. He must have been quite versatile because he also invented the thermos flask and the hot water bottle. The tie (actually, the cravat) was first worn here and was described as 'the most Zagrebian souvenir'. The father of the encyclopaedia was born here in 1534, and his masterwork was titled, *Encyclopaedia seu orbis discipilarumtam sacrarum quam profanorum epistlemon.*

On Sunday I attended an evangelical church that was packed out. Towards the end of the two-hour service, I was invited to tell the congregation about the work of the Bible Societies. The news that so many former communist countries now had their own national Bible Societies was joyfully received, and there was even more joy expressed at the possibility of one being established in Croatia.

I met two Bosnian Muslim men who had been brought to the service. It was the first time they had ever attended a Christian church. They were refugees and one was a photographer. He told me about the horrors of the war, which he had covered for his newspaper. His own family was divided up because of mixed marriages with Serbs. Even though he was a news photographer, he could not bring himself to photograph the dead and dying, and with his family divided, he decided to flee to Croatia. Once again, it was the sadness deep in his eyes that touched me. He wore a winter-weight army camouflage coat and when I commented on its warmth, he said, 'You don't want to wear a coat like this.' My interpreter said of his friend, 'It's the problem of mixed marriages, they are now broken up, children are gone,' he shrugged his shoulders and sighed heavily in despair. 'But I have brought my two Bosnian friends here to church because, if they find Christ, they at least will have salvation for their souls.'

I asked my friend about the stories I had heard of people killing their grandchildren from mixed marriages. Was that true? 'Oh yes, it's true, it has happened a lot. They so hate each other'.

Before leaving Zagreb, I visited two of the twenty or so refugee camps in the city. Only one person smiled at me. I could sense a mood of depression among the people as they perhaps realised that they may never be able to return to their native country. They were housed in tightly packed long low brown buildings. Somehow they would need to rebuild their lives in a new republic that was already overloaded with refugees, and facing serious economic problems and widespread unemployment.

I had spent six days in Croatia and the weather was overcast and dull for the entire period—except for the last few minutes. The week before, it had apparently been sunny and warm or, as one young woman put it, 'Last week it was so hot I only wore a tee shirt and socks.' As I travelled to the railway station in a taxi, the sun came out but it was too late to photograph the beautiful city in this perfect light.

Waiting at the railway station for my train, I was intrigued to see women mopping the platforms. The entire building and platforms were spotlessly clean. The train appeared quite suddenly when a locomotive and three carriages approached the platform at speed. As the engine passed me, I could hear the brakes go into the emergency position. It shrieked to a halt. There were only four passengers that boarded the train for Slovenia. A day earlier, I had enquired about making a reservation, but was assured by the booking clerk that there would be no problem getting a good seat.

The run through to Ljubljana was a pleasant trip as the line follows the Sara River for most of the 160-kilometre route, which includes passing through a picturesque gorge.

The Slovenian people are very friendly, giving visitors a warm welcome. Back in Slovenia, I called in at the tourist information office and was given a vast quantity of literature. The first piece I opened began with a description of the country in inimitable Balkan style:

'A nation of two million, with a distinctive and clear identity, which has preserved its individuality in this treacherous sub-alpine crossroads for 1,500 years, built and preserved during this period 3,000 churches, created a rich artistic heritage, published the Slovene translation of the Bible as early as 1584.

'The old city centres are alive with the drama of earlier times; of the southernmost reaches of European Protestantism, of the northernmost boundaries of plundering Turkish raids against Europe.'

My host had not planned anything for me for the rest of the day, so I took a walk around the city. A few days earlier I had been within range of Serbian mortars and was not frightened, but here, in this peaceful city, I got quite a start when, passing by a tall leather-clad fellow, he pulled out a flick knife and brandished it at me. It had a blade as long as a hand span and was attached to a chain. He laughed and rattled the chain and I moved along smartly.

I began making contact with the various church leaders who were expecting me to phone them on arrival, as arranged the previous week.
The first setback came when the interpreter was unable to help me, as he had classes to attend. The second person who had offered to help was ill. Then all the ministers were either out of town or just about to leave town. A visit to a refugee camp was arranged for next morning, but when I called at 9.00 a.m. as arranged, I was told that my guide was sick and could not work that day. Please could I wait until tomorrow? The Alps were not far away, so I decided to take a bus out to see them. But, by the time we

reached our destination, the weather had changed and was unsuitable for obtaining the colour photographs I needed for the UBS image library.

During the afternoon, I kept an appointment with the Archbishop of Ljubljana, who was able to give me half an hour before rushing off to the hospital to attend an emergency call. It was good to hear him speaking with enthusiasm about the plan to create a national Bible Society of Slovenia.

After that, I spent three hours with a most remarkable scholar who was working on a new translation of the Bible into Slovenian. His office was lined on all sides, from floor to ceiling, with books. He was able to speak the following languages: Slovenian, Latin, Biblical Hebrew, Modern Hebrew, N.T. Greek, Phoenician, Aramaic, German, French, Italian and English. He was also able to read several others. He had earned three separate doctorates, covering different aspects of Biblical Hebrew, with all three theses having been published. They were written in English, French and German and he had translated a summary for one of them into Hebrew. Tears streamed down his face as I told him stories of people I had met around the world who had come to know God just through reading the Bible. He took a bottle of white wine from a cupboard, saying, 'this is our most famous white wine, we even send it to the Queen of England. We will now drink it together in rejoicing over the wonder of the Bible'.

After a considerable wait, I was at last able to visit a refugee camp. First we had to meet with the official in charge of temporary camps. The government office was in the upstairs room of a bank building, protected by an electronic lock. We punched a couple of buttons and a light came on but there was no response. My guide, a pastor's son, was impatient and suggested we give up. I insisted we try some more. After about ten minutes, a voice from the wall asked what we wanted, then let us in. A lady in the office explained that they had to protect themselves from people coming to visit them.

The camp officials provided a press pack that outlined the situation of refugees in Slovenia. They insisted on calling them 'temporary refugees' in the hope that one day these displaced people would be able to return home. However amongst ordinary people, it was generally regarded that this would be impossible.

On the outskirts of Ljubljana were a number of summer camps that the government had provided for harvest workers. These had since been utilised as camps for Bosnian refugees. The camp director handed me over to an English speaking volunteer and to the social worker based in this camp. There was a class for fourth graders going on, and their volunteer teacher, Sabina, said that the children were excellent students and learned quickly.

Another lady had a group of a dozen teen-age girls and was teaching them to make greeting cards. With Easter approaching, she was showing them how to trace Easter eggs and Easter bunnies onto their cards.

'Are you teaching them the real meaning of Easter?' I asked.

'No, they just learn to make cards, like for Mother's Day and Christmas'.

'But don't you tell them something about these special days?'

'No, I don't teach them anything like that'.

'I think you will find that they will be very interested in the story of Easter because as Muslims they will know only a little about Jesus Christ'.

'No, I don't do that'.

Seated in a circle on the communal kitchen floor, a dozen young people were reciting passages from the Koran. They sang long passages from the Koran in a kind of monotone, using handwritten notes.

Back at the camp office, the social worker asked me about the Bible Societies. I explained that we find that refugees, be they Muslims or of any other faith, are often very happy to receive a Bible or a New Testament. She said she understood this very well and that they would love to have some for the camp. 'We can just put them here and they can take if they want, and they will.' I felt like giving the pastor's son a withering look because, on our way to the camp, he had been telling me that the refugees from Bosnia did not want Bibles because they are Muslims.

I was given permission to take photographs and some of the refugee families with young children were very happy about it. The older ones were not so keen. I didn't even attempt to take photos of young women, as that would be asking for trouble.

A large room was provided for each family. One I visited was home to a family of six, including an eight-year-old boy, three young women, their mother, and an aunt. They all looked as though they could do with a bath. Their room was a complete shambles. There were clothes lying all over the place, on the floor, beds and chairs. Someone was asleep on a bed, completely covered from head to toe with a sheet. The mother of the family came in from doing some washing, clad in a grubby blue dressing gown held together with a single safety pin. On a small table was a collection of unwashed plates and cutlery. They were people living in chaos and they looked it. I felt like giving them a lecture on the fact that if they cleaned up their room and themselves they would feel a lot better, but I kept quiet and didn't attempt to take a photo.

The father of the family was still in Bosnia, and they had no idea whether he was still alive or if they would ever see him again. It wasn't unusual for men to be separated from their families while they took work in other parts of the country, or even in other countries around Europe, so their separation at that time wasn't too traumatic for them. My interpreter said that when the realisation sinks in that they may never be together again as a family, depression will set in.

Next to them was an elderly man suffering from a psychological disorder because he had lost his entire family in tragic circumstances in Bosnia. He wouldn't, or couldn't, give us any details, except that his wife and children were all killed before his very eyes. Every one of the 30,000 refugees in this camp, and the other 45,000 around the country, had a tragic story to tell. Some had endured great hardships in their escape, and there were a few who had paid large sums of money to be taken out of Bosnia.

All the Slovenian Christians I spoke to loved the new translation of the New Testament that had recently been published. The old version had been translated in 1914 and was now no longer used by Protestant and

Catholic Christians. Imagine my surprise when the pastor asked me why we were printing 120,000 copies of the old version of the New Testament for the Gideons. 'This will be a terrible waste of paper and money to use this version,' he said, 'only the J.W.s and Mormons use it here. I've sent faxes to the Gideons and your office telling them to stop the order and change the version.'

I explained that if this was an order from the Gideons, then only they could change it, but I promised to look into the matter. It wouldn't have been the first time that something like this had happened. There had been a number of cases when the advice of local evangelical leaders, let alone the Bible Society, had not been taken as to the most appropriate version to use in any given locality.

Later in the day, the manager of the printing press recognised me in the street and said, 'I want to talk to you. That New Testament I am printing for the Gideons is the wrong one. Nobody reads it. I am not a Christian but I know about this book. Tell your people in Stuttgart to stop it'. I called our office in Stuttgart and asked them to verify the order.

On the day I left Ljubljana, the taxi driver taking me to the airport decided to drive me through a couple of small villages rather than along the main road. He wanted me have a better view of the Alps. He spoke very little English, but as we approached the mountains, he said, 'Slovenia is very beautiful'.

8

ALBANIA—what godlessness can cause

May 1993

'There's something quite different about the people now', said my Italian interpreter, Valdo, as we walked along the main streets of Tirana, Albania. 'When I came here two years ago, just after the revolution, the people didn't smile, they walked around with their faces to the ground and never looked at you. Everyone wore the same drab clothes, there was no colour in their dress, they looked shabby and poor and they all had the same lost look of despair'.

These were strong words and I reflected on them. It was exactly what the few books and descriptions I had read about Albania had indicated. Albania had been sealed off from the world for thirty years with no communication possible. A TV aerial pointed in the direction of Italy was a serious offence, and short wave radios were not permitted. There were certainly no newspapers or magazines from the outside world, and no films, videos or DVDs.

Should a foreigner ever appear on the streets, it was not wise to even greet that person, let alone speak. Anyone who tried engaging in conversation was immediately accosted by the security police or informed on by the myriad of people trained for such a purpose. It was necessary for the individual to personally report to the security police any contact whatsoever with a foreigner. One government leader told me that you actually had to go to the police and say, 'This morning I saw a foreigner on the street and he greeted me. I answered with a "good morning" but said no more'. Usually a written report was required.

A map of Albania that I bought in a bookshop had several pages describing the country, including some notes on the constitution. It said,

'The constitution guarantees the inviolability of the person. Nobody can be arrested without the decision of the court of approval of the prosecutor. The home is inviolable. The secrecy of correspondence and other means of means of communication cannot be violated, etc'.

When I showed this to someone who knew better, there was just a snort of disgust—he was lost for words to comment on what he obviously considered to be absolute lies.

It was fascinating to compare two different histories of the country—one was an official publication issued during Enver Hoxha's tenure as the communist leader of Albania, and the other by a guidebook editor. It was as if two different countries were being described. The official communist line was that Albania was a 'people's republic', in which all state power was based on the unity of the people and was derived from and belongs to the people. 'The electors have the right to recall their representative at any time when he has lost their political trust'.

Nothing could be further from the truth.

There had been no private trade. There were no lawyers, because Albania's communist society was deemed so perfect that they were not needed!

When the communists took over in 1945 they declared that Albania was the most backward country in Europe. Fifty years later, although illiteracy had largely been eliminated and the longevity of the people had increased from thirty-two years to seventy-two, the country was still the poorest in Europe, with an unemployment rate of about 70% with a low standard of living. The roads were practically empty of cars. Most of the vehicles that were in use would never pass a road test in other countries, and were driven in the main by unlicensed drivers.

The footpaths of Tirana were crowded with pedestrians. Hundreds of people lined the curbs, their feet in the street, chatting and smoking and watching the world go by. Along the footpaths were private dealers selling illegally imported candy bars, beer, small cakes, soft drinks, and small bags of pumpkin seeds.

When we visited the Roman Catholic Archbishop of Tirana, he told us about a regular meeting that the Pope holds with twenty-five senior cardinals to discuss problem areas of the world. The discussions are kept confidential, but one cardinal said that when they came to the subject of Albania, 'The Pope's face clouded over with intense sadness, he bowed his head, waved his hands and said, "Albania is just hopeless, there is no hope"'.

The Archbishop, an Albanian who had been living in the USA, had just returned to Tirana to take up his post. After discussing the fall of the atheistic dictator and the possibility of establishing a Bible Society in Albania, we went on to discuss the horrendous problems he was facing in restoring the ministry of his church. All the churches had been closed, with many turned into storage barns or factories. As the meeting drew to a close, I picked up the Good News Bible that we had presented to him along with other Bibles, and turned to Psalm 37 and read out verses 35 and 36:

'I once knew a wicked man who was a tyrant; he towered above everyone else like a cedar of Lebanon, but later I passed by, and he wasn't there; I looked for him, but couldn't find him'.

As I placed the Bible on the table, he lunged forward and grabbed it saying, 'Don't lose that, that's what we need'. He beamed with delight at the unexpected and fresh revelation of this message from the Lord. One of my colleagues laughed with him and said, 'That's going to be Sunday's sermon'. The Archbishop then said, 'Sometimes you look for hours for a suitable message from the Bible for the people, but what you've read is the one for next week'.

The one who had 'towered above everyone else like a cedar of Lebanon' in Albania was Enver Hoxha. He became head of state in 1944 and created a Socialist Republic along strict Marxist lines. In 1966, a Chinese-style Cultural Revolution was staged and there was a massive shake-up of the administration. Formally trusted administrative officers were transferred to remote regions and young cadres were placed in leading positions. All agriculture was collectivised and the total farming area of the country became twenty-nine gigantic state farms.

All organised religion of every sort was at first severely restricted then totally banned. Albania became the only country in the world where all religion was completely outlawed.

When Russia invaded Czechoslovakia, Hoxha told his people that it was also likely to happen to them. He built a million concrete bunkers and pillboxes that looked liked small igloos. They were twelve to eighteen inches thick, and used enough concrete to house all of the homeless in the country, if the building materials had been used for that purpose instead. All the borders, the airport and approaches to towns were lined with these structures. Because the bunkers had been constructed so strongly, they were now almost impossible to demolish. I saw some that had been converted into chicken coops.

Under Hoxha's regime, the country went downhill economically and fell far behind the rest of Europe.

After Hoxha's death in 1985, Albania passed through a turbulent period, which resulted in a democratic state being established in 1992. The new government, that for the first time really was a *people's* government, inherited an exceedingly impoverished nation and two generations of browbeaten humiliated people. They had been completely isolated from the outside world and had absolutely no understanding of personal freedom and liberty.

Allison Denbury of International Teams, working with a mission service organisation called the Albanian Encouragement Project, met us at the airport in a nice new van and took us to our hotel. Our United Bible

Societies team comprised Terje Hartberg, Bishop Alberto Ablondi, Michael Roshak, Valdo Bertalot and myself.

The Hotel Tirana, where we were to stay, was booked out because of the forthcoming World Cup football match, Ireland versus Albania, so we put up at the Hotel Alberni nearby.

We were just as well off, but at a third of the price. I heard one American visitor at the Hotel Tirana respond to a question about her room by saying, 'Oh the room is ok, but the toilet doesn't work'. Perhaps she didn't persevere as much as I did in our hotel, because I discovered that by lifting the entire lid of the cistern, the toilet would flush.

We were assigned single rooms rather than the ones described as 'matrimonial', which we took to mean 'double'. When handing me my room key, the receptionist said very sternly, 'There are two beds but we charge for only one. Make sure you do not touch the other bed'. Later I noticed that despite the fact that I did not touch it, the room girl dutifully changed the sheets of both beds every day. Despite that, she wasn't a very good housekeeper, and never cleaned the hand basin, shower or toilet. Our toilet roll ration was about a tenth of a full roll for a week.

I asked the housekeeper about a laundry service and she took my clothes then pointed to the coat hooks on the wall saying, 'Dollar, dollar.' I gave her a dollar and she bundled up the clothes and put them under her jacket. Later that day, they appeared on the coat hooks, washed but not dry—apparently it cost more for drying and ironing. I guessed that they had probably been washed in the ladies' bathroom at the hotel.

There was a brand new TV, which was placed, not on a table, but on its original carton. Unfortunately, the TV didn't work because there was no aerial. There was also a brand-new telephone, but that wasn't connected. In fact, there wasn't a single telephone in the hotel that worked. Instead, it was a kilometre walk to the post office to make a phone call. Water was available for about three hours in the morning and four hours in the afternoon. Electricity, though, was on 24 hours, which was a considerable improvement over recent times.

We had a meeting with the leaders of the Albanian Encouragement Project. They provided services for about 30 evangelical missions and organisations operating in the country. They were very supportive of the idea of a Bible Society being established in the country, because of the sheer chaos that reigned when it came to providing Scriptures for Albania. For instance, two different groups had printed 500,000 copies of the New Testament in Albanian and there were several other editions sent into the country. There were at least six different translations of the New Testament in Albanian. Some had been done very quickly and were deficient in one way or the other.

There were also at least three different translation teams working on new editions. The only complete full Bible published had been sponsored by the European Christian Mission, and was set in a very simple form of the language. The group agreed that this was useful, but another translation was needed for serious study purposes. If a national Bible Society was established, it could sponsor a new interconfessional translation that would be acceptable to all the churches. Just a few days before we arrived, Brother Andrew of Open Doors had presented a copy of the new full Bible to the president of the country, which was in itself a remarkable thing.

The leaders of the Encouragement Project entertained us over dinner that evening and I discussed with them the possibility of visiting some churches in the country. I knew that Albania was suffering from a surfeit of Christian visitors—not tourists, but groups coming on fact-finding visits to study and survey to see what they could do. Many of these visitors would make big promises but nothing would eventuate. This was a sadly familiar problem at that time in so many countries of the former Soviet Bloc. I wanted to visit a place that was off the usual Christian visitor track. One man said to me, 'Of all the people who come here to visit, and I think we can say that there have been hundreds, you are the first one to show any sensitivity to this problem of too many visitors'. He was only too willing to help, and suggested a people group living five hours away in the mountains near the Macedonia border. So many people come to visit that there are churches and missionary groups who refuse to see any one who comes uninvited and the AEP service organisation is under instruction not to give out names and addresses to people without their express permission.

We called on the Minster of Sports, Culture and Religion to discuss the requirements of setting up a national Bible Society in Albania. We first had to see the person responsible for 'foreign contacts' but after hearing what we wanted to do, he called in a man whom he said was the 'Chief of the Christian Church' in the Secretariat of Religion, a Mr Sokol Mirakaj.

These men proved very helpful and even appeared to be a little excited at the prospect of a Bible Society being set up, as they could understand the need for an organisation that coordinated Bible publishing. For two hours we discussed the likely procedures, until it was decided that, instead of waiting for a new law on religion to be promulgated, we would register as an association under the old law.

Mr Sokol assured us that he would try and sweep away unnecessary bureaucracy and red tape, and go straight to the Prime Minister to ask for our proposed society to be given top priority. He gave us a list of questions to be answered when drawing up the statutes of the society. As we prepared to take our leave, I whispered to my colleague, 'Let's ask Bishop Ablondi to pray'. For a second Terje looked doubtful, then spoke up. 'Before we leave may we ask Bishop Ablondi, the vice-president of the United Bible Societies, to pray?'

The secretary bowed his head and quietly said, 'Yes.'

After the prayer, Mr Mirakaj raised his head, his eyes brimming with tears, and said, 'Do you realise what we have done? Do you understand where you are? It was in these very rooms that so many bad things were planned against the people, and here we are praying together. In this room plans were made for people to be condemned, imprisoned, tortured or even killed because they believed in Jesus. My family was held in a prison camp. I went there at the age of three years and came out only two years ago when I was forty-three'.

We were stunned at this revelation and left the building in a subdued mood of wonder at the changes that had taken place. Later in the day, people told us more about the terrible sufferings endured by the Mirakaj family during a lifetime in the prison camp.

After the government banned all religious practises in 1967, relentless persecution erupted. Hoxha used a savage expression to describe the way religion ought to be cut away, when he said that 'the sharp knife of the party' should be used to destroy all religious idolatry. 'Religion is the opium of the people and we must do our utmost to ensure this truth is understood by all the people even by those who are poisoned by it. We shall have to cure them.'

In his propaganda, Hoxha cleverly related the three main religions to the various invaders of Albania over the centuries. The Turks had brought Islam, the Orthodox faith came through the Greeks, and the Roman Catholic Church by the Italians and the Austrians. 'The people would do well to remember their history and muster their patriotic spirit to fight and clean out all religions.'

The Muslims lost 1,300 mosques, which were completely destroyed with only one being left in Tirana and put to government use. All the Christian churches were either destroyed or converted into warehouses or factories. The Orthodox Church Cathedral was destroyed and a hotel put up in its place. Another important church was turned into a restaurant. A Roman Catholic Church became a cinema. A total of 2,196 religious buildings were destroyed or converted to secular use. Nearly all of the nation's one hundred and eighty Catholic priests and many Protestant pastors, as well as a countless number of ordinary Christians, were executed or died under torture.

Vast numbers of Christian believers suffered long years of imprisonment. I heard one story of a man in the Ministry of Culture who, as a lad of eleven years, was caught trading prison bread for tomatoes through the barbed wire fence with a farmer outside. He was punished by being made to sleep outside at night for many years—even during the cold winters.

The Papal Nunciate of Albania (that is, the Vatican's ambassador to a country) assured us that he was 'all for it' when it came to setting up a national Bible Society. He told us about a peculiar problem that he had.

There were five bishops, and three of them were elderly Albanian priests who had suffered long periods of imprisonment in total isolation from the outside world.

These three bishops had never heard of Vatican II, when the Catholic Church decided to allow believers free access to the Bible and to encourage the translation and distribution of the Bible. The liturgy of the church services was to be said in the vernacular and not the incomprehensible Latin of the past. These old priests had absolutely no knowledge of these dramatic changes, and knew nothing about the ecumenical spirit of cooperation among churches around the world.

The Papal Nunciate explained to us that he had a tremendous task on his hands to train his bishops in the modern ways of the church. This wasn't easy for men who had suffered untold miseries, pain and torture simply for being priests of the church. During their time as prisoners, they were not allowed to pray, speak or sing. Even to give the sign of the cross while in prison was enough to have their sentences increased by ten years. Men like this, who stood up against such treatment from evil doers to preserve the faith, were not easily going to change their beliefs just because a senior bishop told them to.

We went to visit the Roman Catholic Church in Tirana and there met an old priest, Father Anton Luli. He had an amazing story to tell us and, seated among the pots of paint and bags of cement of the contractors who were refurbishing his church, we listened spellbound as he recounted his experiences at the hands of the communists.

He began by saying, in the words of my Italian colleague's translation, 'After 17 years of prison and many other sufferings of all kinds, the Lord is really good.

'He has after 50 years given us the chance to taste the delicacies of His heart in the contact of God's people who are really thirsty and hungry for His Word. It is a pity that not many of us priests are now left. We are all now old, sick and filled up with medical problems, physical problems, after constant suffering, both physical and moral.

'In July I will be 82 years old but I feel in myself that I am strong. Notwithstanding during my jail period three times I have approached the border of eternity. A situation, which I really desired in order to free myself from the torments, from the sufferings that were incessant.

'Often I joined Jesus in His prayer in Gethsemane. Probably it is useful to know something of my long odyssey.

'Anyhow I don't do this in order to please myself because I have so many pities in front of my Lord. I do it just in order to console you in order or better for our spiritual advantage. I assure you that I don't add to the reality or exaggerate in what I am going to say to you.

'When our college in Skutani, in northern Albania, was closed, I was named parish priest at Skrele about twenty kilometres north of Skutani. After one year and a half I was arrested on 19th December 1947. The accusation was "agitation and propaganda against the Communist government". This was the normal accusation against the clergy. It was their consistent practice in order to make us disappear. As the president said, "I will persecute the pastors."

'I was taken to Kopleek, a small village in the mountains of Skutani. The guard opened a small room and threw me in against the wall and shut the door. It was dark. In the door was a small window and a weak light came through. To my great surprise I realised that it was a bathroom where the toilet was filled up with faeces that were becoming solid. It was never cleaned during the nine months that I stayed there, night and day.

'This was nothing in comparison to what happened afterwards. Never in my life have I realised the true presence of the Lord as in that moment. But very soon began my Calvary. Over that small room half of the police were living. There was an army officer who had a very ugly face, but he was even more brutal than the others in his behaviour and attitudes. The policemen took me to him and he welcomed me, his face was very angry and almost diabolical. He punched me in the face and then he called three or four policemen. They surrounded me, pushing my body, which was very weak, one to another as a football, screaming and bellowing at me.

191

'And then with his two hands he tried to throttle me with all his strength almost suffocating me. I fell to the ground as a dead body falls. Then a giant policeman jumped on my body with boots, heavy boots, many times, breaking my left rib and for this I suffered for many years without having the chance to fully rest any more.

'The officers requested that I should confess all my sins that I had committed against the people. Naturally that meant against the Communist Party. As I refused he placed the electric power in my ears, which is a torture horrible, you cannot stand it, it is unbelievable. And to some people this kind of torture they have done it to the genitals.

'I will not speak about the regular knockouts and all the beatings and the many times they used the electric power on me during the next following nine months.

'I could go to the bathroom just twice in a day, in the morning at six o'clock and in the evening before the sun set. Outside those two moments, I was not permitted to use the toilet. And this was one of the most terrible tortures, especially when you had colitis. More than once I had been obliged to act physically in exactly the same receptacle, in the very same plate, where I usually had my portion of miserable food. And then at the given time with the cup in my hand seen by fellows I had to go to the Turkish toilet to wash it and then go to have my lunch. What humiliation and what suffering for me, and for my fellow prisoners, trying to put up with that cup near the bed all night.

'In the stagnant swamp pools we worked without shoes, always fighting against the leeches which suck your blood. They usually fastened themselves to the naked parts of the body. In order to free us from them the only way was the lighted cigarette put on the body of the worm. Many died from lack of food and drink and from the sufferings.

'I usually behaved with great caution in my working relationship with my fellows, because I did not trust anybody. Each day from home to work, then work to home. Each day I prayed in my room, without the knowledge of anybody, the Mass, using only the Canon of the Mass. And

I was afraid to pronounce confession or prayers, except in a very rare case and only for people I knew.

'I stayed for nine months in one prison without seeing the sun, under the very boring light of an electric lamp.

'It is impossible for me to describe what I saw and what I heard during those nine months in that place of torment. Lamentations, screams, people blaspheming, when you are utterly exhausted you are not even able to say "Yes".

'Well I heard all this with my ears as I arrived in that place. More than twenty rooms were filled up with disgraced people who were there, both men women, and me. A good part of them were young people, stopped just because they talked to their friends confidentially that they were desiring to pass over the border. In these cases the condemnation was sixteen years in a labour camp.

'After a very long nine months in that prison, which to me seemed like eternity, I arrived in the court. The accusation was the normal one. "Father Anton Luli has made agitation and propaganda against the Popular People. And he has also done economic sabotage creating havoc to the economy"—or something similar.

'The chief prosecutor requested capital punishment, the condemnation to death by shooting. After two days the verdict of the head of the judge was capital punishment transmuted to twenty-five years jail. At that time I was seventy years. Now I am eight-two.

'There was serious trouble if someone gave a minimal external sign like crossing yourself or the sign of the cross. You were immediately accused of propaganda of the faith and then even also taken to court and condemned

'Now that is enough of all this misery.

'The Lord has done a true miracle toward me. It is difficult for me to believe that I am alive, that I am free, and that I am able to speak freely, to be able to serve God, to celebrate Mass, to confess and to have a common life with my very good brothers. It has taken one year in order to become satisfied in eating bread without leaving a single crumb.

'I still had ten years of jail to go when they released me. Three times I was at the end of my life and now the Lord has given me the freedom. Now I have everything except the age, which I would like to be forty years old again, in order to work in the vineyard of the Lord without serving myself. How great is the need of these people of my country who during these fifty years greatly missed being able to come to the house of God'.

I wanted to take his photograph and, rather than disturb him by coming too close, I used a long lens and stood a few metres away. He had the worn tired face of a man who had suffered much and his photo was used many times around the world.

The largest church in the country is the Albanian Orthodox Church and this was now slowly being re-established. The Archbishop, a Greek, had been involved in helping to ensure that the Modern Greek New Testament was accepted by all the churches for use in Greece. Now, in his new role in Albania, he willingly agreed to support the idea of a Bible Society being established as soon as possible.

He was anxious to show me what little was left of the church buildings that the government had taken. The largest one in the city of Shkodra was converted into a gymnasium. He offered a car to show me around.

The next day, the Albanian Encouragement Group made arrangements for a taxi to call at 7.00 a.m. and take me to the isolated town I had been told about in Peshkopi, two hundred kilometres away on the border of Macedonia. It had been decided that if a taxi from Peshkopi picked me up, the fare would be a third less than what a driver from Tirana would charge. I waited until 2.30 p.m. but the driver from Peshkopi never showed up, so I resorted to a previous arrangement with a Christian taxi driver from Tirana named Marko, who had a reliable Mercedes.

The journey took five hours as the road wound through and over a series of hills and mountains, some of which towered to over 2,200 metres above sea level. In a river gorge, where there was a hydroelectric dam, the road was cut through solid rock to form two double lane tunnels.

The mountains were beautiful in the late afternoon sun, and across the border in Macedonia they were flecked with snow. At one point, the driver slowed down to show me a railway station without a railway line. It was many miles from the nearest track. We also stopped to look at a prison camp half way up a mountain. It was coloured grey and looked cold and forbidding. The prisoners worked in the slate mines.

In Peshkopi, I visited a missionary couple Geoff and Haille Owlsey of the Pioneers organisation. A few minutes before I arrived, they had returned from a two-week holiday in Austria. They were renting a small house and their landlords gave them a great welcome home. One by one, the landlord's family members, and other neighbours, came to greet them. Albanians kiss a lot—or at least kiss the air beside each cheek—anything up to four times, depending how well people know each other.

There was a packet of mail to read, but my host was kept from opening it until all the neighbours had finally left. In the lounge, I was given the seat of honour—a pure white sheepskin placed on one end of a settee. The lights in the lounge were not working so one neighbour came in to change one of the three bulbs. 'Albanians are wonderful people to live with,' said Geoff. 'They are always so helpful and do what they can to make you feel at home among them'.

Haille told me that she had to abandon her modern American ways and had to work hard to keep up with the standards of housekeeping maintained by her neighbours. Every morning, the cement path in the front of the house and the porch had to be washed. The women work very hard and have practically no leisure time.

The Owlsey's house was a typical Albanian city home but had a strange room at the rear. Running along the entire length of the back of the house was a narrow room about four feet wide. At one end was the kitchen and washing up area, and at the other, a porcelain aperture in the floor known locally as a 'turkish toilet'. Above the toilet was a window. 'Don't worry about there being no curtain,' said my hostess, 'there's no one out there'. It was a case of going to the toilet in the kitchen!

Marko stayed overnight and drove me back to Tirana the next day. Albanians living outside the cities were very friendly and are quite different from their urban compatriots. Strangers walked up to greet me and shake hands and even some of the policemen at the roadblocks shook my hand.

The countryside was beautiful, with much of it under cultivation. But this work had all been accomplished by manual labour. There were huge fields being dug over with short-handled shovels. The communists introduced this type of shovel because, in their wisdom, they felt that the men worked better with them rather than long-handled ones. A short-handled shovel certainly wouldn't be so comfortable to lean on. There were huge fields where men were cutting the grass with scythes. The grass was collected and loaded onto donkeys and horses that looked like small green mountains, with just the animal's nose poking out the front.

The few animals that a person might own are looked after with great attention. Typically there would be a woman, sometimes very old, her head covered with a white scarf, looking after one or two cows; or a child taking care of three or four sheep. One old fellow was actually hand feeding his cow by bending down and plucking handfuls of grass for the beast. Nearer Tirana we came across a horse-drawn cartload of bread. The small brown loaves were unwrapped and the village women came out to buy the bread directly from the baker.

Back at the hotel, I went to the restaurant for some bread and soup. The place was almost empty and, while I waited for the bill, a couple of ragged little girls of about seven years crept in through the door and glanced around. They sidled up to my table, rubbing their fingers together. One held onto my left arm and repeatedly kissed it with wet lips, while the other patted my right arm and begged for money. They were both very dirty, with unwashed hair and, when clean, would probably have had an olive complexion with startling blue eyes. I gave them each a couple of pieces of bread and told them to hop it before the waiter returned. There was one other table occupied and, clutching their bread, they were trying their luck with four Albanian men having a late lunch, when a roar from the waiter sent them scampering away.

The waiter came over to me and apologised, 'These Albanian children are terrible and very naughty'. Such an experience is difficult for a casual visitor, because it is impossible to know whether such beggars are in genuine need. They could be children of families who are learning to live off the growing number of tourists. Maybe they were gypsies who subsist that way. Then there is the Muslim custom of giving alms to beggars. Then again, perhaps these were orphaned children fighting for their very existence. There is no way of knowing. I knew that the children shouldn't be encouraged to enter a restaurant like that, but giving them some bread eased my conscience.

When I left the restaurant, the little girls were standing at the main door of the hotel and the chief receptionist was attempting to shoo them off. I felt sad to see children living like that and thought of a small child of about two that I had seen a couple of nights previously. He was lying on the footpath, half-naked, crying his eyes out. No one seemed to be paying any attention to him. I looked around and couldn't see anyone who might be responsible for him.

The only Sunday that I was in Albania was spent with the Archbishop of the Albanian Orthodox Church. He decided that I needed to see more of the country and his church, so he cancelled his Sunday appointments and took me to Berat. I was picked up by his driver in an old Volvo and taken to the diplomatic building where the archbishop had his home. We transferred to a smart-looking Mercedes 300 and were soon on our way. It was still fairly early in the morning, so the archbishop said his prayers in the car. Another priest travelling with us joined in. 'Do you know Psalm 23?' asked the archbishop. I began to recite it. 'No, please sing it to us', he said. I broke into the famous Crimond tune and we sang the psalm in three parts; I think we sounded pretty good.

Berat is an enchanting, ancient city. It is protected by the government and is known as a museum town. It is also called the 'city of a thousand windows', because of the many windows of the white-plastered houses that are built up the hillsides overlooking the Osum River.

The journey from Tirana took us through beautiful countryside that is carefully cultivated with a variety of crops, including many fields of barley and wheat. All of these fields were dotted with Hoxha's incongruous igloo-shaped concrete bunkers.

We drove into Berat and turned right, across the river, onto a very old bridge of seven arches built in 1780. It was crowded with pedestrians and mules loaded with all manner of goods, making their way to the market in the Christian quarter. Once we had crossed the river, we made our way up to an Orthodox church built in the 1700s.

Young people, carrying crosses that belonged to the church, greeted the archbishop and led him up the roughly cobbled path to the church. I let him carry on with the two and a half-hour service and asked his driver to drive me around the town. We headed for the museum on the top of the hill, and the Mercedes skidded and slipped all the way up the marble cobbled path. On the summit was a remarkable fortress built in the 3rd century by the Illyrians and strengthened by the Byzantines in the 5th and 6th centuries. The driver took the Mercedes through the huge stone gate right into the citadel and up to the museum of Onufri, who was a famous maker of icons. The Church of Our Lady is also part of the museum and was built in 1797. It has an amazing variety of icons, and a most beautifully carved pulpit and wooden screen that separates the public from the *iconostasis* or altar.

It had been suggested that the new UBS edition of the New Testament for the Albanian Orthodox Church should contain a photograph of an icon on the page after the title page. The museum held a very old icon, which was the archbishop's choice for this purpose, so I was asked to photograph it.

The lady caretaker arrived at the same time as we did and was very cordial in her welcome. After we had entered the building she locked the door to keep anyone else out. 'Photography is not allowed in the museum but in Albania you never know what may be permitted', the archbishop had said. It seemed as though special arrangements had been made. The caretaker seemed unconcerned about my cameras, but as soon as I produced my flash she suddenly became very upset. 'No photograph allowed!' she barked.

'But this is for the archbishop'.

She pointed to a sign on the wall, which was a good representation of a Leica camera. She went to her desk, took out an old and very large key, and fiddled with an ancient lock in a door set into the whitewashed wall. She produced a letter from the Ministry of Culture stating that no photography was permitted without the express permission of the minister. So I relented.

After touring the town, we returned to the church where the service was still in progress. The archbishop was just beginning his forty-minute sermon and, by the end of it, I wondered how many people at home would have been willing to stand through a two-hour worship service then a sermon of that length.

At the back of the church an eleven year-old girl spoke to me in perfect English. Her parents stood by beaming at her language ability. By the time the service was over, we had become quite good friends and they were disappointed that I could not accept their invitation to visit their home. However, they were very impressed by the fact that I had come with the archbishop and that I would be having lunch with him and the church council. But this is typical of the Albanian people. 'Hospitality is something that we don't have to teach the Christians', said Anthea Lyndsey of Operation Mobilisation when I met her later on, 'It's the most natural thing in the world to them'.

Lunch with the church council was a happy affair. A huge plate of salad, complete with potato chips, was followed by lamb and rice, then apples and oranges imported from Greece, and coffee that was so thick you could chew it. After lunch, one of the ladies brought a pillow, showed me to a spare room in the office building, and told me to sleep. 'The ooskop (bishop) will sleep and so must you', she commanded. I was wondering whether to or not when two priests came into the room and wanted to talk. The lady host was unable to drive them out, so she gave up and sat down as well, talking her head off in barely understandable English.

Before heading back to Tirana, we visited another church in the nearby mountains. The Mercedes was unable to get to the top of the road because the hill was too steep and rough. A small four-wheel drive bus from town arrived to transfer us to the top. Built in 1804, this building had been taken over by the government in 1967 and turned into a warehouse. It had been returned to the church fairly recently and already the villagers had restored much of it. There were many frescoes and icons painted on the walls that were in surprisingly good condition.

The villagers had a long list of requests for the archbishop and, as we left the place, he lamented the fact that there were hundreds of such buildings around the country that need renovating. The people didn't want us to leave but, after a coffee in the foyer of the church, we attempted to move to the bus. Outside, under a tree, the people stopped the archbishop from going any further and virtually forced him to sit down and talk some more.

Heading back, the rough road was too much for the Mercedes and half the exhaust system fell off. But we were soon on our way again with practically no traffic to hinder our journey.

Although the next day was the end of the Muslim Ramadan fast and was a public holiday, I decided to visit Duress, which is a port town on the Adriatic Sea. I took the train from Tirana, which was packed with young people heading to the beach. My compartment was crammed full with a dozen seventeen year-olds determined to have fun. One of the girls had a newspaper, which had a page of jokes and funny stories, and they all laughed uproariously as she read them out.

As part of their normal education, these teenagers studied four languages—French, Italian, Greek and English. They said that some of their friends were also learning Spanish and German as well, plus Albanian of course.

'Is it possible to learn seven languages all at once and learn them well?' I asked.

'Of course it is', they answered.

Duress is an ancient city dating back to the 7th century that was situated on the Appian Way—the Roman road to Constantinople. I went looking for the Operation Mobilisation team who, according to the directions I'd been given, 'lived next door to a derelict factory and a twenty metre brick chimney'. They were easy to find and I met up with a young New Zealand woman named Anthea Lyndsey who was one of the first missionaries to go to Albania after democracy was established.

I took her to lunch and as we walked along, an old woman approached and asked for some money for bread. Anthea gave her 100 Lek (US$1) and a Scripture tract. The woman wept quietly in gratitude. A couple of young street children also tried too, but were kindly and firmly refused because Anthea knew that this was their 'business'.

A twelve year-old boy greeted us. 'He's a wonderful evangelist'. Anthea told me. 'Many children have come to faith in the Lord because of his witness.' Within a few weeks of the OM team coming to Duress, there were so many people who responded to the gospel that a small church was established. As we walked the street, we passed a number of people who had become Christians in the past eighteen months.

Duress was the last place I would visit before returning home, but it seemed to symbolise what was going on in Albania. Very few of the churches were conducting evangelistic rallies or special meetings, but people were being converted at a significant rate. Most groups I met found that they had enough to do to teach the people who responded to the gospel just through the casual witnessing of new Albanian Christians.

Since the country had thrown off communism, Christian workers of all kinds had rushed to take advantage of the freedom to preach the gospel. Our visit, though, revealed that many of them were enthusiastically going about their work while steadfastly ignoring all the others. It was a bit of a shambles. The leaders of other denominations, such as the Orthodox Church and Roman Catholics, were quite mystified with the Protestant groups.

Maurice Harvey

'Albania' means the 'Land of the Eagle', and in many ways the country was now learning to fly again in the modern world. It was leaving behind the isolation that its communist leaders had forced upon it for fifty years.

People who were once denied religious freedom of any kind were now open to all and sundry. Thankfully, many were responding to the same gospel message that the Apostle Paul had preached on those same Illyrian shores in the first century.

9

INDONESIA—fascinating and frustrating

1972

I knew very little about Indonesia when I was first asked to consider going there. It was the fourth largest country in the world, an archipelago of 13,677 islands that stretch for 5,000 kilometres (3,000 miles) from east to west along the equator, and 3,000 (1,800 miles) from north to south. The latest official count is 17,508 islands! For New Zealanders, though, Indonesia was vaguely referred to as being 'up in the islands'—a term that covered the vast number of mysterious Pacific nations and atolls.

I had visited the country for a couple of days the previous year, and I didn't know how I could possibly expect my wife and family to settle in a place like that. My impression was that Jakarta, the capital city on the island of Java, was very expensive, corrupt and dirty, with chaotic traffic. Indonesia was a fascinating but frustrating country, even though the people were always smiling and friendly. After Nigeria, Lorraine and I, and our young family, had had a wonderful time living in the South Pacific, based in Fiji. It felt like a retrograde step to go from living in an island paradise to living in Jakarta—a city that I considered to be Asia's equivalent of Nigeria's capital, Lagos.

I kept thinking of my first time in Jakarta, when I was taken to lunch at a restaurant not far from a poor part of town. Too much food had been ordered and we couldn't eat it all. As the waiter came to the table to present the bill, a young boy clad only in a pair of dirty shorts, who had been hovering in the doorway, ran in, scooped up a handful of noodles left on a plate and ran out onto the street with noodles dripping between his fingers. I felt humiliated and ashamed that I had not thought to somehow offer him some food.

I was enjoying a visit to the beautiful South Sea Of Tarawa (formerly the Gilbert and Ellice Islands now Kiribati). but wondering about the wisdom of taking my family to Jakarta. The idea had been mooted but not confirmed and was constantly on my mind. The country was in the early stages of the remarkable modern development that has taken place over the past forty years. Then a cable arrived from Lorraine that said, 'Affirmative Djakarta, November if possible.' The United Bible Societies wanted us there in a hurry. But Lorraine had just recovered from an operation, so the move to a new country would be tough for her. In time, though, Lorraine and I both felt assured that it was the Lord's will for us to go there. So we made the move.

On arrival in Indonesia, we took up residence in a church guesthouse in Jakarta until our house was ready. One night at dinner, we wondered why there was a long thick black and greasy looking hose running through the dining room, almost under our table, out to the kitchen and into the back yard. Out on the road was a collection truck and it was busy pumping out the effluent from the guesthouse septic tank. Fortunately the hose didn't leak!

That evening we met a friendly American named Ed Kimball who said he worked for an organisation called Compassion International. I almost laughed at the name. Little did I realise that I would be working for them one day.

In the seventies, it was quite legal to distribute Christian literature in Indonesia. As far as the government was concerned, then under the leadership of General Suharto, Christians played an important role in the life of the country. Open evangelism was permitted, and the churches were growing at an amazing rate. One of my roles as a Distribution Consultant to the Indonesian Bible Society was to organise the distribution of the Bible in all the languages in which it was available.

The first President of independent Indonesia, Soekano, had recognised the role of the church in agitating for independence from the Dutch. So he decided that Christians should be represented in his cabinet. He chose a young Manadanese pastor, Rumambi, and appointed him Minister of Information. Many years later, Rumambi became the board chairman, then secretary, of the Indonesian Bible Society. In October 1965, the Communist Party of Indonesia was implicated in an attempted coup, but the army stepped in and took control, led by General Suharto.

The army quickly laid full blame for the coup attempt on the PKI (Indonesian Communist Party) and instigated an Indonesia-wide anti-Communist propaganda campaign, in which it is estimated that between 200,000 and 500,000 communists were slaughtered. As an anti-communism measure, the government then declared that all citizens had to subscribe to a religious faith (communism is against religion) and it be indicated on his or her compulsory identity card. Many people who had no affinity to Islam, the country's largest religion, opted for Christianity and joined a church. Because Christians are known as 'the people of the book', many of these new 'converts' began asking for Bibles. At the same time, genuine revival had broken out in East Java and Timor Island, and there were large numbers of true converts to Christianity. An edition of *The Renewal Journal* published around that time states: 'These islands have seen many revivals and people movements such as in 1965 amid political turmoil when over 100,000 animistic Muslims became Christian on the island of Java alone. Revival continues there'.

When it was discovered that communism had mainly spread through the use of literature, the government banned the importation of all books in the languages of Indonesia. (Hence the requirement for us to give a detailed list of all books we brought into the country in our personal luggage.) This meant that Bibles could no longer be imported. So the United Bible Societies assisted the Indonesians in setting up a Bible printing press.

Once the press was established, there was a need for a marketing manager to plan and direct the sale of the Bible throughout the country. The

Regional Office of the United Bible Societies set about trying to convince the Indonesians that they needed an expert to come and assist them. They were not sure about having another foreigner meddling in their business, but they agreed 'to look' at someone who might suit them.

I was invited to attend a marketing conference in Singapore and, on the way back to Fiji, was asked to visit Jakarta for a couple of days. The plan, unbeknownst to me, was to give the Indonesians a chance to take a look at me. I had several things in my favour: I was not an American—they considered them to be too domineering. I was not Dutch—Indonesians had had enough of the Dutch, since the Dutch East India Company, formed in 1602, had colonised Indonesia turning it into the 'Dutch East Indies'. Although, I must hasten to add that they chose a Dutchman, Henk Dyum, one of the world's best Bible printers, to head up their new printing plant. So I unwittingly passed the test and was invited to join the work there. Henk and I formed a wonderful working relationship. I would bring in the orders and he would print them. Even when the press seemed to be at full capacity, he would always find a way to produce all that was needed.

The Board of the Indonesian Bible Society assigned me to not just establish a countrywide marketing system and train local staff, but also to visit all the foreign missions in the country. Their staff had some difficulty in relating to the missions due to cultural and language difficulties.

Christians occupied some important government positions. I was often invited to attend meetings of the Christian Businessmen's Association, which included no less that five army, air force and navy generals. The proportion of the population considered to be Christian was about 20%—far more than official government censuses acknowledged.

It took several days to complete the formalities of living in Jakarta. I had been warned about the difficulties of getting a driver's licence; long queues and endless waiting, plus the necessity of a considerable bribe, were par for the course. The person assigned to deal with our affairs assured me that he would make the arrangements. One day, I was called to the lounge of our guesthouse to find him there with an aged policeman. I filled out the various documents that he had, and the policeman produced a rubber stamp and made out our licences there and then. I dared not asked the price!

We were required to provide a complete set of fingerprints for each member of the family to the following government agencies: Immigration Department, Inland Revenue, Jakarta City, our suburban residents office, the local mayor, local suburban police, and Jakarta police. The process started off at the Immigration Department and, assisted by Mrs Rumambi, the wife of the General Secretary of the Indonesian Bible Society, we filled out one hundred and twenty pages of forms, provided six sets of the family's fingerprints (all fingers), and one hundred passport photographs. Clive, not yet five, enjoyed having his fingers smeared black.

We took over a house that had been occupied by another UBS colleague, Translation Consultant Barclay Newman, who when answering my letter of inquiry as to what the house was like, was pretty non-committal. Privately, I took this to be a bad sign and feared the worst.

It was a typical Jakarta suburban house, jammed onto its section with its walls touching those of the houses on either side. It had no yard or garden space at all. With a tiled roof and whitewashed walls it looked appealing enough, but it had a weak electricity and water supply. I called a Dutchman who had a house maintenance business. He had earlier sent me an electrician, who was busy working on the house. Now I was ringing to ask for a plumber. 'He's there now,' said the Dutchman.

'No that's the electrician,' I said.

'He's the plumber too.'

The Dutchman advised that, because the water was off most of the day, we should build a water reservoir and fit an electric pump. During the night when the city water supply began to flow it would fill up the underground reservoir we had built under the short driveway. Then, when water was used either from a kitchen tap or the toilet, the electric pump would come on automatically. We went ahead with that plan, and it was fine—except, if someone was ironing and if the toilet was flushed at the same moment the fridge started up, the main fuse would blow. There were only 2,300 watts of electricity coming into the house, and it was often below 2,000. Everywhere on the streets, there were people picking up cigarette butts.

These remnants were reconstituted or, to use the modern word, 'recycled' into new, cheaper cigarettes. One day while waiting outside a supermarket, Lorraine noticed a man draining the dregs from orange drink bottles and filling a container that he would sell from his little cart.

Once, when we were having toilet problems, we discovered that the septic tank was directly under the floor of the internal garage. But that wasn't as bad as our friends, the McCowans, who discovered that theirs was located underneath the fridge in the kitchen. After we moved out of our house, it was converted into a butcher's shop and the garage was made into a medical laboratory. I wondered if the people working in the laboratory knew how close the septic tank, which was covered with a loose slab, was to all their sanitised instruments and samples. The name of the butcher amused us: *Hasrat* Meat Shop. We giggled together at the thought of the dead rat we found on our back doorstep and of the way these vermin occasionally invaded the house. *Hasrat* in Indonesia means 'longing or desire' so, in this context, we assumed it meant 'we sell meat that you long for'!

Our children, Rosanne and Clive, attended the Joint Embassy School, which was run by the USA, British, Australian and Yugoslav embassies, and Lorraine took up a teaching post there. An argument, that went on for many years between various government departments, meant that this school of over a thousand students could not be registered therefore, the teachers' salaries were not taxed nor could work permits be issued, because the school 'did not officially exist'.

My monthly salary was transferred to a local bank. One month, I received a note from a different bank informing me that a cheque had arrived from my office. It was a salary cheque but I had already received my monthly salary from the usual bank. My New Zealand accountant told me not to worry, as he had only paid me once and it was obviously a bank error. It wasn't worth investigating as it would take days to sort out. So I put the extra amount on deposit at 26% interest and waited, but I was never contacted by the bank to correct the error.

Jakarta is only about seven degrees south of the equator and, being at sea level, the weather was truly tropical. We installed air conditioners in both bedrooms. To get these units started, it was necessary to ensure that all other electrical equipment was turned off and that only the minimum lights were burning. The units had to be started one at a time. After they were running, it was then perhaps possible to flush the toilet without blowing the fuse. The fuses were not modern self-setting ones. They were the old European porcelain type that screwed into a socket. When one blew it became very hot. Lorraine can tell some stories of having to renew a fuse in the middle of the night when I was away. The fuse box was in the indoor garage and, clad in a nightie, trying to hold a torch, and standing on the roof of the car, she would struggle to get the burning hot fuse unscrewed; all the time hoping there wouldn't be a bat flying around, or a rat on the floor, or a cockroach attempting to climb up her arm or, worse, her leg. It was necessary to keep a box of a dozen fuses on hand at all times.

Electrical problems were common even in new houses. The manager of Citibank was to be transferred to Fiji, so he asked me to show some slides of that country to his family. After a good dinner, we set up the projector and switched it on. All of the lights in his house (US$1,000 rent per month) went out. We then blew the fuse again, before eventually getting the projector to work by turning off all unnecessary lights and appliances. Later, it was discovered that the new house next door (owned by the same landlord) was wired to the Citibank house, which meant that the bank was paying the electricity for both places. Another night, we were invited by our New Zealand friends Merv and Beryl Pearce to a New Year's Eve party in their new home. Just before we all left, the New Zealand Ambassador and his wife asked if they could use the hosts' toilet because they had no water in the four bathrooms of the ambassadorial residence.

Although the tiled roof of our house was exotic, it didn't seem so wonderful when, one evening after cleaning my cameras, I left one lying on a table without a lens in it. It rained that night and the tile directly above the camera happened to be loose (probably disturbed by a monkey), and let in a steady drip of water for an hour or two. In the morning a wail from my wife brought me running. My precious Leica M4 camera was full of water. I dried it out with a hair dryer.

Indonesia is a country where servants have servants. Well-meaning colleagues had hired a whole crew for us. There were two maids, a cook, a night watchman, a day watchman and a driver. The cook spoke a little English but none of the rest did. So it was a question of learning the language fast. A private teacher was hired to instruct us.

Are servants really necessary in a country like this? One writer put it this way: 'They are essential to accomplish the daily tasks that would have you hanging over a chair weeping at the end of a week'. The wooden or tile floors need washing every day. Most members of the family will go through two sets of clothing every day. Try washing and ironing them without mod cons. Or try cooking for the family using a tiny oven with one hot plate, plus a gas cooking ring, and a workbench that only comes up to your knees. Eventually, though, Lorraine decided that she didn't need a full-time cook. When she informed the lady we had at the time that her services were no longer needed, the cook wept saying, 'Oh understand, I too have a cook at home. That's why I need a job!'

When we first arrived, there was no furniture available for sale that we could afford so everything had to be made to order. The only wood available for furniture was teak. Even the queen-sized bed was solid teak but, without asking us, they covered the headboard and tables with dark brown teak-patterned Formica. Just like the furniture makers we had used in Nigeria, everyone was keen to make use of this newfangled product—even if it meant covering up beautiful native timber.

We camped in the house until our luggage arrived from Fiji three months later. When you are learning a language different words come to your attention in different ways, and often you remember how some of them were learned. The Indonesian word *rusak* was such a one.

The truck had arrived with our luggage, and scrawled across some of the boxes was the word *rusak*. 'What is *rusak*?' I asked the new cook. A pained expression crossed his face. 'Ahem, ahem, well *rusak* means . . .' It's possible he didn't know the English word but, more probably, he couldn't bring himself to tell me the bad news. He was a true Indonesian and therefore wouldn't want to say anything to the boss that would be disappointing or upsetting. There is an expression for this: '*asal bapak senang*', which means 'the source of father's happiness' or, put another way, 'whatever makes the boss happy'. So he said in a quiet voice, 'I don't know.' I consulted my dictionary.

Standing on the top of the luggage was a old man holding a very old gun. He was the guardian of our goods, but alas his work was made easy because much of our stuff had either disappeared or was damaged. That's it, *rusak* means 'damaged' or 'broken'.

The steel 44-gallon drum had long been the missionary packing container of choice. These drums hold a lot and are easily managed. We had two of them. One was completely empty except for a thermos flask, undamaged, rolling around the bottom. The other was half full. The sewing machine and typewriter were gone, as well as lots of other precious little things. Indonesia's customs people must have had a great time sorting through the luggage, because many of Lorraine's dressmaking patterns size ten had been changed for someone else's size twenty!

I had packed two wooden cases of books, but the books had arrived in a few gunnysacks. Many of them were covered in lamp black—the dirtiest substance known to man. I could joke that I had the dirtiest theological books in the world! We were very subdued when we unpacked our luggage, but I don't think we ever forgot the lesson of not holding on too tightly to this world's goods. To help prevent communist literature from entering the country, one of the unbelievable customs requirements on moving to Indonesia was to provide a list of all books including title, author, publisher, language and price. All the work I'd put into that paperwork now seemed a waste of time.

I wasn't happy with the driver who had been provided; he was unsafe. I had told the Bible Society that I would only have a driver if he were as good, or better, at driving than me. The traffic in Jakarta was so bad that it was important to be able to have absolute confidence in your driver. Having a driver was useful. Parking was difficult to find in the city, and your driver could circle the block while you went about your business. Even more importantly, when a car was being serviced, it was necessary to stay with the vehicle to make sure good parts weren't exchanged for old ones. The driver could be there the whole time to keep an eye on things.

There were no expatriates who drove their own vehicles. Indeed, some American companies would not allow their staff to drive themselves, because they considered the roads too dangerous. All things considered though, I decided I wanted to drive myself, and needed to find a way to convince everyone concerned that I was more than capable of doing so. I knew I would be safer looking after myself than putting my life in my current driver's hands. It would be humiliating for him to lose his job, but I could see no other solution.

Then an opportunity presented itself. I casually mentioned to the driver that I was to go to Jogjakarta next day and, when he asked what time we would leave, I just said, 'Early in the morning'. At midnight, I said goodbye to my wife and set off east, driving the fourteen hours alone. I figured that when he got to work in the morning, he would get the message that I didn't need him, thereby avoiding some embarrassment for him. Ten days later, when I returned safely, the Indonesian boss greeted me with a look of amazement, saying, 'So you are safe. You can drive in Indonesia?' The driver had already been given another job, so everything had worked out well. By the time we left the country four and a half years later, many expatriates were driving their own cars.

The government kept a close eye on foreigners travelling around the country. We were not permitted to be away from our home address without a letter explaining why we had travelled out of our suburb. This 'reason for travel' letter was called a *surat jalan*. When staying at a hotel overnight, our passports were held and our presence in the town was reported to the police. The passport would then be returned on checkout.

Java had long been known as an island with a fascinating blend of poverty and beauty, of culture and chaos. One Indonesian journalist visiting the USA (Mochtar Lubis) noted in an article in *Newsweek*, 15 October 1973, that: 'The amount of wastepaper, plastics, tins, newspapers, plastic bags, bottles left over food etc., that went into the garbage in the condominium where he lived would have given a comfortable living to several families of rag pickers in Jakarta'.

We soon learned that, like Nigeria, nothing should be thrown away. Someone could make use of bottles, tins, clothes—almost anything. There was a place in the house where such reusable things were put, and the servants could take them without having to ask. If a lady wanted to cut off her long hair, it could be given away, or sold by the servants, as there was a hair dealer that passed by our place about once a month. You could hear the hair vendor in the next street as he called out *'rambut, rambut'*—'hair, hair'. Bottles, large and small, were all useful. When obtaining medicine from the hospital pharmacy, the patient had to take his or her own container. The dispensary would simply rinse it in cold water if it looked a bit dirty, and pour in the medicine.

Browsing through a collection of thirty-year-old newspapers published in Indonesia brought back a lot of memories and was a reminder that a sense of humour is a big help in countries like this. A photograph of 'the first ever rugby football game ever held in Indonesia' showed a scrum. The caption read: 'The scrum is one of the exciting performances in rugby where most of the players are hugging each other'.

There was a photograph of a lorry sitting atop a huge pipe lying beside the road and the caption read: 'The truck ran down a water pipe'.

The editors of Jakarta's only English newspaper made use of some very original English. If a woman had her handbag stolen while out on the street, the event was called a 'snatchery'. The headline, 'Three piercers traced by Police', meant that three men accused of stabbing someone had been caught.

One paper carrying the story of a catastrophic bus accident led with: 'Only four people were injured in Indonesia's worst ever bus accident but 70 were killed.'

The 60s and 70s was a period of astonishing church growth in Indonesia. This resulted in an ever-increasing demand for Bibles. Here's a quote from The Renewal Journal: 'These islands have seen many revivals and people movements such as in 1965 amid political turmoil when over 100,000 animistic Muslims became Christian on the island of Java alone. Revival continues there.'

Due to the large number of people becoming Christians, there was a huge demand for Bibles. I found that we could sell Bibles as quickly as the printing press could produce them. Because open evangelism was permitted, my job was to design special publications of Scripture that could be used in evangelism. Many millions of these were snapped up by the churches and missions. My personal goal was to sell 10,000 copies per day to distributors.

I was visiting a missionary who called himself an 'Independent Baptist'. He explained that he preached the gospel from the book of Romans and therefore decided that all the current Bible Society publications were unsuitable for him. I immediately suggested that we design something specifically for him, right there and then. He explained that the people they met were often troubled by the fear of God's wrath upon them because of their sin. They were afraid to die and go to meet God. Within a few minutes we came up with a title 'Who can Free us from Sin and Death?' and selected passages from the book of Romans. He was delighted and ordered 50,000 copies. A month later he asked for another 50,000 and then 100,000. He said that he didn't know the exact number of people who had converted to Christianity as a result of reading this selection of Scripture, but 'there were many'. Someone showed this tract to Billy Graham and he asked permission to print millions of copies in the main languages of India for use in their Good News Festivals.

One Saturday afternoon, there was a knock on the front door. It was a missionary involved in youth work in Jakarta who had also become interested in distributing the Scriptures. He could see that this would be an excellent means of evangelism. We had previously spoken at length about the possibility of him buying a large quantity of Gospel Portions. He had come to tell me that he had found a sponsor who would pay for them. My interrupted siesta was soon forgotten when I clinched an order for one million gospels of John. It was my biggest sale. This book was distributed by Christian young people all over the country. It contained an invitation to enrol in a Bible correspondence course. There were so many responses that a staff of fourteen people were taken on to deal with the thousands of inquiries.

Sales were so great that time and again we had to adjust our budgets and printing schedules to meet the demand. In the first four months, I sold 2,318,000 Scriptures.

In my file on Indonesia I found the following notes written on 2nd October, 1973, describing my first visit to Timor, when half the island was still a Portuguese colony.

The night porter of the Bali Hotel woke me at 3.30 a.m. and by 4.00 a.m. I was on my way by taxi through the dark streets of Denpasar to the International Airport. Even at that hour, there were scores of women carrying baskets of fruit and produce to the central market or setting up business along the side of the road. They carried primitive lamps with naked flames that glowed orange in the darkness and cast an eerie glow over the fruit.

Most of the passengers were already waiting in the unlit terminal by the time I got there. 'No, it's not a power cut,' said one man, 'there's no light bulbs.' We were a mixed bag—a few Timorese, quite distinctive with their sharp features, and a couple of Portuguese soldiers with nine suitcases. They were ninety kg overweight. They argued about this heatedly and were so upset about paying the extra charges that, at one stage, I thought they were going to pass the hat around the rest of us.

There were a dozen or so European hippies who had slept the night at the terminal and managed to appear at the check-in counter looking as dishevelled and grubby as they could possibly be—such a contrast to the always neat, tidy and clean Balinese.

We took off directly into the rising sun and we were soon over a fleet of Balinese double out-rigger fishing canoes, their white triangular sails glistening in the oil-streaked sea. Then came the island of Penida, which rises steeply out of the sea. It is extremely precipitous, with only the tops of the hills being cultivated.

A few more miles of sea, then the island of Lombok. I once had a very long and uncomfortable ride in an ox-cart there. At that time, it had been the only available transport from the small port to the nearest town. In later years, Lombok was converted into a tourist paradise. The island's majestic volcano, Mt Rinjani (2,376 metres), protruded through the clouds as though nothing would dare to cover it. On the return journey, the pilot took us over its spectacular crater lake and circled it twice. This is one of Indonesia's four hundred volcanoes, one hundred of which are still active.

The next island was mostly mountains, with only the very tops cultivated, and the hundreds of valleys were filled with snowy white cloud. There were many miles of white sandy beaches, but most were inaccessible by road. On and on we flew, the clouds obscuring the island chain that stretches two thousand miles to the west, and to the tip of Sumatra a thousand miles in the other direction—all of which is Indonesia.

Finally Timor Island appeared and we landed at Dili, capital of Portuguese Timor. The airport was situated in a dry, barren area and featured a very unpretentious terminal. The Portuguese immigration officer examined my passport carefully, reading every word in it. I never liked it when an immigration officer did that; it gave me an uncomfortable feeling. He reached for his rubber stamp and banged it on an empty page. It was the wrong stamp—he had inadvertently given me 'residency for life'. When I pointed this out to him, he simply sighed and said, 'It doesn't matter,' as if to say, 'You can stay here as long as you like, but I'm getting out as soon as I can'.

The hippies among us were carefully checked, including their inexpensive luggage. The customs officers made sure we all got on the bus for the city a few miles away, then they closed the airport. The manager of the best hotel in town met me and assured me that he had his finest room ready.

The hotel was situated beside the sea, which in the early afternoon sun was a beautiful green. The place was spotless. The town had a population of only 5,000 and is set along the shoreline, with a splendid promenade area protected by a sea wall and lined with a wide garden and lawn. But the town was deserted—the residents were enjoying their four-hour siesta.

The purpose of my trip was to visit the churches in the colony, the main one being the Roman Catholic. The Bible Society in Australia was responsible for Portuguese Timor. The diplomatic relationship with Indonesia was strained, to say the least. After several failed attempts to obtain an invitation to visit, the General Secretary, Jim Payne, asked me if I would try on his behalf.

I had written to the Bishop of Dili and posted the letter on the way to the Jakarta airport. I wasn't going to give him the chance to refuse me. I took a taxi to the bishop's palace and introduced myself. That, in itself, wasn't quite as easy as it sounds, because I don't speak Portuguese, and he didn't speak English. He tried French and Spanish and German. I tried Indonesian. No he didn't understand, but looked a little interested. I tried some Fijian. His eyes lit up. He understood a few words. He broke into a torrent of Tetun, the local language. I caught a word or two.

It turned out that Tetun belonged to the same language family, called Austronesian, as Fijian and Indonesian. It had a completely different grammar, but a handful of similar nouns and verbs. With a few dozen French words, a few Portuguese words that occur in Indonesian and Chibemba, and a few common Austronesian words, we began to communicate. By the time the Chinese priest, who had been called to interpret for us, had arrived, the bishop had understood who I was and what I represented, and why I had called on him. It must have been hilarious to have heard us. I would use say, a Fijian numeral, an Indonesian verb, a Portuguese noun, in English syntax all in the same sentence. 'Chamo-me Maurice Harvey' (my name is MH, in Portuguese), 'I' (patting my chest) 'trabajo' (work, in Spanish) 'Society Biblique' (Bible Society, in French).

The bishop was cordial enough in his welcome but wasn't interested in buying Scriptures for his people. They didn't need the Bible, he said. We talked for four and a half hours, and I employed all the selling techniques I knew. Finally I emerged from his palace all smiles. He had relented and finally given me an order for a Bible for every priest, a New Testament for every schoolteacher, and a Gospel Portion for all the children. He had also ordered some Bibles in different languages for the libraries. Plus, the Chinese priest wanted a few Bibles in Chinese.

When I wrote up my report for the Bible Society of Australia, I gave a copy to the Indonesian Bible Society as well. I described the bishop as 'a crusty old fellow', and later that year, when the Indonesians issued their annual report, they mentioned my visit to Dili. The report was printed in Indonesian and English and quoted my report—including the bit about the bishop being 'a crusty old fellow'.

On Timor, the one Protestant minister lived on an island five miles from Dili. The charter price for a DC3 to see him (there were no boats available) was a bargain at US$40 for the day.

Around town, I managed to get a good set of photographs of Dili and its people. The guards at the Governor's Palace were traditional warriors with feather hats and bare torsos, bearing wicked swords.

My next plan was to go overland to Indonesian Timor, but there was no bus service to take me there. So I hired a car and driver to take me to Maubise. Within four hours we had climbed to 3,000 (914 m) feet above sea level to our destination, where I was deposited at 'the best hotel in town'. It was a small guesthouse run by an elderly Chinese couple with a large number of children, all of whom chewed betel nut. There's nothing pretty about a cute six-year-old girl with the tell-tale red stains around the mouth, teeth and tongue. The nut acts as a mild stimulant, but is known to cause health problems—including mouth cancer. My room at the guesthouse was US$1 per night and I was invited to make myself at home. There was a single bed in my room with a very dirty coloured mattress. No sheets, pillow, soap, towel, toilet paper, water or food. The toilet and bathroom were filthy. And as my notes from the trip say, 'I'm not too fussy when travelling in these parts but I do have an aversion to a bathroom with a quarter of an inch of green slime all over the floor—it's awfully hard to stand up!'

The hired car, actually a Toyota Land Cruiser, then took me on to Baliboa, up over the highest mountain in the island at 10,000 feet (3,000 m). At one point, the road ran out and we finished up in a stream. 'The road,' said George my Chinese driver, 'is a river.' A river it was, but not too deep to travel along or through. We followed it for several hours with the water leaking in through the doors. This was high adventure. The forest came right to the water's edge and was very thick. Here and there were a few monkeys and many species of birds that fluttered out of our way with a variety of screeches and squawks.

The river was fun, but all the same, it was a relief to reach a road of sorts. A breakdown in the river would have meant big trouble. We arrived at

Baliboa, a small town of six shops. The abattoir was at work on the side of the road near the shops, laying out the carcase of an ox on the grass. The baker offered me a bed in his storeroom. That evening, I lay down and George came along and said, 'Move over,' and hopped on too. It was an awful night, what with George's snores, and having to squash bed bugs. Then the baker began banging his trays around. At 3.00 a.m. I woke George up and suggested we get going. He announced that he wasn't going any further and told me to wait for the mini bus.

The mini bus was a brand new Toyota van. We did a tour of the area, stopping at various points to pick up passengers. By 3.00 p.m. we were at the police station to obtain clearance to leave the town. Then we changed drivers and we were off.

We had only moved one hundred yards, when I discovered that the new driver was little less than stupid. He roared through the town in third gear at 90 kph, scattering pedestrians and chickens in all directions. Once on the open road, he soon proved that he was quite incapable of handling the vehicle properly. We had only been on the road for about half an hour when I heard 'hssssss' behind me then, 'flop flop flop'. Our first puncture.

For the most part, the road was unsealed and the driver raced along, ignoring the many stones that jutted up through the dirt. Apparently some time ago an attempt had been made to lay a foundation of stones and this was covered with earth. Much of the earth had washed away, leaving the road in an uncomfortable state. The little bus was overloaded by at least a ton and we raced along and onto a hilly section where we twisted and turned alarmingly. A troop of monkeys scattered in a volume of shrieks as we swept around a corner into their midst, where they were holding a conference in the middle of the road.

This part of the country had not seen rain for six months and all the streams and riverbeds were quite dry. This was just as well, as at least a dozen bridges were under repair. So we simply drove across the riverbed, but the banks were about 45 degrees. That was all right going down but we all had to get out, unload the luggage and push the bus up the other side.

At 9.00 p.m. we arrived at the small village of Ketu, where we stayed at the home of a Javanese woman and her six lovely children. She ran a sort of private guesthouse. It was quite a small house and I couldn't see where the family of eight slept. They played music very loudly on a cassette recorder until 11.30 p.m. The bathroom and toilet were so dirty that I didn't like to use them. At midnight, one of the older boys crept into my tiny room and laid a mat on the floor, in the narrow space between my bed and the wall, and went to sleep. A few minutes later the mother came and lay down on the single bed right beside me. She turned her back to me and was snoring in minutes. An hour later and I still was not asleep. She turned over and, putting her arm over me, said in Javanese, then Indonesian, 'Come, come'. I said, 'Go, go', and elbowed her sharply. So she turned over and almost instantly began to snore. When I woke up in the morning she was gone. So now I can admit to my wife that I have slept with another women!

The driver announced before we retired that we would depart at 7.00 a.m., so I was up ready to go by 6.50 a.m. The driver eventually got up at 8.00 and we left at 9.00. He had assured me that the road to Kupang was good, but in fact it was little better than the previous day. He flew along at 65 kph over the dreadful road and I felt that my hair was gradually turning white, but not just by dust.

Nine kilometres of the road consisted of a riverbed with about a metre of water covering it. Not as exciting as my adventures in the Land Cruiser, but spectacular all the same as the driver moved as fast as he could, sending up huge plumes of water.

The next day was another day of torture, in the sense that the same reckless driver hurtled the vehicle (fully loaded with eighteen people inside, and a mountain of luggage on the roof) over the rocky road. There was no spare wheel and we had three punctures—all of which had to be repaired on the roadside. No amount of reasoning with the driver would convince him that if we didn't hit the sharp rocks so hard we weren't as likely to get punctures. I was in the front seat which, while perhaps more comfortable, was certainly more frightening.

On arriving in Kupang, the capital of Indonesian Timor, I stayed at the only hostelry that had a room to spare. It was a dirty little guesthouse and I tried not to notice the goings on which suggested it was also 'the best little whorehouse in Kupang'. It was the workplace for a number of beautiful young women who were keen to get to know me. The locals call them *kelapalapa malam* or 'night butterflies'.

Kupang was in the grip of a water shortage and there were people rolling 44-gallon drums of water all over the place. The hotel allowed no baths.

When the time came to fly back to Bali, I duly turned up at the airport and waited. Other would-be passengers were there, but there was no sign of a plane. Finally the local Chinese caterer turned up to announce that the flight was cancelled and we should come back tomorrow. He went to his Landrover and produced the food he had prepared for the flight. 'You may as well have these,' he said, and gave us our boxed lunches. This was repeated three times over three days before a plane came.

Aceh is a province in North Sumatra where the people are renowned for their strong Muslim beliefs. The Indonesian Bible Society published a small book of Scripture called a 'New Reader Portion' in the Aceh language. This had been translated by a Christian Aceh who no longer lived among his own people. I was asked to arrange for the distribution of the booklet. One of our distribution staff members was sent to the area with a supply of the Portions, but when the customs control at the border discovered these books, they illegally would not let him enter their area. He was sent back home on the next bus.

So we tried again by sending the same representative by air, hoping that the airport customs team wouldn't be so strict. They examined his luggage and promptly put him on the next plane to Jakarta. Their actions were technically illegal, but the authorities, from the Dutch colonists onwards, have never been able to control the Achenese.

I pondered this problem for a few days then a surprising opportunity presented itself. I had long been a railway enthusiast, and while I was in Indonesia, alongside my Bible Society work, I acted as the South East Asia Correspondent of the International Railway Journal. I was visiting the General Manager of Indonesian State Railways, when he introduced me to the newly appointed manager of the railway in Aceh province. This was a typical military government appointment because he was an army general who knew very little about railways—he didn't even know the gauge of the track.

Soon afterwards, I was in Medan where the Aceh Railway manager had his office, so I decided to call on him. He was delighted and asked me if I would like to visit his railway. I readily accepted the invitation. He was not keen for me to actually travel on the railway, as it was a narrow gauge affair in poor condition with a maximum speed of 20 kph. Some of the passenger coaches were open goods wagons with wooden planks for seats. Instead he offered me the use of a chauffeur-driven car. I insisted on going by train at least part of the way so a footplate pass was issued to enable me to travel on the locomotive. I was fascinated by the 750 mm (2 ft 5½ in) gauge railway, which had been built by the Dutch military in 1876 for the 'pacification' of the area. Three hours up the track, the official car met me. It was a very large American model, and it took me in some luxury on to the next town.

I took a good quantity of the Aceh Scripture Portions along with me in the train and then in the official car. Wherever I went, I handed copies to people whom I thought would appreciate them, and left many copies just lying about where they would be found. The chauffeur of the car was a Batak Christian and he enjoyed the experience.

Several years later, I heard of a man who had come across one of these Portions and read it carefully. It resulted in him seeking out the way of salvation and becoming a Christian. He decided that he would like to translate the complete Bible into his native tongue. Sadly, before he had finished the New Testament, the Muslim authorities threatened his life if he continued. He was forced to leave his home and live in another city in a different part of the country. Quite by chance, I happened to meet him at his work, and it was only after I had taken his photograph that he asked me not to publish his name or photo. That was when the rest of his story came out. I felt utterly privileged to have played a small part in that story.

The second book to be published in Achenese was the Gospel of Luke. In an article entitled 'Holy Fire in Aceh', a local newspaper posed the question: 'Is the distribution of this book being done by people who want to incite Muslims against Christians? If so, it must be a communist who didn't like to see us happy under our own religions.'

One interesting regular event, was the annual visit of a secretary from the Russian Embassy. He came to buy a copy of each of the new translations of the Bible in the languages of Indonesia. These were for the central library in Moscow, where, we were told, they kept a copy of every book published in every language of the world. Whenever he came to visit, I tried to engage him in general conversation, but these were Cold War times, and he kept strictly to business.

The western half of the New Guinea Island became an Indonesian territory in 1971 and was named Irian Jaya. The entire island is home to an astounding number of tribes, probably about one thousand, with about three hundred and twenty in the Indonesian half. Professional missionary linguists assured me that there were some tribes not yet located and 'documented'. I attended a Bible translation workshop held at Pyramid, a Christian and Missionary Alliance mission station in the Central Highlands.

The local people were Western Dani, of whom it can be said, the women don't wear blouses and the men don't wear trousers. It was a challenge for a photographer to obtain good publishable photos of half naked Christian men and women. The men only wore penis sheaths called *horim* or *koteka*, made out of a dried gourd. It would be fair to say that some of these were so impressively long that they attracted more attention than if the man had been wearing nothing! It was really something to see a man thus attired doing the dishes in a missionary lady's home. The women wore grass skirts and went topless. Many had a string bag that hung from the head down the back. Some looked as they were clothed until they turned around. These bags were like their handbags, containing all the things a woman likes to carry, from sweet potatoes to a baby.

Highland weather (2,000 metres above sea level) can be quite cool and wet, and wearing European clothes, which were prone to get damp, had caused all types of medical problems from skin irritation to respiratory illnesses. As a result, the government had all but given up hope of trying to get the people to change their dress habits. The local missionaries decided that it was best to let the people be and not make 'westerners' out of them. The people had their own code of morals. My black and white photos were very successful and, some time later, the photo editor of *TIME* magazine asked to see them for possible use in a story about the territory. My colour slide films did not turn out so well-they were irreparably spoiled in the heat and humidity.

One Saturday, the members of the Baptist church held a market day to raise money for a new roof for their church. There were many hundreds of naked Baptists buying and selling everything from stone axe heads to sweet potatoes. The church was complying with a recent government regulation that required all places of worship to have a roof of permanent materials. Dani houses were made of mud and straw, as were their churches. One church I was in had been roofed with aluminium. It constantly expanded and contracted with loud creaks as the sun was covered and uncovered by clouds.

I was keen to try out my recently purchased movie camera, so I took it out for a walk near Pyramid. Heavy rain in the previous two weeks (36 inches—just under a metre) had caused the rivers and streams to flood. I was standing on a primitive bridge filming the rushing water when the shoulder strap broke and the camera quickly sank out of sight. The insurance company subsequently paid up. Six months later, a parcel was placed on my desk and in it I found my old movie camera, swollen and rusted with water damage. I took it to the insurance company and presented it to the manager saying, 'I believe this is yours, you've paid for it'. Someone had found it after the water had subsided and taken it to the mission station.

The staple food of the Danis was sweet potato. They had more than sixty varieties. Some men I was with simply put them into the fire and took them out when the skins looked charred enough. There were plenty of pigs about, but these were a sign of wealth, not food, and they were a man's most treasured possession. These pigs were killed and eaten only on very important occasions. The people had many strange customs, some of which were very cruel; such as the way in which a woman chopped off a joint of a finger to show her sorrow when a loved one died. This was done to appease the spirit that caused the death. The Danis had their first real contact with westerners in 1954, when the Christian and Missionary Alliance arrived, followed a year later by the Australian Baptist Missionary Society.

As one missionary put it, 'In one generation, the Dani people of Irian Jaya took the dangerous leap from the Stone Age into the twentieth century, discovering the gospel of Jesus and their destiny as his helpers'. The difference between a Christian home and a traditional one was very noticeable. The former would be clean and tidy. The people would also be different in their demeanor. Of course everyone was friendly and there were a lot of smiles, but there was clearly a deeper sense of peace and stability in the faces of the Christians.

Government officials whom I met described the plans they had to make this area a major tourist attraction and stated that before long, it would be come well known. They encouraged me to show and publish my photos as much as possible. This place was surely going to change very soon.

The people of this highland valley, former cannibals so soon out of the Stone Age, contrasted greatly with Indonesians and, at the other end of the economic spectrum, the Chinese businessmen who were doing well in Indonesia. A bank manager friend said that 90% of all money that changed hands every day was passing through the hands of Chinese traders and businessmen. Many of these people could afford the best the world had to offer, and they ran businesses that kept the economy functioning. A Garuda Indonesian Airline official said, '95% of our passengers are either government employees or Chinese people.'

This leads me to the subject of corruption. A good friend, an internal auditor of the Shell Oil Company, whom we met in Nigeria said, 'You will find Indonesia very corrupt, on a par with Nigeria. We used to keep one million dollars in the petty cash at one of our main export centres, just to keep the oil flowing'. In Jakarta, we soon found that, to keep the postman coming, we had to give him a regular 'gift'. He took every opportunity to personally deliver small parcels or large envelopes, for which he would expect to receive about twenty cents. This kind of activity was rife at every level. The president's wife, Madam Tien, was nicknamed 'Madam Ten Percent'. But as blatant corruption increased, a New Zealand embassy official corrected me by saying, 'No, it's Madam Fifteen Percent now'.

Seeing that I had an important railway journalist title, I was given a permanent footplate pass. That meant that I could travel on any locomotive anywhere in the country. There were still a number of steam locomotives operating and these proved irresistible to me. Many of them were one hundred years old, and in the days of the Dutch, some of the fastest narrow gauge railways in the world were running on Java.

Indonesia is a country of fascinating wonders. There are five hundred languages in daily use by the then population of 130,000,000. (Now 238,000,000) In the forests grow at least 3,700 varieties of trees, and 800 types of orchid. It boasts of flying frogs, flying squirrels, flying snakes and fourteen varieties of flying lizards. There are so many kinds of insects at all levels of jungle life that many are unnamed and little is known about them. Animals range from marsupial mice to elephants.

I visited the 1,200-year-old Borobudur temple—the largest Buddhist temple in the world. About one hundred and fifty years ago, a Dutchman studied a perfectly shaped hill in the middle of rice fields and began examining it closely. He discovered this huge temple that is nearly one hundred and twenty metres square and thirty-five metres high.

But there were some tough times in Indonesia, especially for my family. At one point, there was a public revolt against the increasing influence of Japanese products in the country, and crowds took to the streets, destroying everything Japanese. I was far away from Jakarta, in Central Kalimantan, and knew nothing of what was going on. We had a Toyota, and Lorraine was advised by the school driver to quickly go home and lock the car away out of sight in the garage.

My travels to nearly every part of Indonesia enabled me to photograph the country extensively. I produced several series of photos, both for the Bible Societies and for the general public. I made a set of slides that sold very well to expatriates living in the country but who had not been able to travel widely. My photos included the world's largest orchid, insect-eating flowers, the largest flower (Rafflesia), an unbelievable 32-foot (9.7m) python, a day with the orang-utans in Sumatra, the back side of Bali where few people travelled, walking the hills and mountains of Irian Jaya—they were wonderful experiences and it was good to share them with others. It was this body of work that opened the way for me to become the official photographer of the United Bible Societies, the largest publishing organisation in the world.

One day, I received a message from the New Zealand embassy to meet the ambassador regarding 'an urgent matter'. A group of five journalists had been killed in East Timor and, after a long delay, their remains had been shipped to Jakarta for burial.

The New Zealand ambassador, Mr Ray Jermyn, asked me to photograph the burial service for the families. He also requested me to act as the back-up minister in case there was a serious traffic delay that prevented the official minister from officiating at the ceremony. All going to plan, the chaplain to the British Embassy, Rev. Ken Yapp, would conduct the service and would travel with the Australian Ambassador, Mr Richard Woollcott, in a separate car.

Although Ken Yapp read the service well, it was a very reserved affair with not a tear in sight. A representative of the Indonesian media correspondents spoke, and some diplomatic speeches were made, but it was all quite formal. Tender compassion and sorrow were replaced by diplomatic understatements.

After the lease on our house expired, we found another home that was of much better quality. The rent was very reasonable, but there was one catch—it was in a back section right next to a mosque. The property was owned by a civil servant who had been on full pay leave for two years while a problem in his department was sorted out. (He was still on leave when we left two years later.) When the contract was signed, it was necessary to pay the entire two years' rent in advance. We had to decide whether this better quality house beside a mosque was worth it or not. In the end we decided it was. It meant being disturbed at 4.15 a.m. every morning by the call to prayer. In fact, five times a day the speakers on the roof of the mosque would blare out the call to prayer. Saturday morning was ladies' morning, when a woman would deliver an hour-long sermon. There was a large open exhaust flue right above our stove and the preaching would reverberate down into the kitchen. Our small yard was enclosed by a two metre high concrete wall that captured every sound from the speakers. So we chose Saturday morning as our shopping time.

Our four and a half years in Indonesia came to an end. It had been difficult at times, but we had grown to love Indonesia. There was so much about the country and people that we grew to love and it was difficult to leave. Our children, although well travelled, never lost their love for the place. In later years Rosanne fell in love with a fine fellow from Lombok, Lalu Fathur, and Clive has since joined them in their successful land and resort business on Lombok Island – wwwsempiakvillas.com. This gives us the legitimate reason to visit them often. When I said goodbye to the General Secretary of the Indonesian Bible Society, he apologised for the 'weakness of his people and country. But I hope you have found them to be warm and kind and appreciative of the work you have done with us,' he said. 'I think your family have suffered much for being here'.

My response was simple, 'I think my wife cried (inwardly) when we came here, but she will also cry when we leave.'

10

VISIT TO NORTH KOREA—
dirty pictures of a glassless train

1999

I could approach this chapter in two different ways. One, giving the official reason for going to this isolated and little known country; the other, from a purely tourist perspective. All things considered, I had better keep to the latter, as the official part is supposed to be and remain highly confidential.

The idea of visiting North Korea had been first mooted in 1997, but there was no way a visit of any kind could be made by a Bible Society representative. We came under the category of *persona non grata*—non-permissible visitors, viz: Americans, Christian workers, South Koreans and journalists. It was therefore decided that I wait until after I was retired before making an attempt.

My nephew, Brian Harvey, a travel agent in Dubbo, NSW, had indicated that he knew how to secure a visa for me. At that time, there was only one travel agency in the Southern Hemisphere that was authorised to arrange travel to Democratic Peoples Republic of Korea, and it was in Australia.

It was known that New Zealanders who were not Christian workers or journalists were free to visit if they could afford it. But what about retired photojournalists? There was only one way to find out. Classic Oriental Tours, who specialised in out of the way places like Outer Mongolia, Sikkim, Tibet and North Korea, was enlisted to arrange a visit. A month later I received the go ahead.

I flew from Hong Kong to Beijing on Dragon Air, via Shanghai, and was met by a young lady called Sharon Hui, the travel agent's representative. I soon discovered that she was a keen photographer and had commenced study in this discipline at a local university. She was very excited to see my camera gear, and assured me that next day she would take me to some interesting and beautiful places around the city. Sharon was 26 years old and hoped soon to meet a nice man whom she could marry. She would make a good photo model herself, as her skin was like clear porcelain completely unmarked.

My hotel, the Holiday Inn Lido, was very comfortable. It was chosen because the Korea International Travel Service office was directly across the road. Although I was assured that a visa would be granted to me, it would be placed in my passport by this office. I wouldn't be able to relax until I could see the official approval with my own eyes. So it was with some slight trepidation that I called at the office the next day to collect my visa and train tickets.

There were several pages of forms to fill in that required me to cite my entire family history. Getting the birth-dates correct of all eight of my brothers and sisters had always been a challenge. But the real problem was what to fill in for 'occupation'. I simply wrote 'retired', without any further explanation. The consul clerk didn't bat an eyelid. Half an hour later, I had the precious visa stamped in my passport. That cost US$30, and another $120 purchased my return train ticket to Pyongyang. I was to be the first ever Bible Society person in modern history to visit North Korea.

Sharon proved to be a good guide and made sure we kept free of the chaotic city centre seventeen km away. I was taken to some beautiful parks and lakes on the outskirts of the city. The Shichahai antique market was crammed with objects both old and new. Sharon proudly gave me her cell phone and pager numbers. These were becoming more common in China, and she was right up there with the social elite. When she left me for the evening, she begged me to call her on her cell phone 'as many times as you like tonight'. I think she had only just taken delivery of it and was anxious to use it. She had enjoyed our day together, and had learnt more about photography. At every chance she wanted to hold my cameras and, of course, insisted on carrying the nine kg camera bag.

After lunch next day, I was delivered to the Beijing railway station. It was being refurbished and was so crowded that it was difficult to make our way past the hundreds of people and their piles and piles of luggage. Train No 27 Beijing-Pyongyang was waiting at the platform. It was sixteen cars long, and the last carriage was reserved for VIP travellers—I'd be travelling in style. The carriage was air-conditioned and staffed by three Chinese attendants. One took my baggage and showed me to a four-berth cabin. We were due to leave at 4.20 p.m. and arrive in Pyongyang about twenty-three hours later.

One of the attendants, Lee Lee, made it her job to take care of me, and offered hot sweet tea from a thermos flask every hour or so. At dinnertime she escorted me to the dining car where a reasonable meal was served. My new friend stood near my table and barked instructions to the waiters to keep up the supply of food and drink. No one else was getting such attention, not even the other foreigners on the train, and I wondered why she thought I was someone special. She constantly said things like, 'For you sir it is nothing. It is my duty and pleasure to help you sir. I am proud that you are on my train. I know you are important sir, and have good work to do'.

I had a sound sleep in my empty cabin. In the morning another woman attendant appeared. She had her own key to my cabin. She simply unlocked the door and, without a knock, brought me hot tea, then offered to bring breakfast from the dining car. 'Where's Lee Lee?' I asked.

'She finish. You stay. I bring.'

When we arrived at the border, the real test of my visa would occur. Would they let me enter the country? The travel agents had warned that the border crossing would take several hours. It took two hours to exit from China, as the immigration officers did their work on the train moving from carriage to carriage. Then we crossed the platform to join the Korean train.

The train moved slowly from the Chinese border station at Dandon, across the river Yalu and stopped at Sinuiju. This was obviously a new procedure as I had been told that we would have to walk across a small narrow bridge into North Korea. The travel agents had asked me to give them a report on my visit, noting all the new procedures as these were constantly changing.

We were instructed to remain on the train, in our own seats. I was in the last carriage that carried VIP North Koreans and foreigners. After a few minutes an official collected our passports and took them away. An hour later, an officer came into my cabin and sat down on the seat opposite me. He straightened his back and shoulders and, looking me in the eye and said in English, 'What is your occupation?'

'I'm retired,' said I.

'Ok, thank you,' he said and left.

Another hour passed and my passport was returned by a severe-looking immigration lady who, when handing me my documentation, suddenly broke into a warm smile and said, 'Welcome to North Korea'. Phew, what a relief!

My luggage wasn't checked and I had purposely not brought anything that might cause problems (such as my short-wave radio, cell phone, or my personal Bible). My concern was to not do anything that would jeopardise my mission. I didn't even risk bringing the Lonely Planet guidebook with me.

For now my compartment was empty, but Two men joined me later on. They turned out to be a high government official of the Foreign Relations Department, returning from ten days of meetings in Moscow, and his interpreter. The diplomat's stature in the government was confirmed when a large red Mercedes was driven right up to the carriage door to meet him when we arrived in Pyongyang. He and his interpreter had stayed at the North Korean embassy in Moscow and had travelled the entire way there and back across Russia by train. That was almost fourteen days of travel. The Dear Leader (as North Korea's leader Kim Jong-il is known) of the country has a fear of flying and always travels by train. It appeared to be North Korean policy for government officials to follow their leader's example. A couple of years after my visit, the Dear Leader went by special train to Moscow—nine days each way—and had special food flown to three airports along the way.

Travelling in the same cabin as the diplomat was going to be an interesting experience. Was he the man I was officially supposed to meet? He didn't say. I had no idea if he had been instructed to keep an eye on me. In my conversation with him, I prudently took the line that I was a former New Zealand Railway man and I was interested in railways. I didn't mention the fact that I had been the Asia Editor and then Correspondent for the International Railway Journal and had been for twenty-five years. I certainly didn't mention that I was the recently retired International Photojournalist of the United Bible Societies. I was asked lots of questions about the railway and of course I told him about my family history in New Zealand Railways with over fifty years service by my father and brothers. I had to feign ignorance of the world and not let it be known that I had travelled to more than one hundred and fifty countries. The diplomat often sat for long periods of time and gazed at me silently. I had the distinct feeling that he probably knew a lot more about me than he let on.

Although there was a dining car on the train, my travelling companions had brought a large box of food with them. Each item of food was beautifully wrapped in three separate parcels—one for each of them, and one for me. How had they known that I would be sharing their cabin? The plot thickened. There was rice, Chinese sausage, eggs, many vegetables and of course, *kimchi*—the relish that is served with every meal. It was all very nice. I noticed that there was no *kimchi* in my package, but when they found I enjoyed it, they shared some with me. This was yet another indication that I had been expected. Whoever had prepared the meals had obviously assumed that I, like so many foreigners, would not like the famous Korean chutney.

The diplomat through his interpreter, set about explaining to me that the North Korean people were very proud of their country. Against all odds they had preserved themselves against many acts of aggression. They had worked hard in unity for the common purpose of the country. They are very proud of what they have achieved and avoided their deadly enemies who have tried to force themselves upon them.

The other passengers in my carriage included two young men from Belgium, a family from Libya (who were in the diplomatic service) and several Russians. There were a few Korean men as well—some of whom must have been from the secret service. At all times, at least two of them stood in the corridor near our cabin, and I was unable to engage anyone else in conversation. Our carriage was not air-conditioned and the lights weren't turned on in the tunnels. The carriage was locked, preventing me from walking through the train to see who else was on board. Security men unlocked the door so I could enter the dining car that was coupled to ours, but I wasn't allowed to go any further.

We stopped at a small station, and as we pulled in, another local train pulled out. It consisted of four very old, decrepit carriages with broken windows, and a rusty diesel locomotive that emitted clouds of black exhaust like a steam engine. I was standing in the corridor at the time. There were several small boys seated on the roofs and I quickly took a couple of photos of the train.

The countryside was undulating and comprised of large fields of rice and corn that reached to the horizon. Hills were cultivated right to the top. Children, as they do everywhere in the world, waved to the train as we passed by at a stately seventy-five kph. There was no colour in the buildings, everything looked drab and unpainted. Most of the houses in the villages were long and narrow with thatched roofs. The majority of the roads were unpaved. It was going to be a hot summer and when I went for a drink the thermometer in the ancient but clean dining car read 35° C.

When we arrived at Pyongyang, there was no movement until my friend had been driven away in his red Mercedes. There must have been some announcement to the *hoi poloi* to wait for him. Before he departed, he courteously wished me a pleasant visit. I returned his compliment by saying, 'I'm sure you are glad to be home and to be with your wife and children again.' He answered with an unsmiling 'Umppff.'

I could see two well-dressed young men waiting to one side of the platform. One of them caught my eye and came to speak to me. 'Are you the group from Australia?' he asked.

'No, I'm alone and not in a group, and not from Australia.'

He looked puzzled, and began to look around the other passengers—all of whom, including the VIPs from my carriage, had already formed a line to exit the station through a checkpoint.

He returned to me and asked where I was from. He soon realised his mistake, apologising profusely for mistaking me for an Australian. It turned out that I was not the first Kiwi he had met and he already understood the difference between Australians and New Zealanders. We left the station through a side door, leaving the rest of the passengers queued up for the inspection of their documents. Mine were not checked.

Out on the street, the guides introduced themselves. Park Gyong Nam and Han Hyo Sop were their names. It turned out Park was the senior English-speaking guide, and had been featured in a number of foreign-made videos and reports by the BBC and CNN. I saw him myself in a BBC documentary two years later. My new sidekicks led me to a Volvo station wagon and ordered the driver to take us to the hotel.

The wide streets of Pyongyang were clean and clear of traffic, and it didn't take us long to arrive at the Yanggakdo Hotel. This establishment had only been opened a few months previously, and only the twenty-first floor of this impressive-looking forty-eight storey 1,000-room building was operational. My room was called a 'third class twin' and was clean, grey and clinical, complete with ensuite, television and an alarm clock radio. The bath towels, like Russian ones, were the size of small hand towels. The guides apologised that the casino was not yet open nor the massage parlours and mini golf.

The foyer of the hotel was huge, and along with the rest of the place, was illuminated with very low wattage lights. The hotel boasted eight restaurants including one Western one. The gift shop was impressive, with a staff of ten young women in green uniforms standing rigidly to attention beside each counter, with not a smile among them. There was an extensive range of local silver and semi-precious jewellery, as well as artwork of all descriptions. Apart from anything else, it was a stunning display of mirrors and glass cabinetry.

I dined alone in the Western restaurant, where the set meal was served by two young waitresses. The menu described the food as follows: 'Bread with sliced tomatoes, followed by fried poullet of fish, mixed rice and beetroot, mixed chop suey, fried bread crumbed chicken, peas, and Dutch beer and water.'

The TV in my room had one channel and played a film, in English, of the war exploits of the first president. This was followed by an entertaining concert featuring a magnificent marching display in which two or three thousand young people, each one playing a musical instrument, kept perfect time while marching in intricate formations. All of them smiled continuously.

After that, a choir of three hundred soldiers performed, their chests covered in large medals. They reminded me of a joke we used to hear in Russia. 'Why did Brezhnev go to the gym so regularly to expand his chest? So that he would have more room for medals!' The soldiers sang with great gusto and precision, smiling all the time and clearly enunciating the words. The final act was a soldiers' string orchestra. They also played with considerable gusto—each stroke strong and deliberate, almost comical in its effect.

Breakfast the next morning was tinned cold coffee (manufactured in Singapore—the sort you can buy in vending machines), four tiny pieces of fried bread (each about an inch square—that's not an exaggeration), lettuce salad, the thinnest possible slither of butter to go with two tiny pieces of toast, with the crusts removed, and one scrambled egg.

Park and Han arrived at 9.00 a.m. and presented me with my itinerary. I asked for a few changes, including a visit to the two officially approved churches in the city, plus a couple of government people whom I planned to meet. These changes necessitated a complete revamp of the schedule, which was done without question.

As for all visitors to North Korea, the first item on the programme was a visit to a huge statue of the founding president, Kim Il-sung. On the way we stopped to buy some flowers for me to place at the foot of the fifty metre high bronze sculpture. I was told that I should place the flowers, then stand back and bow to the president as a sign of respect. When I explained that, in our culture, we don't bow but nod the head to our leaders, I was told that that was quite ok. I was also informed that to refuse this action, meant that I would be sent home on the next train. When an involuntary look of disbelief crossed my face, the guide said in a serious voice, almost a whisper, as if he was ashamed to say it, 'Yes, that is true'.

A small group of men and women army officers were already there solemnly making obeisance. Later on I asked many questions about the current leader, Kim Jong-il, and for the most part didn't receive satisfactory answers. I asked about his wife. 'We never see her.' Children? 'There are some—one boy is at school here.' Later I discovered that the president's son is mostly incognito.

Kim Jong-il is not technically the 'president'. Kim Il-sung, his father, was made 'Eternal President of the Republic'. The son therefore can't be the president, as his deceased father will forever hold the title, so the Supreme Peoples Assembly (North Korea's equivalent of a 'parliament') gave him what they call 'the highest post of state', making him Chairman of National Defence, Supreme Commander of the Korean People's Army, and General Secretary of the Workers' Party of Korea.

Having paid our respects to the founding father of North Korea, we were then free to look around. First we went to view the sixty metre high Arch of Triumph, a monument to the first president and his victory over the Japanese occupiers in 1945. In reality, although the Korean people resisted their Japanese oppressors for many years, the final victory had mainly been achieved by Stalin's Red Army, which marched into Pyongyang with little opposition. I knew I was going to be given a large serving of the North Korean version of history, and that this would include a lot of hatred towards America. I was told that although New Zealand had taken part in the Korean War, we had been forgiven because the Americans had 'forced' us to join them. New Zealand sent 1,385 soldiers to the Korean conflict. It was important for me to see a special museum, so I was told. This turned out to be the Victorious Fatherland Liberation War Museum. Rather than covering the Korean War period, this museum covered the period between 1910 and 1945 when the Korean people battled their Japanese oppressors. It is an amazing place with brilliantly made moving three dimensional models and panoramas. There were a dozen other places of national historical significance like this, but I was spared any more of them.

From a distance, I photographed what was described as the 'world's largest luxury hotel', the Ryugyong, one hundred and five storeys high, built in the shape of a pyramid. It has 3,000 rooms and no less than five revolving restaurants. My guides would not take me up close because, although the building was begun in 1989, it was still not finished. As of 2011, when I write this, the exterior has been completed but the interior is still under construction.

The Mangsudae Art Studio was our next stop. Here hundreds of people were engaged in drawing portraits of the Dear Leader and making all manner of billboards and posters proclaiming the greatness of the country and leader. Their work ranged from decorating eggs to giant posters that would cover a three-storey building.

The Grand Peoples Study House was a library where many students were studiously working. It was nicely set out and beautifully furnished to accommodate a large number of people. The cleanliness and orderliness of the place was striking. I was told that it contained 30,000,000 volumes and six hundred rooms. We trooped around another six monuments in the city before returning to the hotel for lunch. Most of the monuments we had seen had the word 'grand' in their descriptions, depicting either their physical size or importance. Without exception, they were all quite impressive.

Pyongyang is a beautiful city. It was completely razed during the 1950-53 war and credit must be given for the way it has been rebuilt so attractively. There are many parks and recreational green areas. As you've no doubt gathered, it abounds with monumental edifices and towers, museums, and educational, scientific and cultural institutions. There were also a number of impressive apartment blocks.

The roads are wide and clean, and carefully controlled by traffic police, who have the task of guiding the least amount of traffic of any city in the world. It was amusing to see a grim faced woman, in her immaculate uniform, on traffic duty on the main 100-metre wide thoroughfare. She was signalling a lone car across an intersection, without another vehicle or pedestrian in sight within three hundred metres.

One building in a main street holds the record for the fastest time to build an apartment—4.9 minutes, with two hundred finished in one day. Generally, though, the builders completed the work at the slower pace of one apartment every fourteen minutes!

Like all Communists, these folk love their statistics. As one official publication put it, 'The total area of the important construction projects in Kwangbok Street and other districts in Pyongyang occupies thirty three million square metres and the principal buildings in this area number more than two hundred and sixty. Among them are schools, a children's palace and other cultural establishments whose total building area is over 410,00 square metres, sports establishments with a total area of over 430,000 square metres, welfare establishments over 300,000 square metres and dwellings for tens of thousands of family units.'

But it has to be said the city is now a beautiful place. Well set out, clean, lots of green areas, and well deserving it's title as 'a city within a park.'

The next day after dining alone in the huge restaurant I checked out of the hotel and set off for Mount Myogyang, one hundred and fifty km away to the north. This is one of the five famous mountains of North Korea.

Park and Han were keen to show me the International Friendship Centre, which displays gifts that were presented to the Great Leader

Kim Il-sung. A second large building contained presents given to the Dear Leader, Kim Jung-il. These gifts had come from many countries and personalities around the world. I was particularly interested to see gifts from Billy Graham, and from the Communist Party of New Zealand. Although the New Zealand gifts were nice pieces of paua that would normally have looked quite lovely, they were dwarfed beside some of the magnificent porcelain objects and crafts of various descriptions from around the world. Kim Il-sung's building is a huge six storeys high, with an intricate system of blue tiled roofs; a really beautiful building. Each floor is covered with magnificent carpets that cover 28,000 square metres. It contains 80,000 gifts.

Our next stop was the only 'working' Buddhist temple in the country. I read that there are officially 10,000 practising Buddhists in North Korea. There are three hundred temples in the country, but very few are available for even occasional worship.

That night I was given a room at the picturesque fifteen storeyed Hyangsan Hotel, which is built in the shape of a pyramid. I was informed that I was the only guest in the entire two hundred and eighty-eight-room establishment. I don't know where the guides and driver slept. Nevertheless, the hotel was fully staffed and as Park said, 'They are all here to serve you'.

Six waitresses stood in a semi circle around my table, but at a respectful distance, all anxious to do something for me. I would drink some water, and as soon as I put down the glass, one of the attendants sprang forward to refill it. There were a dozen small brass dishes with different types of food, and one waitress saw to it that as one was eaten, she moved it away and gently moved the other dishes within my reach. These women moved extremely quietly and gracefully. They were dressed in long-sleeved white silk blouses and green overalls, each wearing their personal ID and a badge of the Dear Leader's photo. It is a criminal offence not to wear this badge at all times.

'What happens when you go swimming?' I joked. But they didn't think that was funny.

One of the receptionists tried to encourage me to stay a few days. 'We have so many mountains for you to see. There are thousands of peaks here and it's only one hundred and twenty eight kilometres to drive around them'. She smiled coyly, 'and the birds, there are so many, altogether 115 kinds of them and their sweet singings are so sweet.'

Inside the DMZ

The guides looked very grave as they announced that today we would visit a very important place. 'It's where we are protecting ourselves from the people in the south and their American allies who want to destroy us.' This was the D-M-Z they explained.

The 'de-militarised zone' is probably the most famously incorrectly named place on earth. The place is the exact opposite of de-militarised. It is, in fact, the most heavily armed border in the world. This four-kilometre wide strip near the 38th parallel stretches across the two hundred and eighty four kilometre width of the Korean Peninsular. Running across the zone, equidistant between North and South Korea, is the military demarcation line. This line runs through the buildings spanning the zone and right down the middle of the table in the conference room. No one is allowed to cross it on pain of death—that is, as far as the North Koreans are concerned.

A total of seventeen tunnels have been built by the Northerners in attempts to smuggle saboteurs, assassins and armies into the South. The first one that was discovered extended a kilometre from the line into South Korea. It was properly reinforced and even had a railway line running through it. Each of the four largest tunnels could permit the passage of an entire army division in one hour. When the tunnels were discovered, the North Koreans claimed they were looking for coal! To help bolster their story, some parts of the tunnel walls had been painted black to look like coal deposits.

The Korean Armistice talks had been held at a place called Phanmunjom. Hundreds of meetings took place, until, as the official North Korean guidebook put it, 'the US imperialists bent the knees down before the Korean people and signed the Armistice Agreement'. The hall in which the signing took place was specially constructed by the Northerners—nine hundred square metres built in five days. There are seven buildings in the complex, including the Conference Hall, which is the one with the table that is divided between North and South. The microphone cables on this table are so positioned that they form the line. Grim-faced soldiers, both American and Korean, watch everyone carefully, guarding that line. I tried to cheer them up with a smile. Even the Americans didn't respond, while the Koreans glared even more seriously. This place was no laughing matter.

Americans and South Koreans match the North Korean guards man for man both inside and outside the buildings. It is said that the land in the DMZ is the most heavily defended piece of real estate in the world and is littered with land mines. I noticed that the American soldiers stood at the outside corners of the building so that they had a clear line of sight along both walls.

'I have to tell you the wonderful story about our flag pole,' said Park. The Southerners built one near here that was one hundred metres high. We then built one that is the tallest in the world. It is one hundred and sixty metres high and has a huge flag on it. This flag is the biggest in the world and weighs two hundred and seventy kgs.' Later I learned that the pole is so unsteady that when it rains, the flag has to be taken down, because the pole cannot support the extra weight of the wet fabric!

This was not my first visit to the DMZ—I had previously visited from the south side. One thing I clearly remembered were the anti-tank traps on the road south. These opened up huge jaws to deter the largest vehicle. The south side of the DMZ attracts nearly 200,000 visitors a year, while the north side has as few as 2,000. I was the only Northern visitor this day.

Accommodation that night was provided in a very old and beautiful traditional Korean house in the former capital Kaesong. The city is a thousand years old, and very famous for its ginseng, jewel processing and embroidery factories. My guides decided I would not be interested in the embroidery, so took me straight to my accommodation. It was only after I left the place the following day that I discovered that it was part of the Kaesong Folk Hotel, consisting of nineteen houses with one hundred rooms, set out like a very neat suburban village. Once again, it seemed as though I was the only guest that night.

It was a traditional Korean house in the truest sense, which meant no chairs and no beds. My bedroom had no furniture whatsoever—just a reed mat on the floor with silk coverings and no pillow. But there was one concession to modernity—a TV was hidden in a recessed cupboard. The television was permanently set to a channel playing tourist-type English programmes proclaiming the greatness of the Dear Leader. The lounge was furnished with four armchairs partly covered with large crocheted antimacassars, and there were sliding paper doors out to the porch. Everything was spotlessly clean, and the furniture and woodwork shone brilliantly.

That evening for dinner, as my notes say, 'I sat on the floor in the dining room in lonely splendour served by a pretty young girl'. This was what is called a *pansanggi* meal consisting of nine dishes plus rice and soup. The vegetables are always served in odd numbers. The dishes were made of brass, which Koreans believe enhances the flavour. My waitress carried in a large stone that was red hot; it fairly glowed and it must have been quite heavy. She daintily knelt on the floor beside me and placed it on the mat. She then placed *bulkogi,* small strips of beef, on the red hot stone and motioned that I should cook it myself. As usual, I attempted to make the girl smile. I thanked her warmly and said *kamsamlidah* ('thank you'). But all I got was a look as if to say, 'Are you stupid, what is there to smile about?' These North Koreans are such a serious lot.

A local speciality that the guides had told me about was served with great aplomb—a sesame seed cake. The head chef brought it from the kitchen, walked to where I was seated, solemnly bowed and handed it to the waitress, who placed it before me. He was either too old, not supple enough or too proud to give it to me at floor level.

The waitress then turned on the TV so that I could view an English documentary that featured several people who had personally met the president. They were very emotional as they described the experience. They included a factory foreman, an engine driver, and several men and women dressed in spotless clothes at their workplace. They all rejoiced in the wonderful care and protection provided by the government, as always, under the leadership of the Dear Leader. It was all designed to impress the tourist.

Later I asked my guides if they had ever met the Dear Leader. They answered in very quiet voices, as though they were ashamed of it, that they had seen him, but they gave no details and certainly had never met him. I took that to mean, perhaps, that they had seen him on TV but never in person. That's why that video I had seen was so significant. They just did not want to talk about him. According to the guidebook, up to 1997 he had never given a public speech.

I had been left alone in the house, so I took the opportunity to take a walk around the area. It was still daylight and many people who were on their way home from work passed me in the street. Very few acknowledged my greetings. Those who did, gave me a serious nod and hurried on. This was a residential area but I was struck by the silence. There were no blaring radios or TVs. No talking or laughing. It was quite warm, about 26° C, so a few houses had their front doors open and I could see people inside but they were all so quiet. I was caught in a brief shower of rain. How I wished I could speak the language and thought again of the little booklet I had bought called *Korean in a Hurry*—the most ridiculously titled book I ever saw. One thing's certain, you don't learn the Korean language in a hurry. The script is easy enough because it's phonetic. Sometimes people looked surprised as I spelt out the words of a sign.

The official literature of Kaesong offers many legends of old. One was about a man who was attempting to overthrow the king. He tested his son's allegiance to him by offering him a drink and reciting a poem.

It loses a lot in translation:

What does this mind you?
What does that mind you?
Do the vines of arrowroot that get entangled mind you?
We get entangled like this and live for one hundred years.

Seo Gyeong-deok was a famous philosopher in the 1500s. He made a definite contribution to the development of the materialistic philosophy of Korea in the middle ages. According to the official local guidebook, 'He advocated materialism'. He expressed this in the following poem. Again it suffers from the official translation:

Matter comes into being, constantly comes into being.
I thought now it has come into being, but still it comes into being.
You, matter, I ask you where do you originate?

Matter disappears, constantly disappears
I thought now it has all disappeared
But still it disappears
You, matter, I ask where you disappear?

One evening, I was taken to the Pyongyang Circus that was officially described as 'a comprehensive polygonal acrobatic centre for the performance of water, ice and animal acts as well as of general acrobatic pieces'. The 3,500-seat auditorium was packed with local people and we beheld some of the most amazing acrobatic performances imaginable. The performers had won the world championship the previous year. Some of the balancing feats were beyond my powers of description and memory. I wondered what system the government had devised to allow people to attend a circus. I guessed that it was probably a reward for good work and achieving set targets.

Now that we were back in Pyongyang, Park and Han couldn't wait to show me the underground railway. This is one of the most carefully design systems in the world and feeds out to the main areas of the city. The beauty of the stations that I was shown was astonishing. Some of the most beautiful chandeliers I had ever seen were suspended from the ceilings of these underground stations. The walls were decorated with massive murals. There is one in Yonggwang station that is eighty metres long and, as the guides told me, was made with 10,000 pieces of mosaic per square metre. Although the mural was impressive, that figure sounded like a bit of an exaggeration to me. Every square inch of floor is perfectly clean. When the president opened the metro he said, 'We were building a metro not as a means of making money but for providing civilised and convenient life to the people so that we did not spare money to decorate the inside well and construct in solidly and modernly'. The murals describe 'the glorious path of struggle traversed by the Korean people'.

The trains that service these stations are roomy and also spotlessly clean inside and out. However, as in many cases here, the real story is never revealed. Opened in 1974, in addition to the two public lines, there are said to be several secret lines solely for military use. The Chinese company that built the metro cars were asked to build twice the number that could be used for the public service.

Upon opening the metro, the president also memorably said, 'I think it is difficult to build a metro, but it is not to cut the tape'. A brochure stated, 'Hearing his words who considered the trouble of builders first, the participants in the opening ceremony felt a lump in their throats and gave enthusiastic cheers, waving the bundle of flowers'.

This underground railway line is possibly the deepest in the world—as far down as one hundred to one hundred and fifty metres below the surface in some areas. I heard of a defector who reported that there is a huge underground square that was constructed in 1970. It was built as a bunker for the Supreme Command of the People's Armed forces, for the storage of manpower and equipment in the event of a war. It is reported to be able to accommodate up to 100,000 people. Secret lines connect the President's Palace and the airport.

A defector also reported that there is another secret military command post called 'a wartime secret command post', one hundred metres below, where 5,000 members of the elite will command the anticipated war with the West. Another interesting feature of the underground rail network is that each station is equipped with nuclear resistant steel doors.

I was aware of this 'secret' information before my trip, so it was fascinating to observe how much my guides could or would tell me. For example, they said that the army had built the underground railway, but they didn't mention the use of prisoners to do the labour. I had done my homework, but was careful not let on what I had learned about the system.

The May Day Stadium was another 'must see.' This arena seats 150,000, and we stayed just long enough to get an idea of its vastness.

An important feature of all Communist regimes is the way they attempt to train the young in their doctrines. All children and young people regularly attend camps where they have a lot of fun, but are subjected to periods of communist teaching. North Korea is no different. I went to a campsite in a beautiful mountain area and witnessed the morning activities at one of these camps. A group had just arrived and were dressed in their neat school uniforms. They stood in regimented rows to salute the flag and recite the appropriate slogans. Later I saw some of them swimming in the river nearby.

West Sea Barrage

The name 'West Sea Barrage' puzzled me no end, until I finally discovered that it was really a cofferdam—a huge eight-kilometre-long system of dams, three locks, chambers and sluices. It closes off the Taedong River from the Yellow Sea in order to supply fresh drinking water and water for irrigation. Some say that is about the only sensible project built under the Kim regime; others say that it has helped to cause the famines of recent years. But as far as the guides were concerned, every visitor must see it.

Travelling back to the capital city we came across a huge crowd of people working in a rice field. They were harvesting the rice by hand. It was explained to me that these were not farmers. Apparently many government departments send their people out to the villages to help bring in the harvest.

The Churches

According to the official literature there are 10,000 Christians in North Korea. There was a time when Pyongyang was an important Christian centre. Today, only two church buildings exist for worship—one Roman Catholic and the other Protestant.

In a country where Christianity had flourished after the arrival of the first Protestant missionaries in 1885, Kim Il-Sung's policy of *Juche*, or self-reliance, introduced an elaborate religious mythology. This was centred around a Juche 'Holy Trinity' that placed the Great Leader at the pinnacle. His mother, Kim Jong-suk, and his son, the current leader, Kim Jong-il (aka Dear Leader), form the other members of the holy family worshipped by North Koreans. Following the introduction of the Juche policy, all religions were banned in a country where, until 1950, according to some estimates, there were 2,850 churches, 700 pastors and 300,000 Christians. This eradication of Christianity has been so effective that the majority of North Koreans today have never heard of Jesus.

I attended the Protestant church on the Sunday. It was full for the morning service with many local people and a few foreigners who were employed by United Nations Agencies, such as World Food. A Canadian couple were officially farewelled as they were returning home after several years in the country. One of the pastors proudly showed me copies of a Korean Bible reprinted in the North. It was actually an unauthorised copy of the UBS text, but no one minded; the important thing was that the Scriptures were available. There were plenty of copies of this edition of the Bible available in the church. A Bible and hymnbook were placed on each seat. The Bible appeared to be a reprint of the standard Korean Bible Society Bible, and I could tell by our UBS codes that it was a reprint, albeit unauthorised. Incidentally, the full Bible in Korean first appeared in 1887.

Before the Korean War, two thirds of Korean Christians lived in the North, but most fled to the South during the hostilities. Seoul now has eleven of the world's twelve largest Christian congregations.

After the church service, a UN worker spoke to me about the severe famine occurring in some parts of the country. I could confirm that many of the people I had seen in the country side looked quite unhealthy and undernourished. I mentioned that I had not tried to photograph such people. He looked at me carefully and said, 'That was very wise'. He said that the government had recently admitted that 220,000 people had died of starvation; but the less publicity the better.

During my tour around North Korea, I carried three cameras and five lenses, and was free to use them as much as I liked. However, experience has taught me to instinctively avoid taking pictures of the type of things sensitive governments don't like having photographed. I shot forty-five rolls of film in colour, black and white and transparency. In general, people didn't refuse to be photographed—especially when it was the guide who asked them for permission.

However, on the second to last day there was a little drama. I met Park and Han after breakfast and they both looked quite serious. I sensed something was wrong. After a bit of 'umming' and 'aahing', Mr Park finally said, 'The security people are angry with you. They say that you took dirty pictures of a glassless train.'

'Dirty pictures of a glassless train?' said I. And I immediately knew what he was talking about. I pretended not to understand but further explanation made it clear. The photos I had snapped of the young boys on the roof of the derelict-looking suburban train on my way to Pyongyang were coming back to bite me.

'You have to give me those pictures,' said Park.

I knew exactly which roll of film the pictures were on, but I pretended not to. 'Well, you must give me all your films and we will process them all,' directed Park. 'Right here in the hotel they can do it.'

I thought I better not make any more trouble, so I returned to my room and produced the offending film. The problem was, though, I had shot the pictures on a Canon APS camera and film, as distinct from standard 35 mm film. There were not many places where processing for this type of film was available, but I was assured that they could do the work, so I surrendered the roll to them.

The lab technician broke open the cassette and processed it. He then cut out the three offending negatives, and that evening the remaining negatives were given to me. The processing was actually done quite well.

I found North Korea very difficult to summarise. I had the feeling that we have not always heard the truth about this country—either from North Korean sources or Western ones. There are too many anecdotes of the cruelty of American soldiers during the Korean War for them to all be untrue. It clearly wasn't all like M.A.S.H. According to the guidebook, 'During the entire war the US Army Air Force relentlessly bombed the northern territory in an unsuccessful attempt to force a surrender; they targeted anything and everything, military and civilian . . . until there was hardly a building left standing in all the North.' It's not surprising that the hatred built up against the Americans still remains.

Without a good knowledge of the language it simply isn't possible to understand everything that is going on around you. Government propaganda, of course, can't always be believed. At best it might be half true. I wondered when cell phones would arrive in North Korea, for they would surely create changes. The Internet is unavailable to the general populace, but it will inevitably come one day.

In general, I found the people gave the impression that they were being watched all the time and no one was free to speak up, even if they could speak a little English. I chatted with many institutional guides and none were free in what they had to say. They were certainly different in their demeanour from South Koreans, whose country I had visited and worked in nine times previously.

I wondered if I should tip my guides and driver. After a couple of careful questions, it soon became clear that tips in US dollars would be most acceptable. I wondered if they would hand these gratuities in, or at least a portion. There are undoubtedly ways and means of changing foreign currency in North Korea, even if the practice is illegal.

As far as the Christian church is concerned, there are some signs of a softening in the official attitude. The fact that they allowed me in was significant. But any reports of growth or activity in the church should not be published at present. From my earliest years, I remember being in prayer meetings when people prayed for those behind the Iron Curtain. At the time it seemed impossible that Christianity could survive in those places. But when the curtain fell, we discovered a large community of believers throughout Communist Europe and Russia who had kept the faith alive despite seventy years of oppression. The same was true in China. We can continue to pray that this will be the case for North Korea.

The North Korean government pretends that it provides for the people, those terrible famine statistics notwithstanding, and in some ways the people seem ok. But there was something missing. Apart from their low standard of living and lack of political freedom, that 'God-shaped space' in every human heart was very evident in the people of North Korea.

On leaving one museum, there was a long passageway to the exit, and my local guide, a woman of about thirty, escorted me to the door. Park and Han were some distance behind us. She quietly asked me, 'Do you have a religion?'

'Yes,' I said, 'I am a Christian.' I asked her in return, 'Do you have a religion?'

She sighed, 'No, but I wish . . .'

APPENDIX

COUNTRIES, TERRITORIES AND DISPUTED TERRITORIES VISITED

There is no official list of countries of the world, in fact there are no two lists the same. Many travellers base their count on geography, political state either at the time of visit or later, or whether it issues its own postage stamps or currency. This one doesn't include airports! We could also add Kashmir. (161)

AFRICA

Angola	Benin	Burkina Faso
Burundi	Cameroon	Central African Republic
Chad	Congo-Kinshasa	Cote d'Ivoire
Congo-Brazzaville	Egypt	Equatorial Guinea
Eritrea	Ethiopia	Ghana
Kenya	Lethsoto	Madagascar
Malawi	Mali	Mozambique
Namibia	Niger	Nigeria
Rwanda	Seychelles	South Africa
South Sudan	Sudan	Swaziland
Tanzania	Transkei	Togo
Uganda	Zanzibar	Zambia
Zimbabwe		

ASIA AND MIDDLE EAST

Armenia	Bahrain	Bangladesh
Brunei	Cambodia	China
Hong Kong	Gaza Strip	India
Indonesia	Israel	Japan
Jordan	Kazakhstan	North Korea
South Korea	Laos	Lebanon
Malaysia	Macau	Mauritius
Mongolia	Myanmar	Nepal
Oman	Pakistan	Palestinian West Bank
Philippines	Singapore	Sri Lanka
Syria	Taiwan	Thailand
Timor Leste	Turkey	Uzbekistan
Vietnam		

PACIFIC

American Samoa Australia		Cook Islands
Fiji	French Polynesia	Kiribati
Nauru	New Caledonia	New Zealand
Niue	Papua New Guinea	Solomon Islands
Tonga	Tuvalu	Vanuatu
Western Samoa		

Maurice Harvey

AMERICAS

Argentina	Aruba	Barbados
Bolivia	Brazil	Canada
Chile	Colombia	Cuba
Curacao	Dominican Republic	Ecuador
El Salvador	Honduras	Guatemala
Haiti	Jamaica	Mexico
Netherlands Antilles		Nicaragua
Panama	Paraguay	Peru
St Vincent and the Grenadines		Trinidad & Tobago
Uruguay		United States of America Venezuela

EUROPE

Albania	Austria	Belarus
Belgium	Bosnia-Herzegovina	Bulgaria
Czech Republic	Denmark	Croatia
East Germany	Estonia	England
Finland	France	Germany
Georgia	Greece	Holy See
Hungary	Ireland	Italy
Latvia	Liechtenstein	Lithuania
Luxembourg	Moldova	Monaco
Netherlands	Northern Ireland	Norway
Poland	Portugal	Romania
Russia	Scotland	Slovakia
Slovenia	Spain	Switzerland
Turkey	Ukraine	Wales

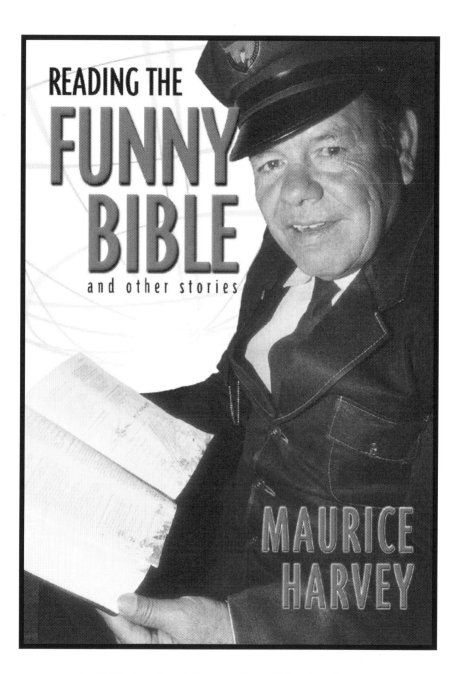

Available in printed form and as a E-book early 2012

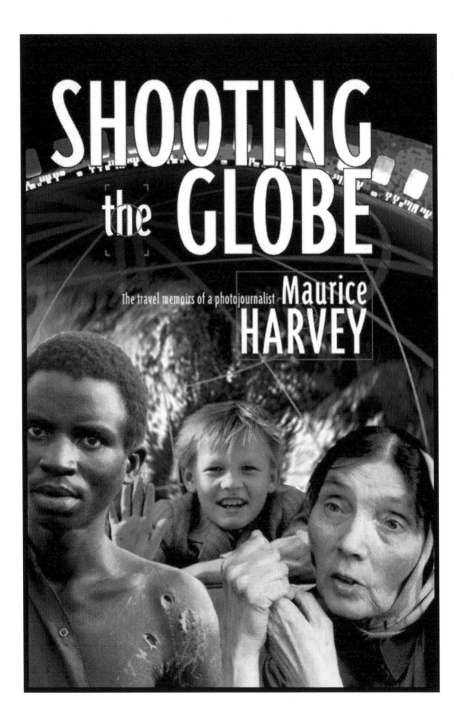

Available in printed form and as an E-book early 2012